Also by Ronald Radosh:
AMERICAN LABOR AND UNITED STATES FOREIGN POLICY

Edited by Ronald Radosh:
DEBS

Co-edited with Louis Menashe:
TEACH-INS: U.S.A.
    REPORTS, OPINIONS, DOCUMENTS

Co-edited with Murray N. Rothbard:
A NEW HISTORY OF LEVIATHAN: ESSAYS ON THE RISE
OF THE AMERICAN CORPORATE STATE

Co-edited with Blanche W. Cook and Alice K. Harris:
PAST IMPERFECT: ALTERNATIVE ESSAYS IN AMERICAN HISTORY

Prophets on the Right

PROFILES OF CONSERVATIVE CRITICS
OF AMERICAN GLOBALISM

Ronald Radosh

 *Simon and Schuster* / *New York*

Designed by Irving Perkins
Manufactured in the United States of America
by American Book–Stratford Press Inc.

1   2   3   4   5   6   7   8   9   10

Library of Congress Cataloging in Publication Data

Radosh, Ronald.
    Prophets on the right.

    Includes bibliographical references and index.
    1. United States—Foreign relations—1933–1945.
2. United States—Foreign relations—1945–1953.
3. Conservatism—United States. I. Title.
E744.R32   327.73   74-20840
ISBN 0-671-21901-4

For William Appleman Williams

For William Appleman Williams

Contents

ACKNOWLEDGMENTS

I am particularly indebted to those two stalwarts of the libertarian Old Right, Leonard P. Liggio and Murray N. Rothbard. As coeditors of the now defunct journal *Left and Right* they were the first to make me aware of the hidden tradition of conservative opposition to the American global empire. Both Liggio and Rothbard have been of immense help in different ways. They have contributed material, made suggestions for research, read portions of the manuscript, and provided me with out-of-print books and pamphlets. Readers will find many of the insights they first hinted at explored fully in this book.

Any scholar working on the noninterventionists will find himself indebted to Professor Justus D. Doenecke of New College at Sarasota, Florida. Author of the invaluable *The Literature of Isolationism: A Guide to Non-Interventionist Scholarship, 1930–1972* (Colorado Springs, Colo.: Ralph Myles, 1972), Professor Doenecke has carefully catalogued every available source. His guide lists books, articles, monographs, dissertations, as well as the location and availability of all relevant manuscript material. I turned to the guide again and again, always with much profit.

Professor Doenecke understands that scholarship holds no secrets, and he has been more than willing to share information, research notes, and ideas. He has encouraged me to proceed with my own study of Lawrence Dennis. My discussion of this forgotten intellectual owes much to Doenecke's own pioneering treatment. He has been an excellent critic, and his comments have undoubtedly saved me from presenting a one-sided and unduly laudatory treatment of the subjects discussed in the book.

Others have been of great help. Senator Robert Taft, Jr., consented to give me permission to consult his father's papers at the Library of Congress; material pertinent to the life of Charles A. Beard was called to my attention by Beard's daughter and son-in-law, Miriam and Alfred Vagts. Their warm, encouraging words were most welcome. David Green, of the University of Saskatchewan, shared material from his own forthcoming study of American conservatism; Louis Menashe read sections of the manuscript, made invaluable criticisms, and offered his friendship and comradeship, which were of great sustenance; a summer research grant from the City University of New York enabled me to travel to various libraries to carry out the research.

9

Special thanks and gratitude are due to my editor at Simon and Schuster, Alice Mayhew. She has asked tough and thoughtful questions. Her probing commentaries constantly forced me to pick up the manuscript for yet another look, to again re-examine and re-evaluate my assumptions and my approach to the subject. Her fortitude and diligent work are reflected throughout the book. She has made many demands; they all reveal respect for the subject and the concerns of the book. It has been a rich and rewarding experience working with her. Also at Simon and Schuster a great deal of help was given by Joanna Ekman and Linda Healey, whose efforts I greatly appreciate.

The book is dedicated to William Appleman Williams. In ways too numerous to list, his ideas and perceptions are to be found herein. Williams is the first historian to comprehend how traditional conservatives launched an attack on America's globalist crusaders. Studying with him years ago, and continuing to learn from him, has been the most important part of my training as a historian and my maturation as an intellectual. He has been a model as a teacher, scholar, and committed radical intellectual.

Finally, thanks to those who have made life a joy to live, and who have given me friendship, warmth, and love—thanks to my children, Laura and Daniel, and to Allis Rosenberg Wolfe for being there.

RONALD RADOSH
New York City
June 1974

Introduction

*An Essay on History and the Questions
to Be Raised in This Book*

THIS VOLUME tries to examine the political thought and, particularly, the attitudes toward foreign policy, and internationalism, of five vividly different men, from the late 1930s through the beginning years of the emergent cold war. They are editor-journalist Oswald Garrison Villard, of the liberal *Nation;* economist and writer John T. Flynn, columnist for the *New Republic;* the noted titular head of the Republican party—"Mr. Republican"—Senator Robert A. Taft of Ohio; the Progressive historian Charles A. Beard; and the self-proclaimed intellectual "fascist," Lawrence Dennis. A thread binds them together—endorsement of "isolationism" before World War II and an adherence to the "conservative" camp at the war's end. To many the descriptive terms that may suggest themselves include "right-wing," "fascist," "isolationist," "reactionary," and most charitably, "conservative."

These men came from different starting places. Beard was part of the old Progressive tradition. Taft was raised to be President, coming from a political family with deep roots in Ohio. Flynn started out as a liberal economist concerned with Wall Street manipulation. Villard was a pacifist and a wealthy publisher, grandson of the abolitionist William Lloyd Garrison. Dennis was a Foreign Service officer who had served in South America. They ended among a group loosely defined as the American right wing. They have often been described as individuals whose ideas exemplify isolationism and extreme conservatism.

Since I am an advocate of a socialist solution to America's domestic crisis, it may appear incongruous for me to have made a study of men of the Right. Some readers may wonder if my partisanship makes me incapable of such a task. To many the politics represented by these men flows from the worst currents within the American tradition.

Our own generation, however, has begun the task of breaking with some long-cherished illusions. In a book about Daniel Ellsberg, Peter Schrag noted that his contemporaries "identified strongly with the actions of [their] nation, [their] government and particularly [their] President." They had, he wrote, "a nearly unshakable faith in the Executive branch." It was Congress "that had been made up of isolationists and America Firsters . . . it was always a recalcitrant legislature that stood in the way of a progressive President."[1]

The "isolationists" were the bad guys—severe nationalists, whose desire to see America first led them to try to prevent the U.S. from fulfilling its international responsibilities. The "internationalists" were the good guys—men of maturity and responsibility, who knew that America could not continue to be an island unto itself. Globalism was an ideology whose time had come. Its opponents had to be stopped.

Now that we know this to be a fairy tale, perhaps it is possible to take another look at the views of those awful America Firsters, whose isolationism has been accused of providing grist for the Axis mill. We will find that the generalized conceptions of what the isolationists advocated were shaped by their opponents. Unity around the consensus was created by branding critics as isolationist at one historical moment, pro-Communist at another. The policy makers and their intellectual allies were concerned with finding effective means to discredit and isolate the critics of the consensus.

Many liberal and radical critics and readers will object to a sympathetic treatment of the politics and ideas of avowed conservatives. The question asked of William Appleman Williams by historian John Higham with regard to Williams' sympathetic treatment of John Quincy Adams, Mark Hanna, and Herbert Hoover, is pertinent: "What sort of radicalism," Higham asked,

1. Peter Schrag, *Test of Loyalty* (New York: Simon and Schuster, 1974), p. 30.

"is it that praises men whom our conservative scholars are also rehabilitating?"[2]

The question is pressing when the list of "conservatives" includes McCarthyites such as John T. Flynn and a proclaimed exponent of fascism, Lawrence Dennis. It is a strange brew of subjects for a radical historian, but only if one sets out to make heroes of the group and villains of their opponents.

That kind of history would be no more satisfactory than the quick judgment made by past generations. Aileen Kraditor has warned against "those on the Left who have endeavoured to find in American history justifications for and forerunners of their own party or movement," since "a historian who looks into the past to find precedents for his own views is irrelevant to a generation that looks into the past for other reasons."[3]

One must go back to the late 1930s, move on through the war and into the 1950s, re-asking the questions these men asked, examining the realities they confronted, and pondering the answers received in response to their probing doubts. If we charge one or another of them with inconsistency, it must not be because he took a domestic position with which we may disagree while making a point about foreign policy of which we may approve. It must only be because within his own context he advanced a clearly contradictory and inconsistent position. One thinks of Taft's failure to effectively challenge the demagoguery of Joseph McCarthy—perhaps because of political reasons.

Those who use history as a means of finding heroes of the past do not consider the lives of avowed conservatives. They decide what is relevant and search history for illustrations. They are, as Kraditor wrote, evaluating "data by present needs rather than by their own past contexts."[4] The point was well made by William Appleman Williams. History, he tells us, "is one of the most misleading—and hence dangerous—approaches to knowledge if

2. John Higham, "The Contours of William A. Williams," *Studies on the Left*, II, No. 2 (1961), p. 75.

3. Aileen S. Kraditor, "American Radical Historians on Their Heritage," *Past and Present*, No. 56 (August 1972), pp. 136–137.

4. Ibid., p. 151.

viewed, or practiced, as a process of reaching back into the past for answers sufficient unto the present and the future." Rather than offering ready-made answers, the function of history "is to help us understand ourselves and our world so that each of us, individually and in conjunction with our fellow men, can formulate relevant reasoned alternatives and become meaningful actors in making history."[5]

History demands that we leave the present, go back "into the heretofore, by beginning again." Rather than stay in the present and look back, we must return to the past and move toward the present, finding out about the "restrictions of our former outlook." If we take that journey, we can "return with a broader awareness of the alternatives open to us and armed with a sharper perceptiveness with which to make our choices." With that method, history offers us rare possibilities: "[It] can offer examples of how other men faced up to the difficulties and opportunities of their eras. Even if the circumstances are noticeably different, it is illuminating . . . to watch other men make their decisions, and to consider the consequences of their values and methods. If the issues are similar, then the experience is more directly valuable. But in either case the procedure can transform history as a way of learning into a way of breaking the chains of the past."[6]

In this volume I have tried to follow the line of inquiry set forth by Williams. It makes little difference to our investigation that Lawrence Dennis advocated fascism, or that John T. Flynn pursued laissez-faire economics. What these men had in common was that they stood outside the consensus, or the mainstream. In historical terms, they lost the battles they waged. How that affected them, and how they responded to developing events tells us much about what Americans were expected to believe and what concepts were regarded as subversive of the existing order. It means a rare opportunity to look at the alternatives. This may move us, in our current predicament, to think carefully about alternative possibilities.

5. William Appleman Williams, *The Contours of American History* (Chicago: Quadrangle Books, 1966), p. 19.
6. Ibid., pp. 19–20, 479.

In this case many of our subjects developed a courageous criticism of the prevailing ideology that America's domestic prosperity and well-being depended upon foreign expansion. Their particular solutions—and our agreement or disagreement—cannot take away from their break with the accepted view. The growth of an American empire was something they foresaw and rejected. Their roots lay in an older nonimperial America—a fact that was responsible for their political isolation as well as for their understanding of what new forces were changing the nation's contours. They called empire by its proper name and rejected its thrust—at a time when their contemporaries scarcely admitted its existence or when they were celebrating its growth as a logical and inevitable development.

These conservatives raised issues and defined problems that, as Williams described them, opened the way for liberals and leftist critics of a future epoch.[7] They offered theories to account for American expansionism; they warned against the erosion of congressional powers by the executive; they opposed military intervention abroad, and criticized what they candidly termed the emergence of American imperialism.

Their criticisms were ignored as Americans centered their attention on whether to enter the war against Nazi Germany, and they were soon branded as apologists for the Axis powers. Their voices stilled by patriotic fervor, they hoped to be heard once again in saner times. But such a time did not come. Even before the end of World War II, the emerging cold war with the Soviet Union demanded a new consensus against the spread of communism. The questions were even more difficult to raise.

It would be left to a later generation to raise them again. If we listen carefully to these individuals, omitting our well-worn ideologies and political biases, we will learn much from their journeys and courage. Whether we agree with all, some, or few of their particular judgments, we may be inspired to act more thoughtfully to reach viable alternatives to foreign adventure and interventionism.

7. William Appleman Williams, "The Critics of the American Empire Open a Door to Create an American Community," in W. A. Williams, ed. *From Colony to Empire* (New York: Wiley, 1972), p. 483.

Charles A. Beard (WIDE WORLD PHOTOS)

Charles A. Beard and American Foreign Policy

"BY ANY STANDARD," the late historian Howard K. Beale wrote, "Charles A. Beard ranks among the most significant historians of the first half of the twentieth century. Many loved him. Many hated him. No one could deny his importance."[1] And few would deny Beale's judgment. The author of thirty-three historical works, fourteen texts, and scores of articles and reviews, Beard was a titan among his fellow historians. He was a scholar who was willing to take history out of the classroom and to apply it to the problems of his own age, who sought to challenge traditional views and interpretations in all areas of history. He stressed social and economic development in an age when most writers centered their attention on institutional and political changes alone.

Beard began to gain prominence as he developed a pioneering emphasis upon the role of economics in the development of political and social change. Believing that men's actions and ideas derived from their economic interests, Beard set out to illustrate this theme in numerous works. In a series of lectures delivered at Amherst in 1916 and eventually published under the title *The Economic Basis of Politics,* Beard offered his basic argument.

"There is a vital relation," he told the Amherst students, "between the forms of state and the distribution of property, revolutions in the state being usually the results of contests over property." Different interests emerged in society around economics; there existed a landed interest, a shipping interest, a railway interest, and many others, all of which grew by necessity and divided into different classes whose members held different beliefs and views. The regulation of these different class interests,

1. Howard K. Beale, "Charles Beard: Historian," in Howard K. Beale, ed. *Charles A. Beard: An Appraisal* (Lexington: Univ. Press of Kentucky, 1954), p. 115.

according to Beard, became the main task of statesmen and political parties.[2]

Above all, it was Beard's book on the framing of the Constitution that became the focus of major controversy. Appearing during the age of Progressive reform (1913), Beard's *An Economic Interpretation of the Constitution* argued that the thrust for the Constitution derived from the upper classes, whose monetary investments had been adversely affected by the government existing under the Articles of Confederation. In particular, a new Constitution was favored by those who had money on loan, by owners of public securities, and by those with an interest in trade, shipping, and the development of manufactures. Those favoring the Constitution were men who had a direct personal stake in the outcome of a new convention. Those who participated in the Philadelphia Constitutional Convention were directly and personally interested in the economic advantages they would gain from a new governmental system.

The propertyless masses, moreover, were excluded from participation in that convention; the members were those directly interested, with an economic stake in its success. Ratification of the new Constitution excluded participation by three-fourths of adult males, who never voted. The Constitution itself was ratified by probably not more than one-sixth of the existing adult males. Thus, Beard concluded, the Constitution was not created by the whole American people, or by the states, but was "the work of a consolidated group whose interests knew no state boundaries and were truly national in scope."[3]

Since many in the Progressive reform movement saw the Constitution as a barrier to social and economic change, Beard's discussion was seen as an impetus toward breaking down an uncritical attitude toward the document. He had insinuated, after all, that the interest shown by the Founding Fathers in the new governmental system arose because they thought that securities

2. Charles A. Beard, *The Economic Basis of Politics* (New York: Knopf, 1922), pp. 62, 70.
3. Beard, *An Economic Interpretation of the Constitution of the United States* (New York: Macmillan, 1913), pp. 324–325.

they held would be better protected under the new system. Beard denied that he had undertaken the study to bolster the efforts of those seeking reform, though he did acknowledge that it had appeared "during the tumult of discussion that accompanied the advent of the Progressive party."[4]

To the present day, historians have debated, re-examined, and modified Beard's assessment of the formation of the Constitution. Beard's methodology and approach have been questioned, his conclusions challenged, and his very approach toward historical research criticized. But the attention given Beard's work in our most recent past is itself an indication of the impact and power which his work in the early part of our century still holds.[5]

It is not our purpose to once again traverse this much developed ground. Beard was eventually to create as much controversy in the area of his studies in U.S. foreign policy. Beard always insisted upon the interdependence of domestic and foreign affairs, and he rejected the commonly held belief that they could be separated into distinct compartments. It was Beard's belief, as we shall discover, that foreign policy developed as a result of the demands and necessities of domestic problems. Domestic events moved policy makers to action abroad. Many times in the nation's past, he would argue, a particular foreign policy emerged from the need felt by statesmen to escape the results of a seemingly insoluble domestic crisis.

Beard had at first been enthusiastic about World War I. But, as was true of many others of his generation, his positive outlook turned to despair. A number of prominent intellectual figures, Bernard Borning wrote, "came to share a common hatred of the war and distaste for the peace settlement that followed it. Disappointed that the war had not safeguarded democracy in the world, that the Russian Revolution was betraying the democratic

4. Beard, in the introduction to the 1935 edition of the book.
5. Some of the most noted critics of Beard are: Robert E. Brown, *Charles Beard and the Constitution* (Princeton, N.J.: Princeton Univ. Press, 1956); Forrest McDonald, *We the People: The Economic Origins of the Constitution* (Chicago: Univ. of Chicago Press, 1958); Lee Benson, *Turner and Beard* (New York: The Free Press, 1960), and Richard Hofstadter, *The Progressive Historians: Turner, Beard, Parrington* (New York: Knopf, 1968).

socialist cause, that Italy had bowed to a demagogue, that international relations appeared to be shaped more by sordid diplomacy and economic greed than by Wilsonian idealism, that Weimar Germany was in danger of slipping from her democratic moorings, and that the foreign policies and domestic politics of France, the United States and the other former Allies seemed to point toward another world catastrophe, numerous American intellectuals were beginning to turn inward and to recommend that America henceforth mind her own business."[6]

As a historian Beard became familiar with the work of Sidney B. Fay and Harry Elmer Barnes. These historians had cited the Allied powers' secret war treaties to attack the theory of exclusive German responsibility for the war, as well as to assert motives of aggrandizement on the part of the Allies. As the war ended, Beard was still convinced that American intervention had been necessary for the national interest. The balance of power that emerged had prevented any one nation from dominating the Continent.

In a short time, perhaps after Beard had traveled abroad in 1921, he began to develop a hope for an America that could remain insulated from the problems affecting Europe. He would later term the vision "continentalism": the belief that if Americans developed their own economy in a self-contained manner, they could "escape the huge burdens of military and naval expenditures necessary to defend trade and investments in all parts of the globe." "Relying upon an economy primarily self-supporting," Beard wrote further, "we cannot be shaken by the disasters of war or the coming revolt of the subject people of the earth against the arrogance of imperialists."[7]

Beard now began to see foreign investments as the source of U.S. overseas intervention. He suggested development of domestic programs that would divert the "surplus of plutocracy" to domestic use. Proposing larger income taxes, road, school, and electric-power development, Beard argued that such a domestic

6. Bernard C. Borning, *The Political and Social Thought of Charles A. Beard* (Seattle, Wash.: Univ. of Washington Press, 1962), p. 117.
7. Beard, "Agriculture in the Nation's Economy," *Nation,* Aug. 17, 1927, p. 150.

program "would reduce our chances of becoming mixed up in the next European adventure in Christian ballistics."[8] Americans had to learn to cultivate their own garden. Domestically, Beard toyed with plans for development of an American corporate state. Desiring administrative machinery that would allow control of the entire economy, Beard proposed a "Five-Year Plan for America." According to this concept, each industrial group would be organized into one unit through a holding company. The corporation formed would receive the status of a public utility and would be allowed to make limited profits. Coordinating the units would be a National Economic Council, which would represent the industries involved. The various antitrust acts would be repealed, and policies would be formulated by a Board of Strategy and Planning.[9]

Beard feared, however, that military interests favoring a big navy were pushing the nation in unwise directions. By 1932 he was arguing that secret plotting by these naval interests might increase the possibility of war. If they were left to make policy by themselves, the militarists would extend America's "strategic frontiers" to the moon.[10] Beard supported Herbert Hoover's definition of national defense: the armed forces existed only to prevent an invasion of the mainland. The armed forces had to protect the nation's continental heritage, not move to defend the American dollar wherever it happened to be threatened.[11]

When Franklin D. Roosevelt was elected to the Presidency Beard hoped that the nation would follow his plans for a self-contained economic course and build a corporatist society that would avoid war by the limiting of foreign entanglements. FDR had been scheduled to participate in the London Economic Conference of 1933, an international meeting meant to stabilize

8. Quoted in Warren I. Cohen, *The American Revisionists: The Lessons of Intervention in World War I* (Chicago: Univ. of Chicago Press, 1967), p. 99.

9. Beard, "A 'Five-Year Plan' for America," *Forum* (June 1934), pp. 332–334; cf. George Soule, "Beard and the Concept of Planning," in Beale, ed. *Beard: An Appraisal,* pp. 65–66.

10. Beard, "Big Navy Boys," *New Republic,* Jan. 20–Feb. 3, 1932, pp. 258–262, 287–291, 314–318.

11. *New York Times,* Feb. 28, 1932, Sec. II, p. 4.

currencies and raise prices. Roosevelt torpedoed the conference, and Beard expressed satisfaction with the President's decision to concentrate on developing a sound internal economic system. FDR's action led Beard to believe that the President sought recovery through a bold domestic reconstruction program, not through foreign trade, investments, and international currency agreements.

The Idea of National Interest summed up different views of the national interest. Beard pointed to a new doctrine that had emerged in the Republican 1920s: "Free opportunity for expansion in foreign markets is indispensable to the prosperity of American business." Diplomacy had become tied to the needs of foreign commerce. Its new chief concern was the "promotion of economic interests abroad." The imperial thrust of the Republican twenties was the use of dollar diplomacy, through which the national interest was to be attained.[12]

Beard had reached the conclusion that the United States had become involved in the First World War because of the activity and influence of commercial interests. These interests were separate from and often contrary to the national interest. The latter could not be narrowly tied to the private concerns of a few special economic interests. Franklin D. Roosevelt, Beard then thought, would act to protect the true national interest of the country. The President's conception was not linked to "the implications of empire or to any duty owed by the United States to 'benighted peoples.'" FDR's solutions to domestic problems were intranational. The Democrats were acting like true Jeffersonians, like those in the nation's past who had emphasized the "national" in national interest and were "essentially isolationist in outlook." The way of life favored by Thomas Jefferson was still a "living and vital force" to those in the new administration.[13]

Beard meant his book on the national interest to serve as an objective study of emerging policy. In his next book, *The Open*

12. Beard, *The Idea of National Interest* (New York: Macmillan, 1934), pp. 87, 107.
13. Ibid., pp. 526–529; see also Cohen, *American Revisionists,* pp. 130–134.

Door at Home, Beard tried to set forth proposals that would advance the national interest. He attacked the belief that the United States had an exportable economic surplus that was pushing it into imperial expansion. He rejected the arguments of those who favored solving domestic problems by adoption of external solutions, be they new foreign loans, increase of armaments, or ideologies irrelevant to the United States, such as communism or fascism. Rather, Beard believed, Americans had to devise means to realize a good society within their own borders. The very title Beard chose suggested historical irony. The Open Door Notes had been issued by Secretary of State John Hay in 1899–1900 as a diplomatic device to announce the American decision to seek an open door to the commerce and markets of China on a basis of equality with other foreign powers. They signified the desirability of commercial expansion, which had become a necessity in order to find markets for the surplus of industrial and agricultural production. Rejecting the attitudes that originally led to issuance of the Notes, Beard simply asserted that the only door to be opened was at home.

What Beard desired was a system of centralized control that would allow the United States to develop by its own resources and that would reduce dependence on foreign trade and commerce. Because America was geographically isolated, it could remain protected with an army that was capable of defending the western hemisphere. "The one policy that is possible under a conception which makes the American nation the center of interest and affection," Beard explained, "is policy based on security of life for the American people in their present geographical home." To give up this position "for a mess of pottage in the form of profits on cotton goods, tobacco, petroleum and automobiles, is to make great policy subservient to special interest, betray the security of the American nation, and prove that we 'deserve to be slaves.' "[14]

If the domestic economy could not absorb what the nation produced, the search for foreign markets could lead to the very type of entanglements and conflicts that might threaten war. He

14. Beard, *The Open Door at Home* (New York: Macmillan, 1935), pp. 261, 267.

preferred to build a society on the model of the older self-contained agricultural community. He brooded about a society that would be based on "manipulation of business" and that would produce a group of urban proletarians trained in "narrow mechanical specialties likely to be destroyed at any time by new inventions." Great wealth would accumulate in the hands of directing classes, a group that would not have the very leadership qualities needed to create a successful community. Even if it was possible, the policy of an open door was "undesirable in terms of consequences."[15]

When Beard wrote *The Open Door at Home* he still thought that the Roosevelt administration was going to create, through its programs of reform, the type of society he advocated. Clues soon began to appear that led Beard to realize that this was not to be the case. Rejecting Beard's chosen path, Secretary of Agriculture Henry A. Wallace responded that a "clear-cut program of planned international trade or barter would be far less likely to get us into war" than various attempts to isolate the American continent. Expressing astonishment that Beard had become an isolationist, Wallace stated bluntly his reasons for opposing Beard's proposals for a corporate state. "Those in the midst of business and political affairs," Wallace argued, could not afford the time needed or arrange the extensive financing that would be required to institute the changes Beard had suggested.[16]

Events in the nation, more than negative responses to his own proposals, began to suggest to Beard that Americans might once again seek recourse from domestic turmoil through the waging of foreign war. Diplomatic conflict with Japan and signs of new economic recession gave grounds for worry. In February of 1935 Beard speculated that war might occur because of domestic causes. Twice before in the nation's past the political party of wealth had been defeated at the polls—by Jefferson in 1800 and

15. Ibid., p. 69.
16. Henry A. Wallace, *America Must Choose* (Boston: Foreign Policy Association and World Peace Foundation, 1934), p. 2, and "Beard: The Planner," *New Republic*, Jan. 2, 1935, pp. 225–226. Cf. Lloyd C. Gardner, *Economic Aspects of New Deal Diplomacy* (Madison, Wis.: Univ. of Wisconsin Press, 1964), pp. 9–10, 95–96.

by Andrew Jackson in 1828. But both times victory had been
reversed by war and the movement of business enterprise. The
War of 1812 undercut Jeffersonian democracy. Later, Jacksonian
measures had been shattered by the Civil War, as the nation
adopted policies originally opposed by the Jacksonians. And
when Democratic reformers won with Wilson, the First World
War destroyed their chances and led to new success for the
political party of business.

Beard believed that the Depression would continue and
worsen. The Democrats, he held, would not deal effectively with
it by radical measures, such as nationalization of the banks. Even
if the Depression came to an end, the extreme concentration of
wealth would reach a new high point. Instead of further domestic
reform, the administration would probably respond much as had
the nation's past leaders. Instead of further reorganization of the
domestic economy, economic chaos would culminate in a new
foreign war. Franklin D. Roosevelt's support to a big navy
program led Beard to believe that the President would opt for
war. Beard emphasized that he did not mean to claim "that
President Roosevelt will deliberately plunge the country into a
Pacific war in his efforts to escape the economic crisis. There will
be an 'incident,' a 'provocation.' Incidents and provocations
are of almost daily occurrence. Any government can quickly
magnify one of them into a 'just cause for war.' Confronted by
the difficulties of a deepening domestic crisis and by the compara-
tive ease of a foreign war, what will President Roosevelt do?
Judging by the past history of American politicians, he will choose
the latter, or, perhaps it would be more accurate to say, amid
powerful conflicting emotions he will 'stumble into' the latter.
The Jeffersonian party gave the nation the War of 1812, the
Mexican War, and its participation in the World War. The Pacific
War awaits."[17]

Seven years before Pearl Harbor, Beard had formulated an
eventual thesis regarding the origins of the Pacific war, an analysis that mainstream historians found hard to accept. To Richard
Hofstadter it meant that Beard argued that "the United States

17. Beard, "National Politics and War," *Scribner's* (Feb. 1935), p. 70.

goes to war not in response . . . to anything other nations do; it goes to war as part of its own cycle of domestic politics, because statesmen who prefer strong foreign policy to strong domestic policy seek war, or at least seek the conditions under which they can stumble into war."[18] Beard, however, was not denying that other nations had imperial ambitions; he was simply saying that America's imperial interests in the Pacific might well lead to conflict with Japan.

Ever concerned that economic necessity would push the nation to war, Beard wanted the nation to move toward war only for a "grand national and human advantage openly discussed and deliberately arrived at," not as a result of a decision meant to bail out capitalists or to rescue politicians incapable of dealing with domestic crisis.[19] Beard was fully aware of "the growing intransigence of Japan on the Asiatic mainland." But the pressures of private greed would require more than diplomatic formulas to avoid the arrival of war. It would require "the sacrifice of immediate special interests."[20]

Beard, like many others, was influenced by the shocking revelations that came out of the Senate hearings, conducted by Senator Gerald Nye in the fall of 1934, on the origins of American intervention in World War I. Nye's committee, as Manfred Jonas notes, combed through State Department files and unearthed "documents that had passed between President Wilson, Colonel [Edward M.] House, Secretary of State [Robert] Lansing, and Secretary of the Treasury William Gibbs McAdoo. These documents seemed to show that concern for America's domestic situation led to the lifting of the ban on credits to belligerents in 1915, to the increasing identification of the United States with the Allied cause, and finally, to the declaration of war itself. When collated with documents taken from the files of J. P. Morgan and Company, and other financial institutions . . . this evidence seemed to prove to Nye and the other investigators that

18. Hofstadter, *Progressive Historians,* p. 328.
19. Beard, *The Devil Theory of War* (New York: Vanguard, 1936), p. 124.
20. Beard, "Keeping America Out of War," *Current History* (Dec. 1935), p. 292.

the United States had been pushed into the First World War by the pressure of greedy bankers on vacillating politicians."[21]

This evidence reinforced Beard's opinions about the economic background of the war's outbreak. In a series of articles prepared for the *New Republic,* and later expanded into book form, Beard set out to prove that "war is not the work of a demon. It is our very own work, for which we prepare wittingly or not, in ways of peace. But most of us sit blindfold at the preparation."[22]

The Devil Theory of War, which Richard Hofstadter called a "tortured little book," was actually a work of popular history. It revealed a Charles Beard who was seeking to reach as wide an audience as possible, a historian seeking to inform the populace of the circumstances that led the nation into war. Citing the Nye Committee, Beard singled out pressures put upon the Wilson administration by American bankers to lift the embargo on loans and to underwrite an Allied victory. Hofstadter, as well as historians Manfred Jonas and Warren Cohen, have argued that Beard "contributed greatly to fixing the onus of guilt on the already suspected parties. It thus has the effect of advertising, rather than refuting, the devil theory."[23] A careful reading of Beard's short book, however, reveals that Beard did not argue on behalf of Nye's vulgar economic determinism.

The determinists contended that the United States had entered the war because it had succumbed to the pressure exerted by investment bankers and munitions makers. Beard's argument was more subtle. He criticized the old Wilsonian view that Germany's unrestricted U-boat warfare caused the U.S. declaration of war. But his rejection of the official administration position did not mean, as Jonas claims, that Beard "strengthened the case of those who placed full blame for American involvement in the First World War on bankers and businessmen."[24]

What Beard did was to place the decision to move toward war (after the resumption of submarine warfare by Germany) within

21. Manfred Jonas, *Isolationism in America, 1935–1941* (Ithaca, N.Y.: Cornell Univ. Press, 1966), pp. 145–146.

22. Beard, *The Devil Theory of War,* p. 29.

23. Hofstadter, *Progressive Historians,* p. 332; Jonas, *Isolationism in America,* p. 153; Cohen, *American Revisionists,* pp. 181–182.

24. Jonas, *Isolationism in America,* p. 153.

the context of over-all American economic diplomacy. He printed Secretary of the Treasury William McAdoo's warning to Woodrow Wilson that American prosperity would dry up if the Allies could not borrow money to pay the United States for their purchases. But it was clear to Beard that the desire of McAdoo and Secretary of State Lansing to reverse the ban on credits was *not* due simply to any kowtowing to the bankers. In their own eyes, as Lansing had put it, former Secretary of State William J. Bryan's conception of the "true spirit of neutrality," which forbade monetary loans to the Allies, stood in the way of America's true "national interests, which seem to be seriously threatened."[25]

Beard understood that American prosperity was indeed tied to the success of Allied war orders; the domestic well-being and prosperity of the American people depended upon continued and growing foreign trade with and exports to the Allies. But once loans were floated, enabling the Allies to pay for the American goods they purchased, the fate of Americans would be tied up with Allied fate on the battlefield. "If the war stopped, American business would slow down from prosperity to dullness, if not calamity. If the Allies were defeated, things would be worse. American millions were at stake."[26]

Rather than risk economic collapse, Wilson had allowed the United States to become entangled in the Allied cause. Renewal of unrestricted submarine warfare had not brought about intervention; it had been the precipitating catalyst. It was only "one of the events that may have predisposed President Wilson in the direction of war." The German submarines had "smashed into the 'profitable' business which the American bankers and traders had built up with the Allies." Beard quoted testimony given by Woodrow Wilson to the Senate Foreign Relations Committee in 1919 in which Wilson admitted that even if Germany had not committed any act of aggression, the United States would have become a belligerent. All that Americans knew, Beard emphasized, was that the actions of the bankers and politicians had

25. Beard, *The Devil Theory of War,* p. 87, quoting Lansing to Woodrow Wilson, Sept. 6, 1915.
26. Ibid., p. 90.

been carried out secretly, without the knowledge of the people or Congress, and that their operations "helped to entangle the fate of American economy in the fate of the Allied belligerents."[27]

The American intervention only postponed the Great Depression for ten years, a fact that was proof to Beard that the Allied cause did not serve the American national interest. It had cost one hundred billion dollars and one hundred thousand lives. Yet it had kept the economy in shape for only a brief duration. In the 1930s Beard supported mandatory neutrality, including an embargo on the sale of munitions and extension of credit to any belligerent nations.

Beard's investigation as to why intervention had occurred led him to stress economic involvement with the Allies, an involvement that developed because of the necessities of American capitalism to obtain export markets. Beard did not shrink from the conclusion that, in order to avoid any possible future involvement, changes might be necessary in the social structure of the capitalist economy. Republicans in the 1890s had tried to make the United States into an imperialist sea power and had plunged the nation into combat with Asian and European imperialism. Quoting Major General Smedley Butler, who had stated that the Republican policy was a "plain capitalist racket," Beard asked that the "racket" be abandoned once and for all:

> Having rejected the imperialist "racket" and entertaining doubts about our ability to make peace and goodness prevail in Europe and Asia, I think we should concentrate our attention on tilling our own garden . . . Tilling it properly doubtless involves many drastic changes in capitalism as historically practiced. Well, with all due respect to the enterprise and virtues of capitalism, I never regarded that "system" as sacred, unchanging and unchangeable. I should certainly prefer any changes that may be required in it to the frightful prospects of American participation in a war in Europe or Asia.[28]

He called for changes in the domestic economy that would diminish pressure to sell goods abroad to belligerent powers.

27. Ibid., pp. 98–103.
28. Ibid., pp. 120–121.

Rather than allow capitalism to lead to war, Beard preferred federal regulation that would allow the United States to extricate itself from the type of trade that would produce involvement in war. If a surplus of products existed, it should not be sold to warring nations. In a flourish of rhetoric unusual for Beard he suggested giving surplus "goods to hungry Americans rather than to fighting Europeans."[29]

Beard's advocacy of mandatory neutrality did not mean blanket approval of American foreign policy or support for total isolation. When the Spanish Civil War broke out, Beard was close to liberal and radical isolationists, who "despite their avowed indifference to foreign quarrels . . . could not fail to see a moral issue in a conflict so clearly pitting Fascists against Socialists." An embargo on arms to Spain meant aid to General Franco's rebel army. A proper interpretation of international law permitted us to continue commercial relations with the legally elected Republican government of Spain, and to bar trade with the fascist forces that sought its overthrow.[30] If neutrality was applied to the Spanish situation, both sides in Spain would be in the same legal position, and Franco's forces would be implicitly granted recognition. Franco was getting supplies from Germany and Italy, and the Loyalists were short of strategic armaments. If the Roosevelt administration applied the Neutrality Act to Spain, the legal government would lose the right to purchase arms. Thus, as Jonas writes, "the Spanish situation presented itself to them as an attack by forces of which they disapproved on a government controlled by men whose political views they shared. The liberals and radicals among the isolationists were torn . . . between their desire to keep America unentangled and their fervent hope that nothing would be done by the United States that would be disadvantageous to the Loyalists."[31] Beard shared the views of these antifascist isolationists.

29. Ibid., pp. 121–123.
30. Jonas, *Isolationism in America*, p. 184.
31. Ibid., p. 186; cf. Beard, "Will Roosevelt Keep Us Out of War?" *Events*, II (July 1937), pp. 2–6. Neutrality had been applied to a civil war, Beard wrote, "without any justification in terms of peril to American interests."

By July 1937 the Japanese had begun their military effort to overrun and dominate China. Roosevelt did not apply the Neutrality Act to the Sino-Japanese conflict, in the hope that that would aid China. In mid-August, after the Japanese had threatened Shanghai, the United States appealed to both China and Japan to make it an open city. Expressing his "hearty appreciation" of the government's policy, perhaps because he thought that a show of restraint by the Roosevelt administration required a great deal of encouragement, Beard cabled the President that his action in the Far East had opened "a grand epoch in American diplomacy."[32]

Beard may have been engaging in wishful thinking, or he may have been merely trying to let the President know what direction Beard thought he should pursue. But Roosevelt's action was temporary. The President was soon to pursue another path. Roosevelt's "quarantine the aggressors" speech in October hinted at a future policy provocative toward Japan. The President shortly thereafter opposed the Ludlow resolution, which called for a constitutional amendment that would require a national referendum on war. By February of 1938, in a printed debate with Communist party chief Earl Browder, Beard opposed the policy of collective security. The Communists, in the period before the signing of the Nazi-Soviet Nonaggression Pact, supported the President's sympathetic attitude toward collective security.

Beard argued that in the event of war against Germany, Italy, or Japan, collective security would not serve as a guarantee of democratic advance. Asking his readers to examine both the Treaty of Versailles and the state of democracy twenty years after the great war's end, Beard noted that he failed to understand how any intelligent person who had looked seriously at the fruits of the last war could see a hope for democracy in the waging of military crusades. War might bring business recovery, but it would undoubtedly be followed by collapse of the economy. The probable end result, he thought, was that America

32. Beard to Roosevelt, Aug. 18, 1937, quoted in Cohen, *American Revisionists,* p. 191.

would find itself with "universal fascism rather than universal democracy."[33]

Appearing a few days later before the House Foreign Affairs Committee, Beard told congressmen that "the Orient from Siberia to Singapore is not worth the bones of one American soldier." Americans, he argued, were "a great and intelligent people, but they aren't smart enough to solve the problems of Europe which are encrusted in the blood rust of fifty centuries of warfare."[34]

By April 1939 Beard was advocating passage of firm neutrality laws. Interventionists wanted the existing Neutrality Act revised to give the President more discretionary power. Beard, to the contrary, desired less rather than more discretion. A tighter neutrality law would merely limit the President's ability to secretly take the nation into war, as Woodrow Wilson had done between 1914 and 1917.[35] Beard had evidently decided that the decision to move toward war had taken place. He now felt so strongly about his position that he bluntly asserted that the United States should stay out of the next European war and any that might follow it. The United States could not take on the job of suppressing all opponents of peace in the world.[36]

Beard rejected such responsibility. There was a threat from Germany and Italy, but the other European nations outnumbered them in population three to one, and were superior in armed forces and material. And, crucially, these nations were not fighting for democracy: France and Italy were quarreling "over the spoils of empire in Africa"; the Tory government in Britain wanted "to let Hitler liquidate Soviet Russia." It was imperial conflicts that were preventing these nations from uniting against Hitler. Beard concluded that the job of preventing German and Italian domination in Europe was that of the powers in Europe.

33. "Collective Security—A Debate," *New Republic,* Feb. 2, 1938, p. 358.
34. *New York Times,* Feb. 11, 1938, p. 14.
35. Beard, "Neutrality: Shall We Have Revision?" *New Republic,* Jan. 8, 1939, p. 308.
36. Beard, "We're Blundering Into War," *American Mercury* (April 1939), pp. 388, 395.

Had they the will, they had the men, money, and materials needed to carry out the job.[37]

Another European war would disturb the economy, but Beard insisted that domestic measures to increase production would be preferable to a search for export markets that would lead to war. The strains of neutrality would "scarcely equal the cost, dislocations and explosions inevitably associated with participation in a European war." The only reason why America might move to war is that war is a godsend to politicians and businessmen who are baffled by the continuation of the economic crisis.[38]

In Europe and Asia many would fight the next war under the banners of social revolution. Would these revolutions, Beard asked, be to the liking of U.S. policy makers? Beard reminded his readers of the farcical American intervention against the young Soviet nation at Archangel in 1918. The U.S. troops sent to Russia fraternized with the Bolsheviks, and the expedition came to naught. It was simply folly to pursue a policy based on underwriting Britain and France.[39]

That same year, 1939, Beard published a short pamphlet intended for a popular audience, *Giddy Minds and Foreign Quarrels*. In it he attacked the type of American interventionism abroad that had become a perpetual adventure meant to subdue the wicked in other nations. The policy had first been developed by imperialists who saw expansion as a means of curbing domestic unrest and populism, a means of restoring domestic tranquillity and getting the nation in working order.[40]

In the 1920s Republican policy makers had joined the old Roosevelt-Lodge imperialism in the Far East and Near East and had turned the government "into a big drumming agency for pushing the sale of goods and the lending of money abroad, and they talked vociferously about the open door everywhere except at home." At the same time they verbally scolded the Soviet Union and sent marines to the Caribbean.[41]

37. Ibid., pp. 392–393.
38. Ibid., pp. 396–397.
39. Ibid., p. 399.
40. Beard, *Giddy Minds and Foreign Quarrels: An Estimate of American Foreign Policy* (New York: Macmillan, 1939), pp. 13–17.
41. Ibid., p. 26.

With the Great Depression America faced a new crisis. Foreign bonds went into default and pump priming took place at the expense of American investors. Roosevelt had at first promised to move the nation away from economic collapse by a New Deal and reforms. But he slowly moved in the direction of interventionism, and now he was seeking to deal with Europe and Asia "as if he were arbiter of international relations and commissioned to set the world aright." In Latin America the New Deal had modified traditional imperial tactics. Public money was to be used to revive the trade which had collapsed when private lending failed, and the administration was trying to line up Latin American governments on the side of the American military. This was a reaction to the attempts by Germany and Italy to enter the South American market.[42]

Beard contended that trade between the United States and China was insignificant and of no vital importance to the United States. Yet the Roosevelt administration continued to pursue the old Republican imperial policy of the Open Door in China—an attempt to gain control of the Chinese market through an open door for commerce and trade. The policy had always been a delusion, yet the Roosevelt administration still sought its implementation. After the Japanese invasion of China the administration tried to cause a national sensation, and at the same time it refused to apply the munitions embargo to the belligerents. Americans were making fortunes selling Japan munitions and raw materials of war—a practice permitted because the United States was in a depression and trade is good for American business.[43]

Beard charged that the administration had shifted its attention to foreign policy in 1936. The Democratic platform promised neutrality and avoidance of war; yet shortly thereafter Roosevelt violated neutrality in Spain by enforcing a munitions embargo which aided the fascist powers. The various measures taken by the Roosevelt administration all proved to Beard's satisfaction that the President expected war in the near future: endorsement of collective security, the call to quarantine the aggressors, the

42. Ibid., pp. 28–32.
43. Ibid., pp. 38–42.

demand to Congress for increased armaments and an increase in naval expenditures. The call for more arms in particular indicated to Beard that Roosevelt sought to wage a holy war, even though he had approved of Munich and had allowed the destruction of Republican Spain. FDR sought to throw the whole weight of the nation on the side of Britain and France, ostensibly through all measures short of war. But these, Beard concluded, would only lead the United States into a full belligerent role.[44]

Beard had already requested that Senator William Borah—a man Beard regarded as having rendered long service in trying to keep the United States neutral—take steps to institute a congressional inquiry into what forces lay behind the development of U.S. foreign policy. Such an inquiry would establish who was developing "quarantine" policy and why.[45]

He had failed to persuade the Congress to hold such hearings. *Giddy Minds and Foreign Quarrels* was his own one-man study and his own appraisal of why the Roosevelt administration had adopted an interventionist position. He rejected world pacification and proposed instead a policy of continental defense based upon the understanding that no amount of foreign trade could set American industries in motion or raise the nation from the depths of depression. The basis of American life was "production and distribution in the United States and the way out of the present economic morass lies in the acceleration of this production and distribution at home, by domestic measures."[46]

Beard refuted the industrialists' argument that foreign trade was centrally important, that though most commodities produced were not intended mainly for the foreign market, that market represented the crucial margin of difference between prosperity and depression.

In 1940 German troops attacked Norway and Denmark, the Netherlands, Belgium, and Luxembourg. These events did not change Beard's mind. In May he published *A Foreign Policy for America,* in which he elaborated the theme of the limitations of

44. Ibid., pp. 48–49, 53, 57.
45. Beard to Borah, Feb. 15, 1938, William E. Borah MSS., Box 417, Library of Congress, Wash., D.C.
46. Beard, *Giddy Minds and Foreign Quarrels,* p. 70.

U.S. power.[47] When Franklin Roosevelt arranged secretly the exchange of American destroyers for British bases, Beard declared his support to the America First Committee—the major umbrella organization of both radical and conservative noninterventionists. The group, he announced, consisted of people who were not simplistic isolationists, appeasers, supporters of foreign powers, or pacifists. Its only goal was to have U.S. policy directed toward preserving peace by concentrating upon development within the American continent, including defense of that zone.[48]

Roosevelt's policy, Beard had long before concluded, would lead to war. "So much was made known through the press in 1941," Beard told Oswald Garrison Villard in 1946, "that I was then convinced that the President was definitely seeking a war (an attack) in the Atlantic. His application of sanctions to Japan was publicly announced and as I have always believed that such sanctions so applied would end in war I was convinced that he was seeking war in the Pacific also."[49]

Beard began to collect material that would prove the President was actively seeking war. In 1941 he suspected that each move to give Roosevelt more discretionary power was a maneuver to bring the nation closer to war. Supporters of intervention were rallying on behalf of the proposed Lend-Lease Act, meant to provide munitions and aid to the embattled Allies. Beard appeared before the Senate Foreign Relations Committee to testify in opposition. The measure would give the President life-and-death power over the lives of Americans, and would hand over congressional authority to declare war to the executive branch of government. It was a measure for waging undeclared war. The United States was not going to send ships and munitions provided by the act to sea and then allow them to be exposed and to stand at the mercy of German submarines. "They will be convoyed," Beard predicted; "the convoys will be attacked by German planes and submarines. Then what? Are we not in the war?"[50]

47. Beard, *A Foreign Policy for America* (New York: Knopf, 1940).
48. *New York Times,* Sept. 9, 1940, p. 7.
49. Beard to Villard, April 15, 1946, Oswald Garrison Villard MSS., Houghton Library, Harvard Univ., Cambridge, Mass.
50. *New York Times,* Feb. 5, 1941, p. 10.

With Pearl Harbor, Beard's effort to keep the country out of war had failed. As his correspondence and the body of his writing indicate, he did not view the attack as an ill-conceived, desperate act of unprovoked aggression. Like other revisionists, Beard judged the attack to be the end to which Japan had been driven by intransigent American diplomacy based on the illusions of the Open Door. He thought that the United States government had maneuvered Japan into starting that Pacific war, and he vowed to devote his energies to finding out how it had been accomplished.

A tentative answer appeared in 1946, with publication of Beard's *American Foreign Policy in the Making*. After 1937, Beard argued, Franklin D. Roosevelt had changed his approach and had begun to look abroad for solutions to America's unresolved domestic maladies. The "quarantine" speech symbolized the abandonment of neutrality and the endorsement of collective security. Outside of a temporary retreat for political reasons, Roosevelt had not worked for peace, in spite of continued assurances that he did not favor war.[51]

Notwithstanding his doubts, Beard supported the war effort. What he opposed was the methods used by Roosevelt to bring the nation into war and the New Deal's messianic impulse to reform the entire world. Beard understood the crucial difference between World War I and World War II. "Personally," he wrote in 1943, "I am in favor of pushing the war against Germany, Japan and Italy to a successful conclusion. Whether it is righteous in the sight of God I leave to our theologians."[52]

Supporting the war effort did not mean that one had to close one's eyes to the questions that remained as to the origins, purposes, and effects of the conflict. He felt it was his duty to confront these questions both as citizen and as historian. Future generations should be spared a repetition. The effort to apply the lessons of the war to end all wars had proved futile. Perhaps future generations would learn a better lesson from examining the events leading up to World War II.

51. Beard, *American Foreign Policy in the Making, 1932–1940* (New Haven, Conn.: Yale Univ. Press, 1946).
52. Beard, *The Republic* (New York: Viking, 1943), p. 300.

Dr. Charles A. Beard, with his wife seated beside him, appearing before the Senate Foreign Relations Committee, February 4, 1941, asks rejection of the Lend-Lease Bill. (WIDE WORLD PHOTOS)

Charles A. Beard:
World War II Revisionist

PERHAPS NO OTHER figure in the historical profession has been treated so unfairly as Charles A. Beard, as a result of his critique of U.S. foreign policy. His later works deteriorated, his critics charged, as he became increasingly identified with isolationism. His work, Richard Hofstadter wrote, revealed an "abandonment of objectivity that can be seen in his impassioned vendetta against the foreign policies of Franklin D. Roosevelt."[1]

This charge had first been voiced in 1944 by Lewis Mumford, who wrote that as "an advocate of national isolation," Beard had become an active abettor of "tyranny, sadism, and human defilement," searching for a way "of reconciling his isolationism with the fact that history has already proved it false in its premises."[2] Beard, Mumford privately argued, had deliberately "suppressed the case for the democracies" and had favorably described "the case for our fascist enemies." His "bias in politics" had undermined his scholarship, Mumford concluded, and Beard had "forfeited completely all respect in his chosen vocation."[3]

1. Richard Hofstadter, *The Progressive Historians: Turner, Beard, Parrington* (New York: Knopf, 1968), p. 316.
2. Lewis Mumford, "Mr. Beard and His 'Basic History,'" *Saturday Review,* Dec. 2, 1944, p. 27.
3. Mumford to Van Wyck Brooks, Nov. 26, 1947, in Robert S. Spiller, ed. *The Van Wyck Brooks-Lewis Mumford Letters: The Record of a Literary Friendship, 1921–1963* (New York: Dutton, 1970), pp. 320–321. Mumford's hostility toward Beard led to a temporary estrangement from his longtime friend Van Wyck Brooks. The issue causing a break was the decision of the Institute of Arts and Letters to award its medal of distinction to Beard. Mumford resigned in protest; Brooks appeared to present the medal to Beard. See letters on pp. 273–274, 321–328, and 333–336 of Spiller's book. Mumford believed that "without being either a traitor or fascist himself, Beard has served the purposes of traitors and fascists, by his manner of presenting and warping the evidence, in supposedly objective works on American history." Open fascists were less dangerous, "for they openly believed in fascism, while Beard's method was to give it the utmost benefit of the doubt while he insidiously attacked from the rear all who were pre-

After the appearance of Beard's last book, *President Roosevelt and the Coming of the War, 1941,* the counterattack was launched by Admiral Samuel Eliot Morison, who accused Beard of a lack of objectivity and of contradictions in his outlook. Since 1898, Morison wrote, Beard "has detested war and has done his best to ignore war, to minimize its results and to deride military men." This posed a problem, since "American liberty, union and civilization would never have been unless men had been willing to fight for them."[4] The implication that Beard's personal hostility to war made it impossible for him to accept war in defense of vital American interests did not, however, engage Beard's judgment concerning the essential inhumanity of war and his belief that waging war damaged the moral fiber of the nation—even when it was necessary.

Because Beard desired "a socialized, collectivist state in isolation," Morison charged, he "was trying to show that Roosevelt dragged the nation into an unnecessary war." If future readers looked only at Beard's book, they "would have to infer that a dim figure named Hitler was engaged in a limited sort of war to redress the lost balance of Versailles; that Japan was a virtuous nation pursuing its legitimate interest in Asia; and that neither threatened or even wished to interfere with any legitimate American interest."[5]

Hofstadter's 1968 assessment was more charitable, but he also agreed that Beard failed to acknowledge the military threat from the fascist powers. Hofstadter accepted Beard's charge that FDR's leadership was "undeniably devious," but he attributed this not to Roosevelt's "Caesaristic aspirations" but to the difficulties he encountered confronting the force and initiative of Germany and Italy.[6]

---

pared . . . to resist fascism" (Mumford to Brooks, Dec. 3, 1947, ibid., p. 325).

Others who turned against Beard included Dean Christian Gauss of Princeton University, Frank Mather, Allen Nevins, and Henry Seidel Canby. See Brooks to Mumford, May 1, 1940, ibid., p. 333.

4. Samuel Eliot Morison, "Did Roosevelt Start the War? History Through a Beard," *Atlantic Monthly,* CLXXXII, No. 2 (Aug. 1948), p. 92.

5. Ibid., pp. 93–94.

6. Hofstadter, *Progressive Historians,* p. 338.

These attacks were wide of the mark. *Beard did not deny the expansionist nature of the fascist powers. His heresy was that he did not exclude the United States from similar charges.* Unlike mainstream historians, Beard did not view the United States as unique, as a nation uninterested in power and concerned only with attainment of peace and justice, playing a world role only when forced to respond to aggression by other nations.

What Beard stressed was the interdependence of domestic and foreign policy, the process of empire building, the inability of relying upon foreign expansion as a method for solving domestic problems. He opposed and criticized the methods used by Franklin D. Roosevelt to bring the nation to war, as well as the impulse of many New Dealers to make the world over. The methods used by the New Deal to solve the domestic crisis would only deepen it in the long run, and the deceptive methods engaged in by Roosevelt would only further undermine democratic ethics and attitudes.[7]

What Beard raised for discussion was the character of America's leadership—a leadership that showed so little confidence in its citizens that it preferred to lie about the issue of war and peace. Beard challenged the policies of deception undertaken by the executive, destined to bring the nation into a state of war against an unpopular enemy. Because the enemy was Hitler's Germany, most Americans, including American historians, proved unwilling or unable to examine Beard's arguments carefully.

Beard did not concentrate on the evils of the Nazi system—he assumed most Americans did not want a fascist system—but on the disintegration of the institutions that made American democracy strong. The one essential difference between American democracy and totalitarianism was that the Constitution did not "vest in the Congress or the President illimitable power secretly to determine the ends of the government in foreign or domestic affairs and secretly to choose and employ any means deemed desirable by either branch of the government to achieve those

7. See the discussion of Beard's foreign policy by William Appleman Williams, "Charles Austin Beard: The Intellectual as Tory-Radical," in Harvey Goldberg, ed. *American Radicals: Some Problems and Personalities* (New York: Monthly Review Press, 1957), pp. 305–307.

ends." The conduct of foreign affairs was subject "to the Constitution, the laws, and the democratic prescriptions essential to the American system of government."[8]

Policies pursued by Franklin D. Roosevelt, Beard charged, violated this basic constitutional tenet. While promising to maintain America at peace, Roosevelt privately exchanged American destroyers for British bases in the Caribbean and Newfoundland in September 1940; Lend-Lease aid was enacted in March 1941; secret American-British military staff talks were held in January–March 1941; naval patrols to report the presence of German subs to British warships were inaugurated in the Atlantic in April 1941; the Atlantic Conference was held between Roosevelt and Churchill from August 9–12, 1941; orders to American ships to shoot German subs on sight were announced on September 11, 1941; merchant ships were armed and sent into the war zones in November 1941; a series of major steps toward war in Asia began with the freezing of Japanese assets in the United States on July 25, 1941, amounting to a commercial blockade of Japan.[9]

It was clear that these acts could have but one effect—to bring the United States closer to military participation in the European war. Yet Roosevelt was constantly asserting that his goal was to keep out of the conflict. The lack of executive candor, the use of deceit by the President, was utterly reprehensible as well as unconstitutional.

Most of Roosevelt's defenders admit his duplicity, but they argue that he had to take secret measures that would have been blocked by an inexperienced and gullible populace whose isolationist sentiments did not allow the United States to play its proper role in the world. This justification was most boldly stated by the diplomatic historian Thomas A. Bailey. Bailey admitted that Roosevelt had deceived the American public before the Pearl Harbor attack. But, Bailey wrote, FDR was acting like "the physician who must tell the patient lies for the patient's own

8. Charles A. Beard, *President Roosevelt and the Coming of the War, 1941* (New Haven, Conn.: Yale Univ. Press, 1948), pp. 581–582.

9. Although most of these charges first appeared in Beard's book, they are neatly summed up by William Henry Chamberlain, "The Bankruptcy of a Policy," in Harry Elmer Barnes, ed. *Perpetual War for Perpetual Peace* (Caldwell, Idaho: Caxton Printers, 1953), pp. 483–491.

good." He acknowledged that Roosevelt revealed "a certain lack of faith in the basic tenets of democracy." But, Bailey added, the "masses are notoriously shortsighted," and statesmen had to "deceive them into awareness of their long-run interests."[10] The truth must be kept from the people to save them from themselves. This policy produces permanent damage to the moral code of a democracy.

A President who took steps meant to make America a belligerent while promising peace and neutrality was engaging in conduct that was morally and politically indefensible. Beard noted that Roosevelt was promising peace *after* the Nazi advance through Europe had led to collapse of the Low Countries and France. It was already clear that fascism threatened the life of the European democracies. Yet Roosevelt had made a covenant with the populace to preserve neutrality, and the events of 1940 did not lead him to argue on behalf of a different course.

If the President felt that his public antiwar commitment had been rendered obsolete by events, Beard noted, he had "constitutional and moral obligations to explain to the country the grounds and nature of a reversal in policy." Before the 1940 campaign France had fallen, the British had suffered disaster at Dunkirk, and Germany seemed on the verge of triumph in western Europe. But it was in the months of desperation for Britain that Roosevelt had made his antiwar pledges. Critics chide Beard for regarding FDR's antiwar pledges seriously. But Beard, who was not a cynic, viewed FDR's statements as "specific commitments to be fulfilled" after victory at the polls. They were, he noted, "the major promises of the campaign."[11]

Beard further charged the administration with duplicity in regard to the Atlantic Conference, the famous meeting at sea between Roosevelt and Winston Churchill, held between August 9 and 12, 1941. In reality, Beard charged, the conference was that between two Allied belligerents. It was called to help FDR find a way to get the United States into war.

Contemporaries agreed that the meeting strongly indicated that

10. Thomas A. Bailey, *The Man in the Street* (New York: Macmillan, 1948), p. 13.
11. Beard, *President Roosevelt and the Coming of the War*, pp. 8–9.

the United States would soon be joining Britain in war against Germany. At his presidential press conference of August 16 Roosevelt was asked by a reporter whether the United States was "any closer to entering the war." To that question the President "replied that he should say not." Later he repeatedly told a group of congressmen that "he had made no *new* commitments for the United States in his conversations with Mr. Churchill." Even during his August 21 speech to Congress, which many observers had thought would be the occasion on which Roosevelt would argue that the United States should assume a belligerent role, the President only reaffirmed his previous statements about the conference. Again Roosevelt stated that he "had made no 'new' commitments at the Atlantic Conference and had reached no understandings that brought the United States nearer to war." Beard summed up the appearances of what was supposed to have transpired: "It appeared, late in August 1941, that apart from arrangements for lend-lease operations, agreement on the noble principles of the Atlantic Charter, and discussions of numerous world issues, nothing had been done at the conference which bound the United States to take more vigorous actions definitely pointed in the direction of war."[12]

The realities, Beard pointed out, were quite different. On December 18, 1945, the Congressional Committee on Pearl Harbor obtained from Undersecretary of State Sumner Welles and the State Department discussions and agreements that actually had taken place at the conference. These included an agreement on parallel and ultimative action in respect to Japan; agreement to occupation of the Azores by U.S. and British armies; the type of world policy to be pursued by the two powers during and after the war; and an agreement on the form and language of the joint announcement on the conference to be issued by Roosevelt and Churchill.[13]

The conference also discussed, as Welles's memo revealed, "the need for a transition period upon the termination of the war during which period Great Britain and the United States would undertake the policing of the world." In a footnote to Welles's

12. Ibid., pp. 121–131.
13. Ibid., pp. 453–454.

memo Beard drew out the importance of the omission of the Soviet Union from postwar plans. Welles explained the omission on the grounds that military experts still thought that Russia would not be able to resist the Nazi onslaught, and that diplomatic relations between the U.S. and the Soviet Union had been at a standstill during the period of the Nazi-Soviet Pact. Whether this "explanation of the failure of President Roosevelt and Mr. Churchill to bring the Soviet Union into the work of 'policing the world' after the war mollified any of the feelings or suspicions the Russian Government may have had on the subject must be left," Beard wrote, "to further exploration."[14]

Beard concluded that the President was well aware of the need to hide the nature of the new commitments to Great Britain. Roosevelt had pushed for a joint statement in which both leaders would say that they had discussed aid under the terms of Lend-Lease and that the conversations had in "no way involved *any future commitments between the two Governments, except as authorized under the terms of the Lease-Lend Act."* FDR had told Churchill that "that portion of the proposed statement was of extreme importance *from his standpoint* inasmuch as a statement of that character would make it impossible for extreme isolationist leaders in the United States to allege that *every kind of secret agreement had been entered into during the course of these conversations."*[15]

Hofstadter agrees that sometime before the summer of 1941 Roosevelt had obviously decided that the United States had sooner or later to enter the war. He agrees that Roosevelt's course of action in the Atlantic "suggests that he was trying, not only to aid Britain but also to create the circumstances and incidents that would overcome public opposition to the final step." Yet he concludes that because Hitler was cautious and did not respond to the use of American convoys and eventual military battles between U.S. ships and German subs with a declaration of war, by the time of Pearl Harbor, U.S. "progress towards full

14. Ibid., pp. 476 ff.
15. Ibid., pp. 479–480. The excerpts are from Sumner Welles's memo. The italics were provided by Beard to stress the importance of Welles's revelations.

scale belligerency was still halting and uncertain."[16]

In general, Beard's critics argue that Roosevelt was extremely reluctant to take the final step that might lead to war. Robert Sherwood, the noted playright and Roosevelt speech writer, blamed the isolationists, because their "long and savage campaign against the President had exerted an important effect on Roosevelt himself. Whatever the peril, he was not going to lead the country into war—he was going to wait to be pushed in."[17] Similarly, New Dealer Basil Rauch, refuting Beard, argued that Roosevelt had to act less boldly than he desired as a precaution against a successful attack on his policy by the isolationist bloc. Roosevelt, Rauch wrote, "was determined to take no avoidable risk of an 'irrevocable act' that might destroy his policy."[18]

A more recent explanation is offered by a contemporary diplomatic historian, Robert A. Divine. Divine acknowledges that in the six months prior to Pearl Harbor, Roosevelt was moving slowly but steadily toward war with Germany. But he notes that the "crucial question . . . is why Roosevelt chose such an oblique policy which left the decision for peace or war in the hands of Hitler."

Divine answers his question by asserting that Roosevelt was the prisoner of his own policies. The nation had been repeatedly told that it was not necessary for the United States to enter the war, that America could defeat Hitler simply by giving all-out aid to Britain. The President had insistently denied that his measures would result in war. Divine then concludes that Roosevelt had "foreclosed to himself the possibility of going directly to the people and bluntly stating that the United States must enter the war as the only way to guarantee the nation's security. All he could do was edge the country closer and closer, leaving the ultimate decision to Germany and Japan." Like other mainstream historians, Divine believes that America acted only after it suffered outside aggression. There were those in the administra-

16. Hofstadter, *Progressive Historians,* p. 337.
17. Robert E. Sherwood, *Roosevelt and Hopkins: An Intimate Biography* (New York: Harper and Brothers, 1948), p. 299.
18. Basil Rauch, *Roosevelt, from Munich to Pearl Harbor: A Study in the Creation of a Foreign Policy* (New York: Creative Age Press, 1950), p. 346.

tion who overtly favored active belligerency, but, he concludes, "it is quite possible that Roosevelt never fully committed himself to American involvement prior to Pearl Harbor."[19]

From Robert Sherwood to Robert A. Divine, the historians agree that Franklin D. Roosevelt was trying, until Pearl Harbor, to find a way out of actual military involvement in the European war. They may now agree that Roosevelt brought the country to the brink, but they add that if the Nazis had not gone over, he would have held back from the final step.

Recent evidence, however, vindicates the accuracy of Beard's insight that Roosevelt considered the United States a belligerent ally when he met with Winston Churchill in August 1941. The British government has finally released Churchill's minutes of the Churchill-Roosevelt conversations at the Atlantic Conference. They indicate that Roosevelt did not intend to sit back until Germany declared war. He told Churchill at the Atlantic Conference that he was looking for an incident that would allow the United States to become a full belligerent. Churchill recorded that Roosevelt "obviously was determined that they should come in. If he were to put the issue of peace and war to Congress they would debate it for months."

At the meeting Roosevelt had informed Churchill that "he would wage war but not declare it and that he would become more and more provocative. If the Germans did not like it, they could attack American forces." Churchill had noted FDR's agreement to have the U.S. Navy convoy British ships across the Atlantic. The President's orders were to have navy escorts "attack any U-boat which showed itself, even if it were 200 or 300 miles away from the convoy. Everything was to be done to force an incident." Churchill had told the President that he thought the Soviet Union might be forced by Germany to sue for peace in the East. If that occurred, the British would lose all hope of the United States entering the conflict. Nazi troops were at that time moving through Russia. Roosevelt, Churchill remembered, "had taken this very well and made it clear that he would look for an

19. Robert A. Divine, *Roosevelt and World War II* (Baltimore, Md.: Johns Hopkins Press, 1969), pp. 46–47.

incident which would justify him in opening hostilities."[20] The agreements between Roosevelt and Churchill explain precisely what Roosevelt had in mind as he pledged formally in the Atlantic Charter to join Britain in working toward "the final destruction of the Nazi tyranny."

Beard was aware that Roosevelt was fishing for an incident. The President cited as possible provocation the alleged German attacks upon the U.S.S. *Greer* in September 1941 and the U.S.S. *Kearny* in October. Attacks on American ships could have been incidents which would justify public belligerency. For Roosevelt and the Democrats had made their antiwar position conditional: the United States would become involved in war only *if it was attacked.* As of July 1941 Roosevelt began to argue that an attack could be construed to mean an attack on any base from which American security might be threatened. Beard retorted that "if this is what the word 'attack' as used in the conditional clause of the Democratic antiwar plank was actually intended to convey by its authors . . . then it is noteworthy that no such explanation of the term was offered to the public by the President during his campaign of 1940 for the votes of the American people."[21]

Roosevelt therefore had to make an incident appear as if the United States had been directly attacked. In September 1941 a German submarine fired two torpedoes—both of which missed— at the *Greer.* Announcing this development, Roosevelt stated:

> The *Greer* was carrying American mail to Iceland. She was flying the American flag. . . . She was then and there attacked by a submarine. Germany admits that it was a German submarine. . . . I tell you the blunt fact that this German submarine fired first upon this American destroyer without warning and with deliberate design to sink her. . . .
>
> We have sought no shooting war with Hitler. We do not seek it now. But neither do we want peace so much that we are willing to pay for it by permitting him to attack our naval and merchant ships while they are on legitimate business . . . In the waters which we deem necessary for our defense, American naval vessels and Ameri-

20. "War-Entry Plans Laid to Roosevelt," *New York Times,* Jan. 2, 1972, p. 7.
21. Beard, *President Roosevelt and the Coming of the War,* p. 137.

can planes will no longer wait until Axis submarines lurking under water, or Axis raiders on the surface of the sea, strike their deadly blow first.[22]

A few days later, however, testimony presented by Admiral Harold A. Stark directly contradicted Roosevelt's claim. Stark, Chief of Naval Operations, reported that the *Greer*'s "legitimate business" was that it had trailed the German sub for three hours, during which time the *Greer* had broadcast the sub's position to a British plane. The plane had then dropped depth-bomb charges in the vicinity of the sub.

A short time later the Roosevelt administration again claimed a German attack upon the United States had taken place. On October 17 the U.S.S. *Kearny* was torpedoed on patrol duty 350 miles south and west of Iceland. Eleven American sailors were killed and several others injured. On October 27 President Roosevelt spoke to the American public on the radio:

> Eleven brave and loyal men of our Navy were killed by the Nazis.
> We have wished to avoid shooting. But the shooting has started. And history has recorded who fired the first shot. In the long run, however, all that will matter is who fired the last shot.
> America has been attacked. The U.S.S. *Kearny* is not just a Navy ship. She belongs to every man, woman, and child in this Nation. . . .
> Hitler's torpedo was directed at every American, whether he lives on our seacoasts or in the innermost part of the Nation, far from the sea and far from the guns and tanks of the marching hordes of would-be conquerors of the world.
> The purpose of Hitler's attack was to frighten the American people off the high seas—to force us to make a trembling retreat. This is not the first time he has misjudged the American spirit.[23]

The critical words were "America has been attacked." This could mean that the shackles were off the antiwar and proneutrality pledges that Roosevelt had offered. Journalists close to the White House, such as the *Times*'s Arthur Krock, made such claims. Two days after the President's speech, however, Secretary

22. *New York Times,* Sept. 12, 1941, pp. 1, 4.
23. *New York Times,* Oct. 28, 1941, p. 4.

of the Navy Frank Knox presented another version of what had transpired:

> On the night of October 16–17 the U.S.S. *Kearny* while escorting a convoy of merchant ships received distress signals from another convoy which was under attack from several submarines. The U.S.S. *Kearny* proceeded to the aid of the attacked convoy. On arriving at the scene of the attack the U.S.S. *Kearny* dropped depth bombs when she sighted a merchant ship under attack by a submarine. Some time afterward three torpedo tracks were observed approaching the U.S.S. *Kearny* . . . the third struck the U.S.S. *Kearny* on the starboard side.[24]

Later it was leaked from other governmental sources that the *Kearny* was actually on convoy duty at the time of the torpedoing and had been engaged in fighting a pack of German subs before being hit by the torpedo. These facts were released the following December by the Senate Committee on Naval Operations. The leaked reports, Beard noted, "dashed interventionist hopes that the *Kearny* attack would now bring full-fledged war in the Atlantic."[25]

Roosevelt's attempt to make good on his promise to Churchill had stalled. The attempts to fabricate an incident had temporarily failed. Beard was infuriated with Roosevelt, not because he now saw fit to bring the United States into war with Germany but because he continued to argue publicly that a belligerent role for the United States was unthinkable.

Interventionist supporters of Roosevelt had argued that passage of Lend-Lease aid the previous March had authorized Roosevelt to do anything he deemed necessary to defeat Germany militarily, including resort to overt war. But Beard noted that when the administration had asked for support of Lend-Lease, they had argued that its effect would be to strengthen Britain, so that the United States would never have to become directly involved. The interventionists now asked for unlimited executive authority to declare war.

Beard did not lose sight of the main issue, that the Constitution "confers on Congress the power 'to declare war,' not to

24. *New York Times,* Oct. 30, 1941, p. 1.
25. Beard, *President Roosevelt and the Coming of the War,* p. 148.

authorize the President to make war when, where, as and if he decides to make it." Only by flouting the Constitution could one argue, as Roosevelt's interventionist supporters were arguing, that Lend-Lease aid provided authorization allowing "the President to wage war at his discretion and pleasure in carrying out its provisions."[26]

If Roosevelt's precedents were allowed to stand, Beard warned, it might mean that a future President "in a campaign for re-election may publicly promise the people to keep the country out of war and after victory at the polls, may set out secretly on a course designed or practically certain to bring war upon the country":

> He may, to secure legislation in furtherance of his secret designs, misrepresent to Congress and the people both its purport and the policy he intends to pursue under its terms. . . .
>
> He may, by employing legal causists, secretly frame and, using the powers and patronage of his office, obtain from Congress a law conferring upon him in elusive language authority which Congress has no constitutional power to delegate to him.
>
> He may, after securing such legislation, publicly announce that he will pursue . . . a policy contrary to war and yet at the same time secretly prepare plans for waging an undeclared "shooting war" that are in flat contradiction to his public professions. . . .
>
> He may publicly represent to Congress and the people that acts of war have been committed against the United States, when in reality the said acts were secretly invited and even initiated by the armed forces of the United States under his secret direction.[27]

Beard's predictions make eerie reading in the light of the Vietnam war. The erosion of congressional authority to declare war did not begin with the administration of Lyndon B. Johnson. But it is the war in Indochina that has led many liberals and radicals to look again at the criticism offered by such men as Charles Beard. In previous war the points made by Beard had been rejected by liberals, who had glorified the powers of the President, especially in the arena of foreign affairs, and had sneered at the obstructions of the congressional isolationists.

26. Ibid., p. 154.
27. Ibid., pp. 582–583.

When a President whom the liberals abhorred came into office, and once he had escalated a brutal war, liberals began to yearn for a Congress more responsive to the people. It is now commonplace to hear complaints about the authority which the executive branch has arrogated to itself, and many voices have been raised to warn of the dangers inherent in the upsetting and distortion of the constitutional process.

The "conservative" critics were not raising irrelevant questions after all. The pejorative "isolationist" had been a smear meant to block opposition to unrestrained expansion. But the "conservatives" had understood that total power to wage war in the hands of the executive could have disastrous consequences for the nation.

Hofstadter is correct when he writes, however, that the "pivot of Beard's book" is not the Atlantic theater but the "Pacific theater, where war finally came." War in the Pacific raises a long and complex debate over whether or not Roosevelt actually knew that the Japanese were going to attack Pearl Harbor, and whether or not he allowed the attack to take place in order to find a "back door to war." Concentrating on this aspect of the Pearl Harbor issue, however, distracts attention from the critical examination of American-Japanese diplomacy during this era. It is in this area that Beard actually made his major contribution.

Most historians acknowledge that American diplomacy vis-à-vis Japan was inept and that a showdown with Japan might well have been postponed. But because of Japan's expansionist aims, Hofstadter finds it improbable that war could have been avoided without jeopardy to the long-range security of the United States. He argues that the Japanese were determined to win American acquiescence to their plans or precipitate war. FDR therefore had the choice of allowing Japan to receive U.S. materials—thereby acting as a partner in her imperialist program—or putting economic pressure on Japan to desist. The second alternative, however, entailed the certainty that Japan would be driven to widen the war.[28]

This interpretation assumes that Japan was the only power with imperialist designs and interests. A contrasting position has

28. Hofstadter, *Progressive Historians*, pp. 337–338.

recently been argued by Bruce M. Russett, who asserts that the belief that Japan would settle only for a plan that gave her everything she could win in a Far Eastern war is highly suspect:

> The evidence, however, shows quite a different picture both of intent and capability. Nor is it enough simply to assert that, because Japan attacked the United States at Pearl Harbor, America took no action to begin hostilities. This is formally true, but very deceptive. The Japanese attack would not have come but for the American, British and Dutch embargo on shipment of strategic raw materials to Japan. Japan's strike against the American naval base merely climaxed a long series of mutually antagonistic acts. In initiating economic sanctions against Japan the United States undertook actions that were widely recognized in Washington as carrying grave risk of war.[29]

Convinced that the United States would fight if Japan moved south toward southern Asia, rich in oil, bauxite, and rubber, Japan turned toward war. According to Louis Morton, former Chief of the Pacific Section of the Office of Military History of the U.S. Army, Japan moved out of "the conviction, supported by the economic measures imposed by the United States and America's policy in China, that the United States was determined to reduce Japan to a position of secondary importance." Japan's leaders believed that their nation was doomed if the challenge was not met. "In their view, Japan had no alternative but to go to war while she still had the power to do so."[30]

Even the attack on Pearl Harbor was a defensive military effort in Japanese eyes. Its objective was to capture the Dutch and British possessions in Southeast Asia, and this was threatened by the American Pacific Fleet stationed at Pearl Harbor. Japan needed to neutralize the fleet before it moved. America's communication lines across the Pacific would be cut by capture of Wake Island and Guam. Once these threats were removed and the rich resources of the South gained, Japan would have estab-

29. Bruce M. Russett, *No Clear and Present Danger: A Skeptical View of the U.S. Entry into World War II* (New York: Harper and Row, 1972), p. 45.
30. Louis Morton, "Japan's Decision for War, 1941," in Arnold A. Offner, ed. *America and the Origins of World War II* (Boston: Houghton Mifflin, 1971), pp. 210–211.

lished a defensive perimeter around her new empire in the South. It would gain control of the resources of Southeast Asia and satisfy its national objective in waging war. There was "no evidence in the Japanese plans," Morton writes, "of an intention to invade the United States or to seek the total defeat of that nation. Japan planned to fight a war of limited objectives and, having gained what it wanted, expected to negotiate a settlement."[31]

Of key importance for the United States was China. Japan's attack on Pearl Harbor, Russett points out, was not evidence of either unlimited expansionist policy or capability by the Japanese. It was the result of less ambitious goals revolving around a determination to hold the position that it had fought for years to establish in China. "When that refusal meant an equal American determination that Japan should give up many of her gains in China, the result was war."[32]

The truth, as Lloyd Gardner writes, is that the only type of agreement with Japan that Secretary of State Cordell Hull would permit was one that consisted of prior acceptance of American principles. The great China market had never materialized. But "many American leaders in the New Deal period . . . *acted upon the assumption* that it would, and this gave them reason enough to oppose Japan's forward movement in Asia. If that were not enough, the fear that the loss of China might mean the loss of all the Far East to Japanese hegemony stimulated others to action, for those who might shrug off the former possibility could not stand by and allow the latter.[33]

The move to intervention and opposition to Japanese efforts in Asia involved more than a concern with American security. Restoration of an Open Door world was of equal importance. Roosevelt and Hull favored a military involvement which would end with a postwar world policed by the United States. "Japan did not want to rule the world," Robert F. Smith explains, "but in 1941 the United States rigidly asserted that any order in Asia

31. Ibid., pp. 194–195.
32. Russett, *No Clear and Present Danger*, pp. 56–57.
33. Lloyd C. Gardner, *Economic Aspects of New Deal Diplomacy* (Madison, Wis.: Univ. of Wisconsin Press, 1964), pp. 150, 328–329.

would have to be in terms of 'the basic objectives of American Far Eastern policy.' Hull's last note to the Japanese made this abundantly clear." The desire of some administration members for a back door to go to war in Europe, the concern of those who favored a militant Asian policy, and the false belief that Germany and Japan were irrevocably united in a conspiracy were all reinforced by British pressure for action, which seemed to confirm a worldwide danger to Britain and to the Open Door world.[34]

The key document of Rooseveltian diplomacy in the days prior to Pearl Harbor was the message delivered by Hull to the Japanese government on November 26, 1941. It revealed the American determination to protect its long-term interests in China.

> Instead of limiting it to the protection of the Philippine Islands, for which the United States still had the obligation assumed after the Spanish War, [Beard wrote] or even to the minimum terms necessary to protect the British and Dutch imperial possessions against Japanese aggression, the President and the Secretary had presented to Japan what amounted to the maximum terms of an American policy for the whole Orient. They called upon Japan to withdraw "all military, naval, air and police forces from China and Indochina"; to recognize only the Chungking Government; to make additional concessions of a similar nature; to observe in China the political and economic practices once covered by the apparently righteous phrase, the Open Door—the old Republican formula for American intervention in China—and henceforth to abide by Secretary Hull's program of international morality.[35]

Beard noted that this program was an expansion of the Open Door to all of Asia. Rather than choose a path of long-range diplomacy through negotiation, and rejecting Japanese overtures for a *modus vivendi,* Roosevelt and Hull had clearly "not limited the issues to primary and essential terms, which, if rejected by Japan, would have given them a pointed *casus belli* to be presented to Congress and the country." They had not directed the emphasis of the memorandum to the southward movement of

34. Robert F. Smith, "American Foreign Relations, 1920–1942," in Barton J. Bernstein, ed. *Towards a New Past: Dissenting Essays in American History* (New York: Pantheon, 1968), pp. 251–253.
35. Beard, *President Roosevelt and the Coming of the War,* pp. 229–230.

Japanese troops, which menaced the Philippines and the British-Dutch possessions in that area.[36]

At no previous moment in America's diplomatic relations in Asia had the United States government ever proposed to Japan, Beard wrote, such a total withdrawal from China under the threat of war and the pressure of economic sanctions. There was nothing in the platform of either major political party between 1900 and 1941 that indicated the American people would support a war against Japan for the purpose of enforcing the aims of Hull's memorandum.[37]

Hull's November 26 memo, Beard concluded, had made it clear that "President Roosevelt had done what Republican imperialists had shrunk from doing: He had supported with drastic economic sanctions the dangerous and shadowy shibboleth of the Open Door . . . Anti-imperialists . . . could readily discern in the memorandum the substance of old imperialism in a new garb of phraseology."[38]

Skeptics and critics of Beard ask why it was wrong to oppose Japanese expansion. Wasn't it necessary to come to China's defense by enforcing the Open Door? Beard preferred the approach and diplomacy of Herbert Hoover to that of his Secretary of State (and Roosevelt's Secretary of War), Henry L. Stimson. After the Japanese invaded Manchuria in 1931, Stimson had favored the use of nonrecognition as a prelude to economic and military sanctions against Japan. Hoover saw it only as a final measure, a substitute for economic pressure or military force. When he became President, Roosevelt pursued the course advocated by Stimson.[39]

In contrast to Stimson and Roosevelt, Hoover had informed his Cabinet that while deplorable, Japan's actions in Manchuria "do not imperil the freedom of the American people, the economic or moral future of our people. I do not propose ever to sacrifice American life for anything short of this. If that were not enough reason, to go to war means a long struggle at a time when

36. Ibid., p. 235.
37. Ibid., p. 236.
38. Ibid., pp. 239–240.
39. Richard N. Current, "The Stimson Doctrine and the Hoover Doctrine," *American Historical Review*, LIX, No. 3 (April 1954), 513–542.

civilization is already weak enough. To win such a war is not solely a naval operation. We must arm and train Chinese. We would find ourselves involved in China in a fashion that would excite the suspicions of the whole world." Hoover realized the imperialist thrust that would be manifest in an armed American intervention in Asia. He recoiled from using military force in defense of empire, refusing to "go along on war or any of the sanctions either economic or military for those are the roads to war."[40]

Hoover also rejected the moral argument that China had to be protected from Japan by armed intervention of the foreign powers. He judged that imperialist Japan would never be able to effectively control China. "We must remember some essentials of Asiatic life," Hoover noted. "While Japan has the military ascendancy today and no doubt could take over parts or all of China, yet the Chinese people possess transcendent cultural resistance; that the mores of the race have carried through a dozen foreign dynastic wars over the 3,000 years . . . No matter what Japan does . . . they will not Japanify China and if they stay long enough they will be absorbed or expelled by the Chinese. For America to undertake this on behalf of China might expedite it, but would not make it more inevitable."[41]

Beard saw Stimson's policy, "with sanctions and war," as one that "was pursued to the end by the Roosevelt administration in the ultimate showdown." Behind it all, Beard wrote to Herbert Hoover, "was Mr. Stimson's career as an old Republican hand of the imperialist school—war for glory and trade and to divert attention from domestic troubles." Beard informed Hoover that he "knew that school and a lot of its history," and that Stimson "belonged to it and stuck to the creed through thick and thin." For Beard it was the "conquest of the Philipines" that was the first step "on the way toward the destruction of our Republic."[42] It is not surprising that Beard thought Hoover's views on the

40. R. I. Wilbur and A. M. Hyde, *The Hoover Policies* (New York: Scribner, 1937), pp. 600 ff. Beard quotes these words approvingly.
41. Ibid., p. 600.
42. Beard to Hoover, Dec. 23, 1945, Hoover MSS., Hoover Institution of War and Peace, Stanford Univ., Palo Alto, Cal. I would like to thank David Green for calling this letter to my attention.

Manchurian situation and China to be "among the judgments of our time most worthy of standing among the permanent memorials of the Republic."[43]

As one who had "rejected the imperialist 'racket,' " Beard found that his reception in academic and literary circles was no longer a warm one. He also detected the beginnings of a selective censorship. Critics of Roosevelt's Asian diplomacy, Beard wrote fellow revisionist Harry Elmer Barnes, were being prevented from using documentary information freely given to "official" historians—men whom Barnes was to condemn as "court historians." These writers, Beard stated, were "the vestal virgins who guard the sacred tradition." Beard was sure that "no big N.Y. publisher will touch anything that does not laud the Saint."[44]

Beard soon formally charged that the Rockefeller Foundation and the Council on Foreign Relations, by their subsidy of William L. Langer's history of the war, were in the process of "preparing the 'right kind' of history of World War II for the education of the American people." Beard cited as evidence the Rockefeller Foundation's annual report for 1946, which noted that the council was "concerned that the debunking journalistic campaign following World War I should not be repeated." They had given Langer a grant of $139,000 so that he could present "a clear and competent statement of our basic aims and activities during the Second World War." This really meant, Beard argued, that the council did not desire anyone "to examine too closely and criticize too freely" administraiton foreign policy. The foundations preferred to try to ensure that Roosevelt's diplomacy would not suffer the same fate that Woodrow Wilson's policies had suffered at revisionist hands after the end of World War I.[45]

Langer, Beard noted, was to present the " 'official case' for the

43. Ibid., Beard to Hoover, Nov. 17, 1945.
44. Beard to Barnes, May 23, 1947, and Jan. 14, 1948, quoted in Hofstadter, *Progressive Historians*, p. 342.
45. Beard, "Who's to Write the History of the War?" *Saturday Evening Post*, Oct. 4, 1947, p. 172; *Rockefeller Foundation Annual Report, 1946* (New York, 1946), pp. 188–189; see also Thomas C. Kennedy, "Charles A. Beard and the 'Court Historians,' " *The Historian*, XXV (1963), pp. 439–450. Kennedy challenges Beard's contention that he was denied access to official records readily available to Langer and other "official" historians.

Roosevelt Administration." He would state it for the council, and his work would be "paid for by the Rockefeller Foundation." Terming this an extraordinary show of effrontery, Beard concluded that "standards of comprehensive, balanced, and judicious scholarship have lost all value and appreciation in those quarters."[46] Langer himself had admitted that Cordell Hull and the War Department had given him selected materials—"not access to all relevant papers." Langer explained that he had done the job as an independent scholar. "Independent scholars," Beard retorted, "don't take such jobs without free access to the relevant papers—if at all in such circumstances."[47] He asked whether the council could "defend the idea of special privileges from the Government in the use of secret documents." Even the Council on Foreign Relations had to maintain that official documents "should be open to all students on equal terms." Or have we, Beard asked, "entered a new age of immorality?"[48]

Beard also complained that he was denied access to copies of President Roosevelt's press conferences for the years 1941, 1944, and 1945. He had written Fred W. Shipman, Director of the Franklin D. Roosevelt Library at Hyde Park, for the transcripts, and Shipman had replied that they were "not available for public inspection at this time." Beard then used stenographic reports of the conferences from the files of a large metropolitan newspaper. "It is an anomaly," Beard wrote, "that a group of journalists are permitted to take notes at the President's press conferences, held presumably for the benefit and information of the public, whereas students of American history are denied access to the official minutes which are supposed to give the authentic version of what was actually said."[49]

In retrospect, it appears that Beard may have been too insistent in his claim that only the "court historians" were able to gain access to official records. A short time after he made this charge the radically revisionist historian Charles C. Tansill was granted

46. Beard statement, Oct. 3, 1947, Oswald Garrison Villard MSS., Houghton Library, Harvard Univ., Cambridge, Mass.
47. Ibid., Beard to Villard, July 17, 1947.
48. Ibid., Beard to Villard, Oct. 3, 1947.
49. Beard, *President Roosevelt and the Coming of the War*, pp. 560 ff.

permission to use State Department archives in preparation for *The Back Door to War,* a study that went further than Beard's work in asserting that Roosevelt had led a conspiracy to allow the bombing of Pearl Harbor.

But Beard was probably correct in charging that the Council on Foreign Relations was subsidizing the work of historians who were expected to "serve a purpose fixed in advance."[50] Beard had much evidence to indicate that the liberal press and mainstream academics were joining together to defend FDR's diplomacy. The *New York Times* and the *Herald Tribune* had both attacked the revisionist George Morgenstern, who had published the first critical account of Roosevelt's Asian policy, *Pearl Harbor: Story of a Secret War* (New York: Devin-Adair, 1947). Beard had written Oswald Garrison Villard that he expected such attacks. "The pseudo-intellectuals who have been trying to terrorize everybody who questions the official myths are now getting frantic," Beard wrote, ". . . for the whole structure is crumbling and the high-brows are tearing one another's hair out." Seeming to suggest that critics of foreign policy might be branded disloyal by the administration, Beard acknowledged that "so far the exercise of critical intelligence is not treason and this Congress seems in no mood to make it treason by law or to permit the President to do it by executive decree over the radio."[51]

The appearance of *President Roosevelt and the Coming of the War, 1941* brought forth the predictable unfavorable reviews. The book was unfavorably discussed by the former revisionist-turned-internationalist Walter Millis, as well as by the budding young dean of mainstream historians Arthur M. Schlesinger, Jr. Nevertheless Beard remarked that "the Roosevelt myth ain't what it used to be." The documents contained in his book alone, he was sure, were "enough to show the public how FDR and his associates were operating behind the scenes." America was "in a mood," Beard wrote, "to consider the question of how we were secretly governed by our great *Fuehrer!*"[52]

The country may have been in such a mood, but Beard's

50. *Washington Post,* Nov. 15, 1947, p. 8.
51. Beard to Villard, Feb. 9, 1947, Villard MSS.
52. Ibid., Beard to Villard, April 13, 1948.

opponents were relentless. Harry Elmer Barnes related one attack by the president of New York City's Brooklyn College, Harry Gideonse. An associate of the internationalist Freedom House, founded by Wendell Willkie, Gideonse had, according to Barnes, addressed the group and had argued for independence of the executive branch of government from congressional control in both foreign and domestic affairs. Adolf Hitler, Barnes remarked, would have applauded Gideonse's remarks.[53]

Groups, such as Andrew Carnegie's Endowment for International Peace, which had been established in 1924 to change people's minds about war through education, had, in Beard's view, "done incalculable damage to mind and morals."[54] In the 1944 presidential election Beard found no choice between Tnomas E. Dewey, "the Peanut of Pawling," and Roosevelt, "the Madhatter of Washington," but he informed Villard that he was uncertain whether he could honestly vote for the only alternative, Socialist party leader Norman Thomas. Thomas too was "a world-saver."[55]

The end of the war, and Roosevelt's death, brought Harry S. Truman to the mantle of leadership. Within a short period America faced what many believed to be a new enemy abroad—the giant Soviet colossus. Disputes over the outcome of arrangements made at Yalta by FDR, Churchill, and Stalin, particularly in regard to the composition of the new Polish government, led to bitter attacks on Russian intransigence and violations of the Yalta agreement. Cooperation with Russia gave way to containment, a policy meant to apply counterforce to Russian strength at critical points of contention. The threat was said to be military, and it became the task of the United States to meet that threat and force it into retreat wherever and whenever it became apparent. The military strength of the United States and its allies had to be built up, and the Russians had to be resisted at any place where they applied pressure. Containment reached fruition in 1947 with the Truman Doctrine of aid to Greece and Turkey. Asking Congress for a large amount of money to bolster those

53. Ibid., Barnes to Villard, June 23, 1948.
54. Ibid., Beard to Villard, Sept. 8, 1945.
55. Ibid., Beard to Villard, Oct. 20, 1944.

governments, Truman developed the principle that wherever anti-Communist governments were threatened by insurgents, foreign invasion, or domestic upheaval, the United States had the obligation to rescue them with all necessary economic and military aid. A new globalism and interventionism was masked by treating a classic struggle between Left and Right within Greece as an example of worldwide forces of freedom being put to the test in a contest with the forces of slavery.

Beard's comments on the emerging cold war were vague in some regard, but it *is* clear that he did not respond to the Truman message with confidence or support. He had come to believe by 1947 that "the State Department is now our prize madhouse, with all the inmates bawling and gesticulating almost hourly as they beat the wind." He thought he detected in Truman's stance "a project to invade Russia by way of Turkey, now that the opportunity to fight Russia in China has exploded."[56] Beard departed from the bipartisan consensus of both Republicans and Democrats who sought to wage the cold war. "The Democrats," he wrote Barnes, "are playing the old game of crisis and trying to wring one more victory out of the bloody shirt! Having brought the country to the verge of disaster, they want to complete the job." He believed that Truman was looking for another "Pearl Harbor in the Mediterranean or Palestine."[57]

Beard, of course, *was* an anti-Communist. But his moral opposition to totalitarian government did not lead him to support a holy crusade against such systems. The Truman administration was arguing that Hitler and Stalin were moral and political equivalents, that the United States had the obligation to act against Russia as it should have acted against Germany in the 1930s. Beard rejected that conclusion. World War II was supposed to have eliminated all foreign devils. Yet Stalin's Russia came out alive and powerful, partially as a result of Western policy during the war. That result suggested to Beard that sacrifices encountered in the war against Hitler had been in vain. For if Germany and Russia were approximately the same type of threat, the goal

56. Ibid., Beard to Villard, Sept. 8, 1947, and Jan. 7, 1948.
57. Beard to Barnes, Jan. 6, 1948, quoted in Hofstadter, *Progressive Historians,* p. 343.

of eliminating such a threat to world peace and stability had not been attained. The war had produced another "totalitarian regime no less despotic and ruthless than Hitler's system," Beard wrote, and its leaders had a "political and economic ideology equally inimical to the democracy, liberties and institutions of the United States."[58] What guarantees were there, Beard asked, that a cold war against them would produce results any different from those produced by the hot war against Germany during the 1940s?

Beard rejected one more crusade against the latest power proclaimed as the new menace. The war we had just fought had not created a new world of peace and justice, and new interventions were not likely to produce utopia. The totalitarian ideology of another nation was not sufficient reason to engage it in cold or hot war.

The policy of interventionism, moreover, had ironically produced an America similar in nature to the very fascist regimes fought during the war. Interventionists had argued, Beard wrote, that if the Nazis won, the United States would become an "armed camp for defense," with a "permanent conscript army, multiplied annual outlays for armaments, a huge national debt and grinding taxes," and the burden of a military effort that would mean "cessation of beneficial reforms at home." In 1948, Beard thought, Harry S. Truman was urging continuation of a tough posture abroad, partially to restrain "the expansion of Russian imperial power."[59] The end result, he implied, would be the same.

He opposed the Truman policy of "an unlimited program of underwriting, by money and military 'advice,' poverty-stricken, feeble and instable governments around the edges of the gigantic" Russian colossus. Beard charged that such a policy, if it was meant to work, was "predicated upon present and ultimate support by the blood and treasure of the United States." This meant an uncertain future for young people in America. "In short," he sadly proclaimed, "with the Government of the United States committed under a so-called bipartisan foreign policy to

58. Beard, *President Roosevelt and the Coming of the War,* p. 577.
59. Ibid., p. 578.

supporting by money and other forms of power for an indefinite time an indefinite number of other governments around the globe, the domestic affairs of the American people became appendages to an aleatory expedition in the management of the world."[60]

Beard concluded that if Roosevelt's precedents were allowed to stand, a future President might, "as a crowning act in the arrogation of authority to himself, without the consent of the Senate, make a commitment to the head of a foreign government which binds the United States to 'police the world,' at least for a given time, that is, in the eyes of other governments and peoples policed, to dominate the world; and the American people are thereby in honor bound to provide the military, naval and economic forces necessary to pursue, with no assurance of success, this exacting business."[61]

In the context of the emerging cold war, Beard's predictions and prophecies were ignored. Hofstadter sees Beard in a tragic position, as a historian whose works "were to become the staple assumptions of the far right wing," whose preconceptions brought Beard to the verge of strange alliances—meetings with Henry Luce, cordial relations with Herbert Hoover, and agreement with editorials in the Chicago *Tribune*. All this indicates to Hofstadter that Beard's responses to the war "were pulling him steadily toward the right."[62]

Beard cannot so easily be surrendered to the political right wing. In his last writings he concentrated upon the abuse of presidential power, and he argued for reassertion of congressional control in the area of foreign policy. He opposed the beginnings of the cold war that he detected in the Truman administration's bipartisan program, a program supported by a coalition of Republican *and* Democratic policy makers. Once again Beard thought he detected an American leadership that was seeking to avoid dealing with domestic turmoil by creating a foreign crisis.

Perhaps Beard could have moved toward the political Left. Perhaps he might have responded to a program for structural

60. Ibid., p. 580.
61. Ibid., pp. 583–584.
62. Hofstadter, *Progressive Historians,* p. 340.

rearrangement of the economy, so that an economy would be created that would not depend upon new foreign markets for domestic prosperity and well-being. An American socialism that called for decentralized economic control of basic resources and that guaranteed a system of political and civil liberties might have had an appeal to him. Beard cannot be faulted for failing to move in this direction. For no such program was advanced in the America of the 1940s. The American Left viewed itself as part of the New Deal. Both Communists and Socialists had given their support to the Roosevelt administration. They had closed their eyes to FDR's violation of democratic morality. Beard was not about to accept any of their postwar proposals as serious alternatives. Even Norman Thomas, as he had put it, was a "world-saver."

It is not strange that Beard moved closer to such a man as Herbert Hoover. As President at a critical juncture in the nation's history, Hoover had refused to take America into war on behalf of the empire in Asia. That act alone allowed Beard to offer Hoover the kind of respect and admiration he could never have toward Franklin D. Roosevelt. Beard honored those Americans who waged a courageous oppositon to unlimited presidential power. The political label attached to them by their opponents did not deter Beard from giving them his support. Beard understood that use of the term "isolationist" as a smear word was meant to discredit alternative proposals and isolate the critics. Refusing to accept isolation and defeat, Beard persistently spoke out, accepting allies wherever he might find them.

Beard knew that the more America overstepped the limits of its strength, "the more likely it is to lead this nation into disaster," even into a war that would be "beyond the conquering power of its soldiers, sailors and airmen." Had Americans read and taken Charles A. Beard seriously years ago, perhaps the nation we have inherited from the bipartisan cold-warriors might have been different. Perhaps we would not have moved toward the very precipice Beard tried to turn us away from, "with no divinity hedging our Republic against Caesar."[63]

63. Beard, *President Roosevelt and the Coming of the War,* pp. 592–593, 598.

Oswald Garrison Villard (WIDE WORLD PHOTOS)

Oswald Garrison Villard and the Emergence of World War II

BORN IN 1872 to Helen Garrison, a daughter of the abolitionist leader William Lloyd Garrison, and Henry Villard, a German immigrant who became a reporter and railway tycoon, Oswald Garrison Villard grew up in a rarefied atmosphere of wealth, good education, and reform sentiment. From preparatory school to Harvard, Villard was given access to the opportunities that would open up a world of success. Although he performed poorly in academia, frequent trips to Europe acquainted him with affairs of the world and gave him an urbanity and cosmopolitan attitude that would reveal itself in his later years.

Tired of academic life and finding little satisfaction in brief flirtations with teaching, Villard chose to enter the world of journalism. The task was not difficult, given his father's ownership of the New York *Post* and the *Nation*. When Villard moved to his father's paper in 1897 he joined with other leading citizens of New England to form the Anti-Imperialist League at the conclusion of the Spanish-American War. The league members argued that acquisition of Hawaii and the Philippines violated the American tradition of self-determination and meant that the United States was setting out on the path of colonial empire.

Villard's introduction to anti-imperialism led him to the doctrine of pacifism, a belief that was to become a life-long commitment. Domestically, he favored the classical liberal theory of laissez-faire economics, and he did not approve of a positive role for the state that Progressive politicians were demanding between 1906 and 1912. He wrote articles attacking political bossism and high tariffs and favoring civil rights for Negroes, women's suffrage, and peace. His views were traditional and acceptable. Only in the area of women's rights and civil rights did Villard show an independence of spirit. Here he pursued the path followed by his grandfather, a path honored by Villard as a founder of the National Association for the Advancement of Colored People.

By the age of forty, Villard was president of the New York *Evening Post* Company and manager of that paper and the weekly *Nation*. It was during his tenure with the *Post* that war broke out in Europe. Committed to pacifism, Villard sought to oppose both German militarism and British violations of neutral rights. When American advocates of preparedness raised the cry for a strong defense budget and armaments production, Villard tried to rally pacifists into opposition. Preparedness, he argued, was supported by arms manufacturers and "masters of privilege" who would benefit from war. War would be the antithesis of domestic reform. It would mean an end to civil liberties and the growth of police-state measures at home, as well as increased powers to a strong central government. War would mean the necessity of abandoning the time-honored tradition of weak government. War and liberalism, Villard believed, were totally incompatible.[1]

When Villard made such statements in 1914, the United States was not yet at war. He still had praise for President Woodrow Wilson, who, Villard argued, was maintaining a nonpartisan position toward belligerent nations. When Wilson refused to take the United States into war after the sinking of the *Lusitania* in May of 1915, Villard praised him for not being stampeded into hostilities by the pressure of militarists. When the German government announced its cessation of submarine warfare in September, Villard took that act as proof of the success of Wilson's cautious approach.

Villard hoped that war would not come to the United States. When the Wilson administration showed signs of shifting toward intervention, Villard felt a profound sense of betrayal and shattered dreams. Wilson's support of preparedness and armaments came to him as a rude awakening. Wilson's turnabout, Villard wrote, would draw America into "the maelstrom of militarism and raise up a military and naval caste dangerous to the demo-

1. Oswald Garrison Villard, unsigned editorial, *Post,* Nov. 18, 1914, quoted in Michael Wreszin, *Oswald Garrison Villard: Pacifist at War* (Bloomington, Ind.: Indiana Univ. Press, 1965), p. 49.

cratic way of life."[2] When Germany resumed submarine warfare in February 1917 Villard still hoped that the United States would not be drawn into battle. Germany's new position was "outrageous and utterly indefensible," he argued. But if the United States entered the war, every movement of domestic reform would come to a quick end. Censorship of the press would be instituted, he predicted, and all civil liberties would come to a halt. Most objectionable, he suggested, was that "the progress of socialism would certainly be great if the war continued for any length of time."[3]

In calling attention to the perils of socialism Villard was making it clear that he held to laissez-faire, that he rejected the idea of some progressives that the war was a mechanism for introduction of national planning. The government controls of socialism would interfere with individual liberty. Advocating a firm course of resistance to war, Villard now placed Wilson in the camp of those captured by militarists. Wilson, he argued, was a pawn in the hands of those old-fashioned diplomats who lived by intrigue and deceit. The President had once argued that America must not become an armed camp. Now he was trying to build the largest navy in the world. Elected on the slogan "He Kept Us Out of War," Wilson was "winning the acclaim of the very business interests that opposed his re-election."[4]

As the war raged, Villard sought to guard American interests against the imperial politics of the Old World powers. When the Bolshevik government of Russia revealed the secret treaties of the Allied powers in 1918, Villard published them in his paper. He also had them issued in pamphlet form, hoping to give them wide circulation in the United States. Woodrow Wilson was not able to gain a liberal and impartial peace at Versailles, Villard later claimed, because he was unaware of the duplicity of the Allies as revealed by the text of the secret agreements. Villard's action in publishing the text met with the objection of the *Post*'s editors, who felt that discrediting the Allied powers was not

2. Villard to Woodrow Wilson, Oct. 30, 1915, quoted in Wreszin, ibid., p. 58.
3. Editorial, *Post,* Feb. 22, 1917, quoted in Wreszin, ibid., p. 67.
4. Editorial, *Post,* April 4, 1917, quoted in Wreszin, ibid., p. 71.

beneficial to the effort to gain peace. Villard sold the *Post* and moved to gain direct editorial control of the *Nation,* of which he became editor in chief in July of 1918.

Under his direction, Michael Wreszin writes, "its point of view became a rallying point for a number of brilliant young writers." Villard "developed a new initiative and fighting spirit which established him as one of America's foremost liberal journalists. Villard continued his discussion of the peace aims in the editorials in the *Nation* and soon brought his magazine into the limelight as one of the most representative and important factions in the great debate over the treaty and the League of Nations."[5]

Under his direction the new *Nation* campaigned for a democratic peace, a peace based upon no annexation of territory, on free trade, disarmament, and an end to conscription, and on the self-determination of nations. Villard found that many of Wilson's actions violated these goals. The Siberian intervention in July 1918 seemed to be an example of the very secret diplomacy Wilson had supposedly repudiated, and was an example of interventionism, to be accepted because it was limited in scope.

Villard hoped, at the war's end, to rally people around Woodrow Wilson's pronounced effort to fight reactionary leaders who sought a victor's peace. Within a short time Villard concluded that Wilson had yielded to those very forces of reaction. He had given in to those who wanted an invasion of Bolshevik Russia, he had agreed to revision of freedom of the seas, and he had given in on his stand against a punitive peace by accepting the Allied demand for German reparations. Villard saw no choice but to have the *Nation* editorially denounce the Versailles peace conference and the peace treaty for ignoring the principles espoused by Wilson in the Fourteen Points. The treaty was harsh; it was a peace of vengeance that flouted the concerns of humanity. The peace treaty sought to destroy Germany, diminish her territory, ruin her economy, and dismantle her defenses. It was a peace in the interest of the wealthy and powerful, those who were the champions of the established order and the opponents of revolution. Villard had the *Nation* oppose membership of the United States in the League of Nations; such membership, Villard

5. Wreszin, ibid., pp. 89–90.

believed, would make the United States an ally of the Old World imperial powers. The alternative he proposed was agreement for international disarmament.

By the 1920s Villard was a confirmed opponent of war and an advocate of neutrality. Domestically, he had also begun to modify some of his older laissez-faire concepts. By 1919, he later recalled, he had "been emancipated from any smug liberalism and social blindness due to the ease and luxury" of his bourgeois upbringing.[6] Although he still believed in private property, Villard felt that nationalization of some industries might be required to meet the demands of new conditions and times. He supported federal laws to abolish child labor and establish government ownership of the railroads. In the area of foreign policy Villard opened up the *Nation* to the writings of new revisionist historians who were beginning to probe the reasons for America's entry into World War I. In 1924 he endorsed the presidential candidacy of Wisconsin's Robert M. La Follette because the third-ticket candidate advocated a national referendum on war.

Villard called himself an internationalist. He favored, he wrote, a "parliament of man and the cooperation of all nations not only to outlaw war, but to grapple unitedly with the monstrous evils of the world."[7] Yet he was happy that America remained aloof from "the daily intrigues and quarrels of Europe," and he believed that America should honor the commitment of the Founding Fathers to stay free of entangling alliances and international political commitments.[8] A later generation would term that viewpoint isolationist, although Villard saw that belief as a logical deduction from pacifism.

As the 1920s came to an end Villard insisted that his magazine was "not even socialistic much less extremely radical, except perhaps in its pacifism." It was annoying, he wrote a correspondent, to find that the *Nation* writers were "constantly por-

6. Villard, *Fighting Years: Memoirs of a Liberal Editor* (New York: Harcourt, Brace, 1939), pp. 461–462.

7. Villard, "Politics and Patriotism," speech, Jan. 31, 1926, Oswald Garrison Villard MSS., Houghton Library, Harvard Univ., Cambridge, Mass.

8. Editorial, *Nation*, March 3, 1926, p. 218, and "The League Unveiled," *Nation,* March 31, 1926, p. 332.

trayed by ignoramuses as extreme radicals," advocates of bloody revolution, exponents of the IWW, causes with which "pacifists have no sympathy whatsoever."[9] Villard was sympathetic to Norman Thomas' candidacy in the 1928 presidential election, yet he refused to give Thomas the magazine's endorsement. Believing that no party bearing the name "socialist" could be a success in the United States, Villard preferred an effort to build a new third party that would unite all progressives.

Responding to the plight of the unemployed and dispossessed, Villard offered proposals that were light years away from his original advocacy of laissez-faire. He now endorsed protection for labor through federal old-age pensions, sickness, accident, and unemployment insurance, greater industrial democracy, and national planning. When Franklin D. Roosevelt won the presidential election in 1932 and announced the institution of a New Deal, Villard responded positively to the effort to create a welfare state. He supported the extension of federal authority and he rejected theories of rugged individualism based upon classical liberal economic theory. Only when government failed to respond to the needs of its citizens did Villard oppose the power of the state. Hence he attacked the power of the state when it interfered with civil liberties. His liberalism, Michael Wreszin notes, "was genuine and compatible with the mainstream of liberal thought in the early thirties."[10]

While Villard did not favor destruction of the entire economic system, as some radicals proposed, he did envision a drastically modified capitalism. He advocated public ownership of basic resources, federal unemployment insurance, massive government-sponsored public works, and federal aid to the unemployed. FDR's first year in office satisfied Villard, and he wrote of a "change in spirit from a government by and for big business to a government dedicated to the public welfare."[11]

As the New Deal progressed, however, Villard began to differ from many of the policies adopted. In particular, he began to express fear of the possible growth of fascism in America. The

9. Villard to Robert L. O'Brien, Dec. 3, 1920, Villard MSS.
10. Wreszin, *Oswald Garrison Villard*, p. 209.
11. Villard, "The Gifts of the New Deal," *Nation,* Jan. 3, 1934, p. 8.

enormous concentration of power in the executive branch of government worried him, and he feared that some administration supporters wanted to make the republic over into a fascist-type corporate state. Some New Deal programs, such as the corporatist National Recovery Act, were viewed as programs whose intent contradicted the basic spirit of the nation's institutions. NRA in particular revealed that corporatism had become part of the American scene. Businessmen in each industry were given exemption from antitrust prosecution and were granted permission to draw up codes of fair competition which the government would enforce as law.

The real break between Villard and the Roosevelt administration came over foreign policy. Villard began to fear executive leadership and initiative in foreign affairs. He, along with his close friend, Yale professor of international law Edwin Borchard, led what William Appleman Williams has called a "conservative assault." They "bitterly attacked the drift toward involvement in another war and repeatedly warned that the Congress and the citizenry would find it extremely difficult to recover the initiative and power that President Franklin Delano Roosevelt was gathering unto himself in order to handle foreign affairs as he wished." Despite the political differences of those who resisted the drift toward war—opponents included radicals, pacifists, reformers, New Dealers, conservatives, and businessmen—they were all "united by a rising anger about the way foreign policy seemed increasingly removed from the influence—not to mention the control—of the concerned citizenry."[12]

Actions taken by the Roosevelt administration late in 1935, Borchard informed Villard, showed that American leaders were taking the nation into war in the name of peace. Secretary of State Cordell Hull had publicly opposed neutrality and advocated aid to the Allied side. Such policy would promote an arms race and would be certain to lead to a new world war. Administration arguments, Borchard claimed, were also being used by European

12. William A. Williams, "The Critics of the American Empire Open a Door to Create an American Community," in William A. Williams, ed. *From Colony to Empire: Essays in the History of American Foreign Relations* (New York: Wiley, 1972), pp. 483–484.

imperialists to get the United States to help them maintain their empires. Although he backed neutrality, Borchard rejected placing an embargo on all trade with belligerent nations. Such a step would only place the fate of the world in the hands of the strongest sea power. Trade had not caused World War I, Borchard concluded; rather, it had resulted from the unneutral and inept policies of the Wilson administration.[13]

Villard agreed with Borchard's attack on administration opposition to neutrality. After World War I, he argued, Presidents had adopted policies that led to international commitments, and had usurped congressional prerogative in the area of foreign policy. The right of the people to declare war or peace was the most fundamental power any self-governing people would reserve to itself. For that reason Villard supported the Ludlow Amendment for a nationwide referendum before war could be declared. Until such an amendment passed both houses of Congress, Villard wanted to take every possible precaution to prevent "men in high places" from making decisions that would lead to war.[14]

Villard also favored compulsory neutrality without allowing for modification. The new editors of the *Nation,* an editorial board to whom he had turned over active management of the magazine late in 1932, disagreed with their publisher's analysis. They favored giving the President authority to direct an arms embargo against aggressor nations. Restrictive laws would harm America by prohibiting active support to the threatened democracies. They favored sanctions, arms embargoes, and extension of the neutrality ban to all materials that could be used for purposes of war. They favored collective security through action with League of Nation powers against Mussolini. For America to meet its responsibilities, the *Nation* editors favored economic sanctions against aggressors.[15]

Villard had already retired as active editor of the *Nation.* Growing indication that the new editors now were actively op-

13. Borchard to Villard, Nov. 7, 1935, Villard MSS.
14. Villard, "Who Makes War in America?," speech, n.d. (1928), and Villard to Alanson B. Houghton, Aug. 22, 1927, Villard MSS.
15. Wreszin, *Oswald Garrison Villard,* pp. 240–241.

posed to his policies led Villard to sell the magazine to a liberal New York stockbroker in April of 1935. Under the agreement of sale Villard was to continue to write his weekly column. International events only widened the gap between Villard and the magazine's editors. They were particularly incensed about Villard's endorsement of noninterference in the Spanish Civil War. The *Nation* favored sale of arms to the Spanish Republican government, a measure that even many Left isolationists supported. Villard, however, refused to support a curb to the arms embargo in the Spanish case. He continued to insist upon strict neutrality, even though Germany and Italy were aiding General Franco and even though Villard's own sympathies lay with the Spanish Loyalists. The editors finally ran an editorial proclaiming that Villard's words were aiding the cause of the Nazi dictator.[16]

To this attack Villard replied that Hull's decision to allow Roosevelt to decide between aggressor and aggrieved would only assure that the nation would end up fighting a war in which the people had no concern. Villard was preoccupied with the nation's experience before World War I, when the populace was "deceived by lying propagandists, the entanglement of big business-men with the English war machine and the false Wilson slogans." He believed that the past was again being repeated and that Cordell Hull and Franklin D. Roosevelt were playing the old Wilsonian game.[17]

At this point Villard stopped his attacks on Hitler and Nazism, and he became obsessed with the necessity to keep America out of war. When others argued that 1937 was not 1914, and that America clearly needed discriminatory neutrality, Villard asked, "How do they know that we ought to be on the side of the democracies, that the cause of the democracies will be any juster than that of the allies in 1914–1917?" The Allies might turn out, he argued, to be "aggressors for their own evil ends."[18]

Like other defenders of neutrality, Villard continued to hope that Roosevelt's commitment to domestic reform would keep him

16. *Nation*, Jan. 2, 1937, p. 2.
17. Villard, "Issues and Men," *Nation*, Jan. 2, 1937, p. 19.
18. Villard, "Another Word on Neutrality," *Nation*, May 1, 1937, p. 508.

away from fruitless foreign adventures. After the 1936 election Villard continued to hope that the President would continue the further reorganization of economic and social life. He was aware that the conservative Supreme Court was blocking critical New Deal programs. To deal with that problem Villard favored a constitutional amendment that would give Congress the power to pass new laws without judicial review. The President rejected that path. Instead he proposed in February of 1937 to produce a New Deal majority on the court by enlarging the number of justices and by forcing the resignation of some of the members.

Villard responded negatively to Roosevelt's course. He detected in Roosevelt's attempt to "pack the court" a high-handed maneuver that was politically expedient but probably unconstitutional. The bill had been drafted in secret, he wrote, and the President sought to jam it through Congress by political pressure. Such a procedure, if regularly used, could end with the downfall of Congress and the birth of dictatorship.[19]

What Villard objected to as well was the possibility that strong executive power might be used at a later date to bring the nation closer to war. The President might be tempted to take steps that led to involvement. It was even worth delaying the passage of New Deal programs if one result was a weak presidential power in the area of foreign policy. Once again the *Nation* editors were aghast that Villard joined anti-New Deal conservatives on the court issue. The charge that Roosevelt was showing fascist tendencies was a slander coming from the Liberty League, public utility barons, industrial spies, and big industrialists. What was Villard doing, they asked, when he echoed their spurious charges?[20]

Heywood Broun used his column in the *Nation* to attack Villard for echoing the arguments of FDR's conservative opponents. Villard retorted that Broun would have desired a rote opposition to the conservatives, regardless of their case. Broun and AFL President William Green were political enemies, yet they were both enemies of fascism. According to Broun's present logic,

19. Villard, "Issues and Men," *Nation*, Aug. 7, 1937, p. 152.
20. "Purging the Supreme Court," *Nation*, Feb. 2, 1937, p. 173.

Villard argued, Broun should have editorially come out in favor of Hitler, since Green was his adversary.[21]

Villard found support from the ranks of the isolationists. Senator Burton K. Wheeler, an opponent of intervention, wrote Villard about a speaking tour of the Midwest in which he had called for an American retreat from Asia. "We went to war to make the world safe for democracy and we have had less democracy than we did before." As for lining up with England and France to stop fascism, a position supported "by some radicals as well as conservatives," Wheeler feared that it might mean that America would end up with a fascist government. It might also mean a war in which the United States fought European nations over control of African colonies.[22]

Villard accepted such information as proof that most Americans agreed with firm neutrality and did not wish to risk the possibility of war. His position was still supported by Edwin Borchard. *New York Times* columnist Arthur Krock was writing that it was not possible for the United States to attain neutrality in the modern world, and he favored executive discretion in applying embargoes. Such authority, Borchard argued, really meant power to be unneutral, and it amounted to discretionary authority for intervention.[23]

After the Munich conference the *Nation* published a letter from Albert Guérard, a noted professor of French literature and supporter of collective security. He asked Villard what path he would advocate if the United States adopted measures short of war against an aggressor nation and eventually it became necessary to fight. Villard responded: "I should never fight under any circumstances. . . . I should not withdraw any non-intercourse or boycott measures to which any dictator country might object." But he thought the question hypothetical, since he believed that "neither Germany nor Japan nor Italy, the 'so-called' aggressor nations, could make war upon us whatever we did to them."[24]

21. Villard, "What Is the Nation Coming To?" *Nation,* March 27, 1937, p. 352, and "Those Liberals Again," *Nation,* March 6, 1937, p. 269.
22. Wheeler to Villard, Dec. 16, 1937, Villard MSS.
23. Ibid., Borchard to Villard, Jan. 12, 1937.
24. Letters to the Editor, *Nation,* Feb. 18, 1939, p. 216.

Villard's position was in some respects contradictory. He was willing to support European nations in a fight against Germany, and he continually condemned Britain for pursuing the policy of appeasement. His case seemed to rest on the desirability of having European democracies resist so that the United States could remain militarily uninvolved. Villard claimed that he was an isolationist only insofar as he was opposed to the United States entering another European war, and he backed U.S. support of Britain and France if that support did not mean measures that would lead to war.

Villard did interpret every measure actually taken in the name of aid to the Allies, however, as steps that might end in American intervention. He attacked Roosevelt in 1939, asking that the President turn his "eyes away from Europe, cease announcing that war is just at hand over there and cease joining England and France in their great power politics game of seeking to maintain peace by overawing and bluffing the dictators."[25]

Villard antagonized pro-Soviet readers in the *Nation* audience when he signed a statement issued by the Committee for Cultural Freedom criticizing intellectuals who attacked fascism but apologized for the Nazi-Soviet Pact and the Soviet totalitarian system. The pro-Soviet group saw the statement as one that would sow suspicions between the Soviet Union and antifascist forces in the West. To Villard the Nazi-Soviet Pact only offered more evidence that "America must keep out of the whole revolting European mess and free ourselves from the delusion that we have got to back England and France in order to save democracy."[26]

When some began to argue that FDR should run for a third term, Villard responded that such a suggestion was treason to American institutions. The citizenry had to be protected against an abuse of executive power. A defense of traditional liberal values meant dedication to the very institutions that lay at the core of American democracy. It was incorrect to claim that opponents of a third term had become conservatives.[27]

25. Villard, "Don't You Know, Mr. President?" *Nation,* Aug. 5, 1939, p. 149.
26. Villard, "Issues and Men," *Nation,* Aug. 5, 1939, p. 149.
27. Villard to Burton K. Wheeler, July 19, 1939, Villard MSS.

Villard's outspoken criticisms of the Roosevelt administration proved to be too much for the *Nation*'s new editor and publisher, Freda Kirchwey, who had purchased the magazine in 1937. At one time she had taken a poll of readers and had found that most disagreed intensely with Villard's position. Now his column was receiving even more vehement protests. She proclaimed that "to attack Roosevelt, even by means of a series of questions, at a time when he is fighting tooth and nail against a reactionary coalition in Congress seems to me a serious error in judgment" and also was unfair.[28]

Villard did not see the necessity of compromising principle for the sake of being part of a broad liberal coalition. He saw himself as trying to gather support for far-reaching change. "The pseudo reforms, the waste, the extravagance, inefficiency and militarism of Roosevelt," he wrote editor Kirchwey, were the forces destroying what both he and the new editor sought to accomplish. FDR, he thought, was "just another Ramsay MacDonald," who was "opening the way to either Fascism or collapse of the forces of reform, precisely like the Socialists in Germany."

Villard believed that the New Deal was failing, not because of the obstructionism of congressional conservatives but "because of the failures of Roosevelt." As for the charges that he had changed his cherished liberal viewpoint, Villard argued that he was only trying to maintain principle. "I have lived through so many disasters to liberalism like the one I see coming now," he explained, "that I cannot sit silent and overlook wrongdoing in Washington without protest." It was Kirchwey, not he, who was "playing right into the hands of the Fascists by not standing out against the President on his abominable militarization of the country." One million people were already mobilized in a new war machine, making up "the most powerful lobby in Washington," which could offset everything "that the New Deal should stand for." It was Roosevelt's own policies, as far as Villard was concerned, that had created a conservative politics.[29]

Villard, moreover, argued that Roosevelt's desire to meet force with force complemented Hitler's own philosophy. The United

28. Ibid., Kirchwey to Villard, July 31, 1939.
29. Ibid., Villard to Kirchwey, Aug. 2, 1939.

States had assumed responsibility for defending Central and South America, and the nation's doctrine was now that of a country in arms. America had become committed to Hitler's doctrine of reliance upon the use of force. FDR claimed that force would be used only in defense, but that was exactly the argument made by Hitler. Both the language and policies of powers that used force were similar. FDR's militarization made the United States indistinguishable from Nazi Germany. Americans did not stop to inquire whether the means they were adopting would destroy the very democracy they sought to preserve.[30]

Villard opposed Roosevelt's interventionist measures, but that did not imply approval of what was going on in Germany and Italy. In August 1940, after France and Britain had declared war, he visited both England and Germany. He was disgusted with what he found in Berlin and publicly reaffirmed his hope that England would win. The belligerents were not moral equals; but he did not relate this opinion to the issue of American entrance into the war.

Even if Hitler won, he believed, there would be no threat to American security. "Roosevelt, like Woodrow Wilson, was deliberately conspiring to whip up hysteria along with other conspiratorial elements in an effort to put America into the war and thus to divert attention from the domestic failures of his administration."[31]

By May of 1940 the conflict had reached a point of no return. Kirchwey informed Villard that his contract with the *Nation* would not be renewed. She would keep him on only on a weekly basis and would cut his fee from fifty to thirty dollars per column. The magazine had come out in favor of aid to Britain on an extended level, along with universal military training. This

30. Villard, "Hitler Wins in Washington," n.d. (1940), Villard MSS.; see also Wreszin, *Oswald Garrison Villard,* p. 259. Wreszin writes that Kirchwey was justified in her critique, that Villard's criticisms reflected the traditional accusations of conservatives who harped on waste, extravagance, and inefficiency of the administration. Calling Villard's views conservative, however, does not take away from the validity of his critique.

31. Wreszin, *Oswald Garrison Villard,* p. 261.

meant, Villard wrote, that Kirchwey had joined hands "with all the forces of reaction against which the *Nation* has battled so strongly" in the past. Roosevelt's policies, he protested, would "destroy the New Deal, subjugate labor and enthrone reaction, precisely as did our last adventure into war . . . which finished the New Freedom." War and liberty, Villard insisted, do not mix. Kirchwey and the *Nation* would have to "bear a heavy share of responsibility" for new reactionary measures. "You will be wailing because of the new crop of Mitchell Palmers and J. Edgar Hoovers who will be doing to death the causes for which you have stood." Villard promised to touch lightly on these themes in his last column and to part amicably for the sake of the magazine. But privately he let Kirchwey know that he thought she had "prostituted his once liberal journal."[32]

Judging from the way Kirchwey was treating him, Villard undoubtedly thought that she was accusing him of pursuing a pro-Axis policy. From the aim of building an antifascist Popular Front—a goal that Kirchwey sought along with liberal administration supporters and Communists—any criticism of Roosevelt and the New Deal was fuel for the Nazi engine. Villard kept his promise to depart from the *Nation* quietly. "America is to be safeguarded not by guns and by warships . . . but only by greater economic and industrial wisdom, by social justice, by making our democracy work, and not by creating a state rivalling Hitler's in substituting guns for butter."[33] His association with the *Nation* had begun in January of 1894, and had come to an end forty-six and one-half years later.

Freda Kirchwey did not let Villard's statement go unanswered. His final column, she believed, represented a politics of "escape and Appeasement." Villard was living in a dream world. His writing was "a danger more present than Fascism." Though he supposedly recognized the challenges to democracy from abroad, he claimed that they were "our concern only if we choose to make them so." It was a "retreat from the grimmest reality that

32. Villard to Kirchwey, June 13, 1940, Villard MSS.
33. Villard, "Valedictory," *Nation,* June 29, 1940, p. 782.

has confronted our nation in many generations." Pacifism meant support to appeasement.[34]

Condemned as an advocate of appeasement and tainted with the brush of pro-Nazism by his former colleagues, Villard, not surprisingly, was welcomed by some old-style conservatives. But some responsibility lay with the staff of the *Nation,* who decided they could no longer print his antiwar and old liberal views. Seeking an outlet, Villard joined the anti-interventionist America First Committee. Interventionists fought the committee as best they could. In June 1940 the playwright and presidential speech writer Robert Sherwood took a newspaper ad asking whether the Nazis would "considerately wait until we are ready to fight them." Any American saying that they would, Sherwood wrote, "is either an imbecile or a traitor." Villard exploded when he saw the ad. He answered by addressing William Allen White, the journalist who had formed the Committee to Aid America by Defending the Allies. There were millions of Americans, Villard retorted, "who are not fifth columnists nor imbeciles or traitors who do not agree that we are going to be 'alone in a barbarous world' and that we are in jeopardy." Acknowledging that he and others might be wrong, Villard stressed that critics had a right to be "treated as just as loyal, just as sincere, and just as earnest Americans as Sherwood or anyone else."[35]

Villard disagreed with the America First Committee's support for building an "impregnable defense for America." He had joined only on the ground that he had "the right to differ with the Committee as to what constitutes an impregnable defense."[36] Nevertheless Freda Kirchwey used that plank of the committee's program to embarrass Villard, pointing out to him that "many of the other persons on the board are extreme reactionaries."[37]

Villard rejected the use of guilt by association. He admitted that he had joined a group whose members did not see eye to eye

34. Freda Kirchwey, "Escape and Appeasement," *Nation,* June 29, 1940, pp. 773–774. For commentary, see the valuable book by James J. Martin, *American Liberalism and World Politics, 1931–1941,* II (New York: Devin-Adair, 1964), 1156–57.
35. Villard to White, June 12, 1940, Villard MSS.
36. Ibid., Villard to Douglas Stuart, Aug. 21, 1940.
37. Ibid., Kirchwey to Villard, Oct. 4, 1940.

with him on all policies; but his major objective was to keep the United States out of war. He was willing "to be associated with any non-Communist group that is working sincerely for the same end." As for the reactionaries, they seemed to favor that goal, while the liberals were working "to put us in."[38]

If the conservatives were going to stand for the principled liberal position, Villard would be glad to work with them. There was some substance to the charge that the America First Committee was made up of reactionaries and was dominated by businessmen. But the America First Committee was an umbrella antiwar organization, composed of both Right and Left isolationists. Both groups wanted to avoid war and to reject international entanglements. The left wing "sought to insulate America against the historical forces they associated with monopoly capitalism and its internal contradictions. By so doing, they expected to assure this country of the independent opportunity to work out a just and democratic Socialist solution." Unlike the isolationist Norman Thomas, such conservative isolationists as Herbert Hoover hoped to restore the economy "to its pre-Depression vigor and thus to save democracy by saving capitalism."[39]

Villard acknowledged that many businessmen in America First held a position similar to his own. But he no longer argued, as he did before World War I, that bankers and businessmen were taking the nation into war. "Yet one cannot say," he emphasized to Porter Sargent, "that the business men are putting us into war." The responsibility for that lay with Franklin D. Roosevelt. Villard thought that the President would "put us into the war before election day if he thinks that Willkie is licking him, and then we shall have the cry raised: 'A vote for Willkie is a vote for Hitler.' "[40]

Villard feared that five years hence Americans would be "living under a totalitarian machine," since once war arrived, civil liberties were invariably curbed. William Graham Sumner

38. Ibid., Villard to Kirchwey, Oct. 5, 1940.
39. Manfred Jonas, *Isolationism in America, 1935–1941* (Ithaca, N.Y.: Cornell Univ. Press, 1966), pp. 98–99.
40. Villard to Sargent, July 30, 1940, Villard MSS.

had shown a previous generation that after the Spanish-American War, Americans ended up practicing the very evils they had sought to punish Spain for. "We were torturing, concentrating, burning villages and crops—doing every single thing for which we had denounced the Spaniards. So it will be when we go to war with Hitler." Villard regretted that to point this truth out meant that one was subjected to being called "a 5th Columnist, a pro-Nazi, a traitor."[41]

Having lost his audience, Villard began to talk with others about "the possibility of starting up the old *Nation*." Interest was expressed by John Chamberlain, George Leighton, Norman Thomas, John T. Flynn, and others. The difficulty was lack of money, because "many of the liberals and Jews who supported The Nation are now for war, particularly the Jews." Villard thought of trying to gather backing from the middle class in the Midwest, which opposed intervention. He wanted to avoid appealing to "the sophisticated intellectual group to which The Nation and The New Republic now appeal." This group, which unfortunately comprised exactly the reading public for magazines like the *Nation,* he now defined as a "small minority who would put their own country into war . . . in opposition to the wishes of their fellow citizens."[42]

Pearl Harbor ended his career as an opponent of war. Now he was to concentrate on trying to help his countrymen avoid the evils he thought were imminent. Villard wanted the citizenry to gain control over the direction of foreign policy. Those who *had* control branded their critics as reactionary. Even Villard's biographer concludes that once Villard made his decision to oppose American entry into World War II, his writings became "hardly distinguishable from the utterances of the most reactionary forces in America." Charging Villard with having "completely abandoned his idea of principle over political expediency," Michael Wreszin argues that during the war Villard "continued his association with reactionary elements."[43] To repeat the charges of

41. Ibid.
42. Ibid., Villard to Mauritz Hallgren, Feb. 12, 1941; Villard to Lincoln Colcord, Feb. 28, 1941.
43. Wreszin, *Oswald Garrison Villard,* pp. 264, 269–270.

reaction only obscures the nature of Villard's critique and provides an apologia for those who argue that policy must be left to the experts. Villard believed that no one was as expert as the people, and he thought they had not been allowed to make their will known.

Oswald Garrison Villard, representing the "Committee on Militarism," testifies on the subject of compulsory military training before the Senate Military Affairs Committee, July 11, 1940. (ACME)

Villard Confronts the Cold War

IT IS NOT SURPRISING that Villard's biographer saw Pearl Harbor as an event that led to Oswald Garrison Villard's "spiritual death." Opposition to the war had supposedly made his values irrelevant. Yet the war in no way led Villard to cease his efforts, though he was unacceptable in the intellectual community. After Versailles his articles in the *Nation* had established Villard as a figure to be reckoned with. After Pearl Harbor he was to be ignored and often misread.

Old family friends, such as Eugene V. Rostow, chided Villard for his claim that the interventionists were blind to the moral issues of the war. Rostow saw the only way out through victory, and he accused Villard of producing arguments that broke down into vague abstractions. Rostow may have differed from his older friend, but Villard was anything but vague.[1]

While administration loyalists saw the war as a fight on behalf of Four Freedoms, Villard argued that it was "rapidly becoming a war for other things as well." In an article, "Head on for Imperialism," Villard presented an analysis that resembles post-cold-war revisionist writings of historians such as Gabriel Kolko. He pointed to the partnership of government and business in the development of Mideastern oil resources. "At least," Villard explained, "we are not going to let any chance to garner some rich pickings pass us by as we wend our triumphant way toward the new world order."

The desperate need for oil, Villard feared, meant that the United States government would itself jump into the oil business. He predicted that the U.S. "will strike hands with these ancient domestic foes and take part of their Arabian holdings to assure

1. Rostow to Villard, Dec. 5, 1941, Oswald Garrison Villard MSS., Houghton Library, Harvard Univ., Cambridge, Mass. Unless otherwise indicated, all citations in this chapter are from the Villard MSS.

us of bigger and better oil supplies when the next generation grows up." Those who saw this as socialism did not realize that "we live in new times. The policy for America from now on is to take any oil field or foreign harbor or Atlantic or Pacific island that we deem essential to our national safety."

America was sending 1,500 tons of lend-lease supplies per day to Russia over "the Persian railway in American cars, pulled by American locomotives, run by American engineers." The U.S. Army had rebuilt the railroad, increased the water supply, built highways, rehabilitated two Iranian harbors and one in Iraq on the Persian Gulf. The U.S. government had "taken over practically every activity of the Persian Government except on the educational side." The demand now was simply "that we shall not get out of there without some share in Persian oil." The problem was that 95 percent of the Iranian oil supply went to Russia and England. The demand to obtain that oil meant the real possibility of "serious involvement with Russia and England in care of whom Persia asked us to take over."

Oil in Venezuela and the Caribbean was already controlled by Standard Oil. The problem there was simple: "If the time ever comes when the inhabitants of the countries involved decide, as Mexico decided, that they want the right to their own natural resources, there will certainly be a great furor in this hemisphere. Perhaps our government may take over there also so that it can legitimately send in marines when trouble comes."

America's oil imperialism proved that the United States was not involved in an idealistic war. Actually, the war was being used to move America toward "becoming an imperialistic power interfering in concerns of others and grabbing natural resources all over the globe":

> We are to have permanent conscription and a seven-ocean navy, the largest ever dreamed of in the world, and a merchant fleet of 50,000,000 tons . . . to be prepared for our next wholesale effort to save the world for democracy or from other countries, white or yellow, which we may have to put in their places. A prominent American who has just returned from Russia and stopped over at many American encampments, including some in Persia . . . de-

clares that at every stop American soldiers asked if he didn't think
that we should have to fight Russia next.[2]

What some called an American Century Villard saw as a
movement toward imperialism. The South American states were
already secure and delivered, and now the United States wanted
the entire Western world. He ended with what he envisioned
would be the new battle cry: "Long live the American Empire!"

Villard renewed a dialogue with *New Republic* publisher
Bruce Bliven. Like Freda Kirchwey, Bliven had supported intervention, and he had removed antiwar columnist John T. Flynn
from the *New Republic*'s pages. By 1943, however, Bliven had
second thoughts about the war's effects and wrote in an editorial
that "nearly all American liberals have been profoundly unhappy
about the political aspects of the war." Bliven was concerned that
some public figures wanted an imperial settlement and that ad-
justments with Russia would not be so simple. He reminded his
readers not to assume that Russia would quickly and lightly
declare war on Japan. Why, he wrote, "should Russians die to
maintain the British, Dutch and French empires in the Far East?"
And why, Villard retorted, "should American boys die for the
same purpose?"

Bliven also feared that in the war's aftermath, unfulfilled social
revolutions in France, Greece, and the occupied countries might
produce changes not to America's liking. In that case the U.S.
government might try to freeze the *status quo* by perpetuating
fascist regimes. Bliven was now asking some of the same questions Villard had asked before the United States had gone to war.
Bliven had even discovered, Villard noted, that "Mr. Roosevelt
has never been more of a liberal than he felt he could afford to be
at any given moment," and that the men who advised him at the
right moment always turned out to be generals and business
executives with billion-dollar war contracts.

But while Bliven wanted the war fought on to a successful
conclusion, and believed that "the slow forces of time extending

2. Oswald Garrison Villard, "Head on for Imperialism," *Christian Century,* Nov. 10, 1943, pp. 1300–02.

over the centuries after all justify liberals in their aspirations," he was angry that not all American leaders had abandoned conservative postwar visions. But he thought that they would gradually accommodate themselves to common sense. The war was not even over and already such a liberal as Bliven was disillusioned. Bliven, Villard wrote, had hauled "down the flag that was hoisted as a signal to all good liberals to seize their arms for the certain victory of all their aims and aspirations." The death of their sons was to be atoned for by "consolation that the mills of the liberals' gods grind exceedingly slow." Bliven no longer desired a new world created out of the deaths; he desired only the rescue of England and physical defeat of the Axis.

Such disillusionment began, Villard argued, when "the peace of Versailles was written to be lost." In World War II it was apparent while the fighting continued, "when we are believed to be on the high tide of victory, flushed with surety of a glorious triumph over the forces of evil." Bliven's pained words demonstrated to Villard that both liberal and conservative camps now admitted "that the idealistic catchwords with which our rulers of the democratic nations have led their peoples to the war are about as real as the Wilsonian slogans of the war to end war."[3]

Villard's skepticism was reinforced by his friend Edwin Borchard, who saw American entrance into the Pacific war as an imperial adventure, meant to preserve the *status quo*. State Department policy was created to protect so-called world order, particularly the British Empire. Terming that policy "imperialism gone wild," Borchard argued that American defeat of Japan would produce worse chaos than in Europe. The United States would claim the right to police Asia, and the result would be perpetual war, as well as a sharp struggle over control of the old European colonies.[4]

Borchard agreed with Villard that the peace emerging out of World War II would be "as unbearable as that of Versailles, and that the population of this country will have to pay the penalty." A harsh policy would only lead the Germans to support the

3. Villard, "Hauling Down the War Flag," *Christian Century,* June 9, 1943; pp. 692–693.
4. Borchard to Villard, Jan. 8, 1943.

Right. Believing that inflation and the "follies of Versailles" had led the Germans to accept Hitler, Borchard argued that a similar postwar policy would produce similar results. "I fear," he informed Villard, "that we are leading up to a pax romana in which the United States will attempt, under British guidance, to dictate the fate of all parts of the world. Starvation and bombs seem to be the favored sanction."[5]

Revisionist historian Harry Elmer Barnes agreed that a fight had to be waged against harsh postwar treatment of Germany. The best means of prevention would be to "get the present gang out of Washington before the War is over or as soon as possible, even if we have to support the devil to bring about the result." For Barnes a ticket of Chicago *Tribune* publisher Colonel Robert McCormick and anti-Semite Gerald L. K. Smith was preferable to Roosevelt and Henry A. Wallace, though he hoped he would not have to make such a choice. But because the Soviet Communists would oppose Western policy toward Germany, Barnes thought that Stalin might turn out to be "the least repugnant figure" among the potential opponents to FDR and Churchill.[6]

Villard himself had few doubts about the disastrous course America was on. Harry Hopkins had made it known, he claimed, that the United States was determined to be a great imperialist nation with naval bases, airfields, and army garrisons throughout the world. Another Warren G. Harding, he thought, was waiting around the corner.[7]

The Harding around the corner turned out to be Harry S. Truman, whose accession was received by Villard with skepticism. Villard saw Truman as an incompetent small-town politician reared to national leadership by the Roosevelt forces in the Democratic party. Truman, he wrote conservative journalist Frank Hanighen, did not know what was going on around him. A letter of the President's which had been shown to Villard revealed "a perfect example of a small-town, lower Middle Class American Legion mentality, kindly, ordinarily well meaning and wholly unfit to play the greatest role in the world. Truman was

5. Borchard to Villard, May 21, 1943.
6. Barnes to Villard, July 20, 1943.
7. Villard to Charles A. Beard, March 6, 1944.

talking about unification of command of the armed forces. This was particularly dangerous with a President in the White House who gave the military full speed ahead. Congress could move in an anti-militarist direction, but it could not be relied upon when the President moved in the opposite direction and declared that the national safety is in peril."[8]

Postwar developments justified his skeptical attitude. Because of the duplicity of the Roosevelt administration, he expected the worst. FDR's 1944 victory had given him a "clean bill of health for all his dirty skullduggery in putting us into war and deceiving the American people." Villard thought it meant that FDR had carte blanche to do what he wanted without consulting Congress, since "so much was made of his fitness to deal with our foreign affairs single-handedly."[9]

Villard did not find the results of the Yalta Conference to be encouraging. Detecting no signs of any move toward disarmament, Villard saw the administration moving toward a more belligerent military stance. According to Villard, Harry Hopkins had stated that the United States was going to establish a naval base on Formosa, and then move to encircle the entire world.[10]

Skepticism about New Deal foreign policy aims had led Villard to view internationalist liberalism with grave suspicion and had moved him closer to an uneasy alliance with certain elements on the political Right. Villard was upset to find that his friend Eugene Rostow supported war-crimes trials for captured Nazi leaders, even though the Nuremburg trials violated *ex post facto* law. He was also angry to find that Rostow backed French separatist schemes for undermining Germany, a policy that Villard saw as a criminal performance worthy of Adolf Hitler.[11]

The policies supported by such liberals as Rostow led Villard and Edwin Borchard to dub their opponents totalitarian liberals. Borchard pointed out that Rostow was willing to tolerate if not endorse "totalitarianism at home," even though Rostow acknowl-

8. Villard to Hanighen, Jan. 3, 1945.
9. Villard to Albert Jay Nock, Nov. 20, 1944.
10. Villard to Helen Alfred, March 8, 1945.
11. Rostow to Villard, n.d.; Villard to Rostow, Feb. 14, 1945.

edged that money spent for Lend-Lease aid, Bretton Woods, UNRRA, and U.S. foreign trade would carry the American debt to an amount higher than three hundred billion dollars. Borchard and Villard reasoned that the crucial interventionist decisions had been made at Yalta. The charge found welcome echoes among many on the Right. "At Yalta," Borchard noted, "they agreed ostensibly on the permanent intervention of the United States in all European elections, so that nonintervention, which Stettinius promised in Greece, Italy and . . . Poland . . . is now to be replaced by a universal intervention the outcome of which can only mean universal war." It was "one of our misfortunes," he wrote, "that the liberals upon whom we had a right to depend have adopted totalitarianism without realizing where it would lead." Henry L. Stimson stood at the head of the greatest war machine in history. Censorship was so vast that it was impossible to talk freely about what American policy should be. In 1945 Borchard wrote Villard that "a man would be hounded if he dared to tell the truth. And yet the critics are the most loyal and honest Americans of all."[12]

Franklin D. Roosevelt at Yalta had repeated the crimes of Woodrow Wilson at Paris, and the outcome could only be a resurgence of intervention. The anti-communism of some members of this group led them to support interventionist measures aimed at stopping the Soviet colossus. But to Villard the menace to peace came from the leadership of the United States. Villard dared to criticize what was surely an emerging consensus in favor of a cold war. He had at first hoped that the White House would be safer under Truman, and that the new President would prove a better negotiator at Potsdam than FDR had been at Yalta.[13] But events were not comforting.

Villard remained skeptical about the possibilities for success of the new United Nations Organization, which privately he regarded as the post World War I dissidents had viewed the League of Nations—as an unworkable alliance of imperial nations whose wranglings would increase the danger of war. Publicly, he ex-

12. Borchard to Villard, Feb. 24, 1945.
13. Villard to Congressman Lawrence H. Smith, July 12, 1945.

plained to Charles Beard, he had decided to accept it with reservations, but not to oppose it. "This time I don't want kooks and knaves to say that we have wrecked the league by not going in."[14]

Villard was horrified at the news that an atomic bomb had been dropped on Hiroshima and Nagasaki. At a time when most liberals viewed the event as a necessary military maneuver to end the war against Japan, Villard responded that "such monstrous slaughter of innocent human beings was certainly never dreamed of." He could not but feel that America would "pay a terrible price for it in the loss of our own morale, in the economic destruction we are inflicting on the whole world, and in our complete destruction of every ethical teaching which this connotes."[15]

But Villard's worst fears were confirmed by the results of the Potsdam Conference. That summit meeting, he contended, showed American leaders repeating the errors made at Versailles and making new ones. The Potsdam Agreement revealed how hollow the peace really was, and showed that U.S. negotiators would not criticize the Russians no matter how outrageous their actions were. At this point a major contradiction in Villard's outlook became apparent. For while he opposed the Truman administration and the cold war, he agreed with those who depicted the Russians as the new international villains. He disliked the fact that when he and other opposed Russian policies, they were accused of desiring a war with Russia.[16]

As he saw Potsdam, it went Versailles one better. After World War I the Allies took Germany's naval and merchant fleets from her, but they never said that Germany could not sail another ship. As Villard read the Potsdam declaration, "this particular bit of vengeance we reserved for 1945." He saw a major source of revenue and employment being stripped from the 75,000,000 Germans who were supposed to support themselves without sufficient income, as well as support four occupying armies, while they had lost most of their heavy industry. "We are going to

14. Villard to Beard, July 16, 1945.
15. Villard to Felix Morley, July 16, 1945.
16. Villard to Irving Dillard, Sept. 11, 1945.

make the Krauts understand this time," emphasized Villard, "that they lost the war."[17]

Here again Villard's emphasis dovetailed with that analysis presented by the anti-Soviet postwar revisionists. This group believed that the United States had fought the wrong enemy during World War II, that Russia, not Germany, was the power that should have been opposed. They attacked what they called Germanophobia—the tendency to blame all wrongdoing on the particular characteristics of the German people and nation. Although Villard parted company with the Right on evaluating Soviet foreign policy, he saw eye to eye with them on the German question.

He perceived Potsdam as a master plan to bleed Germany to death. German exports and imports were to be paid out of taxes levied against export profits. As soon as trade brought in more money than the Germans needed for a minimum, the Allies would take the greater surplus from enslaved German labor for their own reparations. In reality, Villard felt that the Allies were putting an end to German shipping in order to eliminate the chief competitor to British and American shipping.

Like J. M. Keynes after World War I, Villard predicted that the attempt to carry out the Potsdam Agreement would collapse within one year, if not sooner. The effort to fix terms for what Germany could produce was fallacious, since there existed no basis for determining this.

. . . If the heavy German industry is largely destroyed, if her textile plants are not to be allowed to produce far more than the German people need, if she is not to mine much more coal than before the war and turn out a much larger iron production, and if she is to have no shipping, she will not be able to support her own people, import the necessary goods for them which she does not herself produce, and earn anything like the sums we Allies propose to squeeze out of this utterly wrecked country, which 12 American generals have just jointly declared cannot be resurrected to fight another war in one hundred years.

17. Villard, "The Coming Collapse of the Potsdam Pact," *Progressive,* No. 26, 1945, pp. 8–9.

Such conditions would produce a German nation that would move sharply toward either the Left or the Right. Germany had to be allowed to develop a shipping industry and factories for peaceful purposes, and the Allies had to give the Germans far more economic rights than they contemplated at Potsdam.[18]

Potsdam was a pact of vengeance imposed over innocent and guilty alike. The Allies were trying to control the Germans until they accepted subservience to their new conquerors. Germany was once again a vanquished subject power, and its condition demanded sympathy. Unlike other antifascists, Villard did not wish to bleed Germany white in atonement for Hitler's sins. Moreover, it was not yet clear whether Russia had agreed to enter the ongoing war against Japan, and no provisions had been made for Soviet withdrawal from "Stalin's puppet states." Hence Villard demanded firm "inter-Allied supervision of the promised election in Poland." Here he revealed anxiety over what he saw as American acquiescence to Stalin's territorial demands. He charged that the Big Three had violated their Atlantic Charter commitments, and that "Anglo-American acceptance of Stalin's settlement for Central Europe is bound to plague us—and the next generation even more so." The Potsdam Agreement, in other words, was underwriting Russian influence in Poland. The truth was that "reformation can never be imposed upon a people from the outside."[19]

Villard actually misread the nature of what had occurred at Potsdam. From a one-sided analysis of the pact he argued that the peoples of the world had been prevented from determining their own destinies because of Big Three machinations. He saw Potsdam participants tearing "to shreds their solemn promises under the Atlantic Charter to permit no territorial aggrandizement and to make no territorial changes which do not conform with the freely expressed wishes of the people concerned."

He agreed with the anti-Communist revisionists that the Western nations had by "the Pact of Potsdam underwritten the Russian rape of Poland under the Ribbentrop-Molotov Pact, and

18. Ibid., pp. 8–9.
19. Villard, "The Potsdam Pact: Disaster for Europe," *Progressive*, Aug. 13, 1945, p. 1.

sought to compensate Poland by handing over huge areas of Germany to the Polish. By this single stroke we have created two perilous areas of discord and bitterness and scheming and plotting which can only explode in bloodshed again." The Polish settlement alone had proved the pact's "folly, its impossibility, its shamelessness and above all its threat to all of Europe."[20]

Villard's concern for an industrialized Germany actually paralleled the concern of leading businessmen, as well as the majority

20. Ibid.; see also Walter LaFeber, *The Origins of the Cold War: 1941–1947* (New York: Wiley, 1971), pp. 124, 129–131. In fact, the pact revealed a different set of priorities from those claimed by Villard. LaFeber notes: "Germany was the central issue at Potsdam, and the final agreement was reached only after long, angry debates. . . . Part of the American problem was Russia, but another difficulty was contradictions within the U.S. position. The President, for example, could not have both a 'whole' Germany and a Germany which would be rapidly reconstructed economically, for if the nation was governed by the Four Powers as a whole, Russia would extract reparations from the entire area. . . . The United States had to choose: it could have either a united Germany under four-power control, or a large portion of Germany safe from Soviet reparation demands, a portion which would serve as the seed for an economically revived Europe and a buffer zone separating the Communists from Western Europe. The United States chose the latter. At Potsdam . . . the nation was in fact divided. The final reparation settlement illustrated the division. Whereas at Yalta the Big Three had agreed to a total reparation sum of $20 billion to be extracted from a united Germany (with half going to the Soviet Union), the final settlement at Potsdam mentioned no specific figures. Instead, it gave percentages and recognized explicitly the strength of the Soviets and the Western powers in their respective occupation zones of Germany. Poland's occupation of Eastern Germany (the territory east of a line formed by the Oder and Neisse Rivers) was also recognized, although it was to be only 'temporary.' "

Stalin was concerned that Germany should not be allowed to pose another military threat to Russia. This aim was accomplished partially by giving portions of Eastern Germany to Poland in compensation for territory which Russia had absorbed from the Poles. Truman and Churchill at first bitterly objected to this.

The view that Germany had to be allowed rapid economic recovery was *actually held* by leading American businessmen and statesmen. Both the State Department, Henry L. Stimson, and others favored keeping Germany industrialized and economically viable. Alfred P. Sloan, chairman of the board of General Motors, told financier Bernard Baruch that Germany had to be industrialized. Like Villard, Sloan argued that the Potsdam pact too closely resembled the proposed Morgenthau Plan, which advocated a de-industrialized and partitioned Germany. Morgenthau's plan was never accepted by the administration or put into effect.

of policy makers within the government. Villard's concentration upon the betrayal of the Poles led him to distort what had actually taken place at Potsdam. The Potsdam Agreement was different from Secretary of the Treasury Henry L. Morgenthau's proposed plan for Germany. He favored a nonindustrialized and partitioned Germany that would have an agrarian economy. Like Villard, major administration leaders saw the folly of not allowing Germany to get back on its feet.

Villard still remained aloof from the hard-line anti-Communists. He may have been looking at Potsdam through the eyes of one who had lived through 1919, but he felt that Russia was not evil incarnate. The enemy were the "military lords and masters" within the United States. Leaders of the armed forces, especially of the navy, were preparing to rearm America. These groups, "swollen by their magnificent successes in the greatest of wars, are plainly proposing to capitalize heavily on their achievements and to continue to call the tune in the expectation that a militaristically inclined President and a subservient Congress will obediently give them exactly what they want." Admiral Nimitz' desire for more ships, and the apparent merger of the army and navy, were to Villard "a great danger to the American Republic." It was almost as if, he noted, "instead of being supreme victors, we had a menacing enemy immediately around the corner against whom we must arm without the loss of a moment. No question of the cost to the American people is allowed to enter the discussion, just as neither President Truman nor General Marshall ever gave an exact estimate of what the army, plus peacetime conscription, will cost."[21]

Villard could not have been more clear. There was simply no menacing enemy waiting to attack. The heralded Russian menace was nonexistent. Behind the move to build up the armed forces, he believed, was the concept articulated by Truman that force alone counts in international relations. Quoting a Truman statement of October 23, 1946, in which the President had said that America could assure peace only as long as it remained strong and that peace must be built upon power, Villard wryly com-

21. Villard, "Our Military Lords and Masters," *Christian Century,* Feb. 13, 1946; pp. 204–5.

mented: "How the Kaiser and Hitler and Mussolini would cry Amen to this!" Villard saw this as a militarist attitude straight from the White House. He accused Truman of "openly entertaining such imperialistic plans as the domination of the Pacific and the north Atlantic."[22]

It was no surprise to find Villard writing a friend to complain that in America the tension against Russia was growing steadily. He had been told by an associate in New Mexico that "to call a man a Communist is to use a fighting word, that no one speaks of Russia any more as an ally, but as a future enemy." He found it prophetic that William Bullitt had written a book in which he almost demanded an immediate war against Russia.[23]

Yet on some issues Villard supported hard-line anti-Communist policies. He had a close relationship with Syngman Rhee and supported the creation of a pro-Western government in Korea. During the war the United States had favored an international trusteeship for Korea, rather than immediate independence. This irritated nationalists such as Syngman Rhee, who had been warning the State Department about the dangers of Russia's using Korean Communist divisions to communize Korea. By May 1944 the State Department favored Four-Power trusteeship, and it supported this position at Yalta. The United States was meant to play the dominant role in the occupation government at the war's end. Conflict was ironed out when it was specified that Japanese troops south of the 38th parallel would surrender to the United States, while those above that line would surrender to Russian troops. Russian troops already in Seoul then withdrew north of the parallel and informally acknowledged the American partition of Korea into two zones.[24]

As far as Villard was concerned, there was little hope ahead as long as the United States did not straightforwardly aid Korea and those peoples who were Stalin's other victims.[25] At first Villard had hoped that Russia would be kept out of Korea, "but

22. Ibid., p. 205.
23. Villard to Edward Groth, Aug. 8, 1946.
24. Gabriel Kolko, *The Politics of War* (New York: Random House, 1968), pp. 601–604.
25. Villard to Frank Hanighen, Jan. 3, 1945.

after reading of the secret bargains with the Soviets as to Sakhalin and the Kuriles I am prepared for anything." As an "appeaser," Villard wrote to Syngman Rhee, "Franklin Roosevelt made Chamberlain look like thirty cents."[26]

Acceptance of the Yalta myths became a staple item in Villard's world view. Soviet-U.S. agreement on the status of Korea was the equivalent of Chamberlain's acquiescence in the destruction of prewar Czechoslovakia by Hitler's Germany. On this point Villard's analysis was encouraged by some of his traditional right-wing contacts. *Human Events* editor Frank Hanighen wrote him that "Roosevelt and Churchill at Yalta faced a Stalin demanding Manchuria and Korea," and because of FDR's indecision, "Stalin doubtless felt he had an assent." Hanighen asserted that the State Department, moreover, had "never made any preparations for the government of Korea."[27]

From that point on, Villard befriended the cause of conservative nationalism espoused by Syngman Rhee. Villard chided the United States for failing to assure an independent Korea, a pledge it had made to the Philippines and other Japanese victims. "Why is it that the Russians have taken the northern half of Korea while we occupy the southern," and we allow the southern half to be run by Japanese officials? This decision, he asserted, meant that the United States was portraying an "incredible American attitude of continuing in office their hated conquerers."[28]

Villard supported but one principle for Korea—that a "people demanding freedom" be given the right to govern themselves when they demand that right. He saw America seeking to deny Koreans their right to gain independence. He was upset that the Korean provisional government established by Rhee was getting a cold shoulder in Washington, and he did not buy the official excuse that the State Department could not tell which group of Koreans really represented the Korean people.

Villard favored having the State Department choose one group

26. Villard to Syngman Rhee, Sept. 6, 1945.
27. Hanighen to Villard, Sept. 12, 1945.
28. Villard, "Showdown in Korea," *Progressive,* Oct. 1, 1945, p. 4. The decision to maintain Japanese occupation troops was made to keep Korea in non-Communist hands until surrender to Western troops could be arranged.

of Koreans and aiding them to temporarily take over until a plebiscite could be held. United States indecision revealed that no plans had been made in advance, which led to dependence on Japanese administrators. This was a great affront to the proud and independent Koreans, who desired a free nation that would stand as a buffer state between Russia and China as well as between the latter nation and Japan. Only independence would prevent a Russian effort to occupy Korea, and the United States had to stop using the argument that the Koreans were too inexperienced for self-government.[29]

Villard's assessment was accurate in terms of the inconsistencies he disclosed in U.S. policy. But the solution he proposed was that eventually decided upon by the Truman administration. They would move to back Rhee as a stable non-Communist nationalist, who would build a South Korea favorable to U.S. interests. Villard viewed support to Rhee as commensurate with a long-standing commitment to colonial independence, and he did not understand the conservative role played by Rhee. His stand on Korea put him squarely on the side of conservative nationalism within Korea and domestic reaction within the United States.

Villard's Korean tie undoubtedly was the factor that led him to be among the original public supporters of Alfred Kohlberg's "China lobby" group. The executive committee of the American China Policy Association included Benjamin Stolberg, Isaac Don Levine, Max Eastman, Sidney Hook, Claire Boothe Luce, A. Philip Randolph, Freda Utley, Louis Waldman, and Villard. Kohlberg, an industrialist who imported Chinese lace into

29. Ibid., pp. 4, 10; cf. Joyce and Gabriel Kolko, *The Limits of Power: The World and United States Foreign Policy, 1945–1954* (New York: Harper and Row, 1972), pp. 277–299. The Kolkos' modern revisionist account bears striking similarity to Villard's analysis. They point out that at the war's end American authorities were worried about the revolutionary character of the people's committees established in Korea during liberation from Japanese rule. To prevent surrender to these popular forces the U.S. Supreme Allied Commander asked the Japanese authorities to keep order. Japanese rulers were kept in office as official U.S. policy, and President Truman publicly stated that Koreans could not rule themselves until "time and patience established them for expertise needed for self government." The Kolkos differ only in that they do not see Rhee as a viable alternative to enforced Japanese rule.

America, was the instrumental figure behind the new association.

On August 6, 1946, Kohlberg had addressed a letter to the State Department charging that the United States was trying to force Chiang Kai-shek to give in to Communist pressure. Trying to create a Nationalist-Communist coalition would make China a Soviet satellite. Kohlberg also charged that concessions to Russia had been made at both Yalta and Potsdam, and that Truman had agreed to a pro-Communist partition of China.[30]

Shortly after this letter was released to the press Villard resigned as a director of the China lobby. Noting that he could not go as far as the other members in supporting the cause of Chiang's government, Villard stressed that he was as "strongly opposed to the Communists as anybody can be," but he realized that Chiang's government was "as bloody and dictatorial as most dictatorships." Villard, moreover, registered himself as being totally and "absolutely opposed to the employment of American troops in China." He understood that an excuse for their presence was the fear that if they got out, Russia would move in. But Villard did not believe that American foreign policy could be dictated by fear of Russia.

Maintenance of U.S. troops in China would only do great harm to the reputation of the United States. The effect would be to increase the drift toward imperialism and overseas conquest. Villard also feared that if American troops were kept in China they would be fighting the Chinese Communist army before long. As for the Communists, they had "substantial grievances against us since it is openly admitted that we have trained and equipped well over thirteen divisions for Chiang." Villard even feared that the U.S. could be drawn into war with Russia over an incident with the Chinese Communists. Already one marine had been killed. Continuation of the present course assured the worst kind of disaster.[31]

Kohlberg did not agree. Accusing Villard of having swallowed Communist propaganda, Kohlberg described Chiang's government as composed of "the most forward looking of Chinese." The danger was that fellow travelers, such as Theodore White and

30. Kohlberg to Dean Acheson, Aug. 6, 1946.
31. Villard to Kohlberg, Nov. 20, 1946.

Edgar Snow, might succeed in getting the United States to abandon Chiang. Once China fell, the rest of Asia would follow.[32]

Villard was not convinced by Kohlberg's logic. On February 20, 1947, he formally resigned from the board of directors of the American China Policy Association, simply noting that he was not in complete sympathy with their position.[33] When the Nationalist Chinese government was on the verge of collapse Villard saw Chiang's demise as an event of major significance. If the U.S. proceeded to arm other Western nations and got involved in China's civil war, he noted, the result would be militarization and dangerous military alliances with other powers.[34] After the revolution had taken place, although he thought he might shock a friend of his, Villard approved of Chinese Communist efforts to throw out foreigners and retake Hong Kong. "When you think how they have been exploited," he explained, ". . . they are entitled to run their own country the way they see fit."[35]

Tacit support to the Chinese Communists, however, did not mean that Villard supported insurgency when he thought the Russians stood behind it or when he believed they acted in opposition to independence movements. He tied Russian movement into northern Iran with British imperialism in the Far East. "It is a terrific test of us and the English," he wrote. "Can you tell me the difference between the British destroying Javanese villages with long-range naval guns, and the wiping out of Lidice? Both were certainly acts of revenge because of revolutionary activities." Despite his opposition to the imperial activity of Western nations, Villard did not suppose Americans should sit "idly by and watch Russia inflict more horrible cruelties and injustices upon nearby peoples."[36]

Villard thought the Koreans were threatened by Russia's attempt to gain influence in Asia. He supported the struggle for liberation of the Chinese Communists, *and* the conservative nationalism of Syngman Rhee. When the State Department fi-

32. Kohlberg to Villard, Nov. 29, 1946.
33. Villard to Kohlberg, Feb. 20, 1947.
34. Villard to DeLancy Howe, Nov. 7, 1948.
35. Villard to Howe, May 5, 1949.
36. Villard to Howe, Feb. 21, 1945.

nally made up its mind for Rhee, and he became Premier of South Korea, Villard was overjoyed: "right triumphs some of the time." He wanted to take a tough line. If Washington put sufficient pressure on the Russians, he wrote Rhee, "they finally do yield."[37] It is hard to see how Villard would have worked out the contradictions in his politics if he had lived to witness the Korean war and the intrusion of Chinese Communist troops. In 1949 he did not have to confront the possibility.

Generally Villard was in opposition to Truman's cold-war policies, and he was sympathetic to some of Henry A. Wallace's criticisms. Wallace had written Truman in March of 1946 opposing an aggressive posture toward Soviet Russia and suggesting that mutually advantageous trade relations could create a basis for negotiations and help end political misunderstanding. Conflicts with Russia over growing Soviet control of Eastern Europe might be solved if economic arrangements were worked out first. Wallace believed that Soviet behavior was the "result of their dire economic needs and their disturbed sense of security," and he argued that "we can disabuse the Soviet mind . . . by proving to them that we want to trade with them and to cement our economic relations with them."[38]

As Secretary of Commerce, Wallace was expressing these opinions until the furor that resulted from his speech in Madison Square Garden on September 12, 1946, when he told his audience that "Russian ideals of social-economic justice are going to govern nearly a third of the world. Our ideas of free-enterprise democracy will govern much of the rest. . . . By mutual agreement this competition should be put on a friendly basis, and the Russians should stop conniving against us in certain areas just as we should stop scheming against them in other parts of the world." It was a spheres-of-influence concept. The United States, he insisted, had to acknowledge that it should stay out of political

37. Villard to Syngman Rhee, Aug. 30 and Dec. 16, 1948.
38. Wallace to Truman, March 14, 1946, in Harry S. Truman, *Memoirs,* I (New York: Doubleday, 1955); Wallace to Truman, July 23, 1946; *New Republic,* Sept. 30, 1946, p. 404; also see Ronald Radosh and Leonard P. Liggio, "Henry A. Wallace and the Open Door," in Thomas G. Paterson, ed. *Cold War Critics: Alternatives to American Foreign Policy in the Truman Years* (Chicago: Quadrangle Books, 1971), p. 80.

affairs in Eastern Europe, just as Russia had to accept that it must keep out of political affairs in Latin America.[39]

Secretary of State James F. Byrnes was in Paris negotiating European peace treaties with the Russians. Wallace, he charged, was undercutting his hard line. On September 19 Truman asked Wallace for his resignation.

"Beyond question," Villard commented, "Henry Wallace is stronger out of the Cabinet than in it." Villard understood that Wallace attracted a large potential following. "Many Americans who don't like what is being done in Europe in our name as a nation may turn to Wallace to see if he can offer leadership of the kind they desire. All who favor making the nation's policy one of absolute refusal to be drawn into another war, and all who dislike England, may turn to the Iowan full of hope that at last there is a spokesman for their views."

Wallace had a great appeal; however, this did not mean that Villard agreed with all of the Secretary's views. Wallace was not a clear anti-imperialist. He favored a world divided into blocs controlled by the great powers. He wanted Russia to have control of Eastern Europe, and he argued that the Russians had as much right to it as the United States had under the Monroe Doctrine to South America. In Wallace's view, Eastern Europe was meant to be a Russian sphere.

Wallace was beginning to attack British imperialism, but at a time when England was being forced to withdraw from her former colonies. Villard thought Wallace inconsistent; before the war he had been "one of those who insisted that the American people must sacrifice their youth and their wealth to preserve England and its imperialist policies!" He saw his break with Truman prompted purely by ambition and thirst for power. Wallace had remained quiet even when Roosevelt had dropped him from the Vice-Presidency. If Wallace was to succeed in his new crusade, he would have to put forth a detailed program on foreign policy. He would have to courageously define an independent policy toward Britain and Russia and pledge to stand by his proposals.

39. Paterson, ed. *Cold War Critics,* p. 86; also see *U.S. News and World Report,* Sept. 20, 1946, p. 65.

There was a chance that the bipartisan cold-war consensus could be broken apart. If Wallace stood up and led a large portion of the electorate, and if the labor movement joined him, Villard predicted that possible success. Wallace's campaign might then become the vehicle for a popular referendum on foreign policy. The people should not be compelled to accept policies worked out in secret by the administration's own experts, or even by those of its critics. If Wallace championed the right of the American people to formulate their own foreign policy, Villard concluded, the people would rise up to support him.[40]

Privately, Villard and his friends were pessimistic. Edwin Borchard wrote to express his agreement with Villard's 1946 articles. Believing that American foreign policy had degenerated, Borchard agreed that Congress had abdicated its power to control foreign affairs. The United States had become as militaristic as any power on earth, Borchard concluded, and was acting in as evil a fashion as any aggressive nation.[41]

Villard did not favor catering to Stalin's imperial appetite, which included the Dardanelles, as had that of the czars. But he concluded that the American response was as dangerous. It was ironic that the Allies, who had promised in secret treaties between 1914 and 1918 to give the Soviet Union what it sought, should now be willing to go to war over the Dardanelles, "thousands of miles away from our shores." State Department opposition to Russian influence there would only produce fear and enmity in Moscow. Secretary of Defense James Forrestal had announced the presence of navy units in the Mediterranean, an action that appeared threatening to the Soviets. Villard thought that if the situation exploded, the United States would rush to battle, using the threat of the atom bomb as an instrument of pressure.[42]

The remnants of the old British Empire might be threatened by Russian penetration, but any war to protect them was unthinkable. Villard favored internationalizing the Dardanelles under UN auspices, but this was an equally myopic solution. The UN

40. Villard, "Wallace on Trial," *Progressive,* Sept. 30, 1946, p. 44.

41. Borchard to Villard, July 20, 1946.

42. Villard, "Dynamite in the Dardanelles," *Progressive,* Oct. 21, 1946, p. 42.

was under American control; the United States would have fiercely resisted Russian proposals to internationalize the Panama or Suez Canal. Villard thought, however, that an American gesture at neutralization would prove that the United States was acting like a great power, and that it was willing to move toward international cooperation.[43]

The Truman administration was thinking along different lines. Truman was not going to even contemplate proposals along the lines suggested by Villard. The historic Russian desire for control of the Dardanelles became to the administration part of a universal conflict between freedom and slavery. The answer was the Truman Doctrine of aid for Greece and Turkey.

On that critical issue Villard did not stand with the majority of his countrymen. America had "gone completely militaristic under Truman's guidance, or rather with his assent, for I don't think he knows what is going on or understands often what he signs his name to, and there isn't the slightest sign of any magnanimity toward the conquered people." The trend of his administration was simply to "overawe Russia and threaten them."[44]

The plans for aid to Greece and Turkey horrified him. "Where in the world will this venture not lead us?" The Spanish-American War had taken the United States from Cuba to Asia, and Villard predicted similar repercussions from the new interference. It was "the beginning of the payoff for our going into the war . . . As other countries are hovering on the verge of disaster one must ask . . . how much can we really put up to keep the world afloat?"[45]

The Greek-Turkish intervention was opposed by some on the political Right. *Human Events* editor Felix Morley wrote that "we may be at this moment deciding for war with Russia just as we decided for war with Germany when Lend-Lease was passed. People ought to understand that this decision is being made, and, if they want, express themselves on this subject." Morley, who was sure that Russia possessed an atomic bomb, saw "no sense whatever in trying to bolster peripheral spots like Greece while

43. Ibid., p. 4.
44. Villard to Horace Eaton, Feb. 24, 1947.
45. Villard to Irving Dillard, March 5, 1947.

we are simultaneously pursuing a policy which destroys the heart of Europe." Morley, like Villard, favored a policy of rebuilding a strong Germany, starting with a $100 million loan.[46]

Villard understood that some were advocating aid to Greece for humanitarian reasons, but that the policy would lead "straight to empire and entanglements as far reaching as was our taking over the Philippines, to which we owe our war with Japan and many other troubles." The Communist menace was real, but he predicted that once we were in Greece and Turkey, the United States would spend billions of dollars to keep the Communists from taking control.[47]

Moving into Greece, his friend Edwin Borchard wrote, meant that the United States was lining up for combat with Soviet Russia. Borchard didn't think that Congress would grant Truman the funds he requested, and he doubted whether any amount of funds could "prevent communism [from] prevailing among the poverty stricken. We have made sure there will be much poverty in the world and we seem determined to lend people money when the consequences of poverty show themselves."[48]

Villard's answer to the Truman Doctrine was an assertion that Russia ruled the United States. Every action in foreign policy was dictated by fear of Russia; to move into Greece and Turkey because of such fears was preposterous. It was bad enough "that we are now definitely mixed up with the exploitation of oil in Iran and Saudi Arabia, that the Government is playing oil politics in that distant section of the globe." To replace Britain elsewhere meant a movement into "the most dangerous tinderbox in the Near East."

Once economic aid was given, troops might later be sent. Having assumed financial responsibility for a nation, "if we don't send troops, I'll wager my best hat that in no time at all the U.S. Army will be insisting that Greek and Turkish armaments be standardized according to our own so that there may be full

46. Morley to Villard, March 11, 1947.
47. Villard to Morley, March 7, 1947; Villard to Edwin Borchard, March 6, 1947.
48. Borchard to Villard, March 12, 1947.

interchange of weapons and ammunition." He called attention to the 100,000 troops in Japan and the 90,000 in the Philippines, stationed there only to impress Russia that the U.S. had great military strength.

Villard could not see any danger of revolt in the world, especially in what remained of Germany. But military leaders, he said, were glad that Soviet Russia existed, because it gave them an excuse to militarize the United States on an unprecedented scale. American officers were "devoting their days and nights to planning the war with Russia when they are not spending their time endeavoring to put over universal military training."

Villard still thought Franklin D. Roosevelt had been an appeaser of Russia. America was hanging on in China because it had been warned that if American troops were not maintained there, Russia would "try to make permanent the occupation of Manchuria which Mr. Roosevelt so stupidly and shortsightedly granted to Stalin."

He believed that America had abandoned its policy of pursuing a foreign policy based on justice, "without any show of force," in favor of the militarist theory that Russia responded only to military pressure. Villard preferred exertion of moral influence. America's case did not have to rest on the strength of arms. He looked back nostalgically to the days of Grover Cleveland, when, supposedly, U.S. policy was framed purely on the grounds of morality. America then stayed within its own hemisphere, and conventional military powers respected it. "It was not until William McKinley and Theodore Roosevelt," he claimed, "that we had to have secret diplomacy and embark upon overseas adventures and bloodshed."

It was ironic that Americans expressed fear of Russia. For Russia had every reason, given U.S. military preparations, to be terrified at America's threats. Villard made it clear that he was ashamed and humiliated by America's new imperial policies, "by the sacrifice of those magnificent ideals we held when we were utterly opposed to militarism and war and refused even for a time to annex Hawaii." America should use its moral influence to create a free world. But the only way to check Communist imperialism was by democracy, not emulation of Russian imperial policy.[49]

The Republicans had not presented an alternative to Truman's interventionism. Instead, they had almost reassured his re-election by going along with the Truman Doctrine. The bipartisan unity on foreign policy gave Truman the chance to produce an atmosphere of crisis and to argue that successful confrontation with the Russians demanded his continuance in office.[50]

Villard was impressed with Senator Robert A. Taft. He was his own man, not an individual with reactionary ties. His character had been proved by his courageous attack on the Nuremberg trials.[51] Villard let Taft know that although he had never voted for a Republican for President, he would do his utmost to let the American people learn how incompetent and dangerous the Truman administration was. Villard hoped the senator would gain the Republican nomination. Thanking Taft for his opposition to universal military training, Villard hoped the senator would take a stronger position against the cold war. He asked Taft to "denounce the deliberate efforts being made to put us into war with Russia, even if thereby you parallel Vishinsky's, in the main, just attack upon us." Villard told Taft that the Russian UN representative's charges were accurate; the United States was now a military state beside which "the Kaiser's and Hitler's will seem of a kindergarten variety."[52]

Villard now looked more positively on Henry Wallace's efforts "to prevent war between the United States and Russia and to assail the militarization of this country by President Truman." The military influence was now so pervasive, he concluded, that it extended to industrial life, education, the economy, and scien-

49. Villard, "Russia Rules America," *Progressive,* March 17, 1947, pp. 1–2.
50. Villard to Peter Grimm, April 29, 1947.
51. Villard to Irving Dillard, Feb. 3, 1947.
52. Villard to Taft, Oct. 14, 1947. Taft answered that he would do all possible to block UMT, which he saw as "the key to militarization of the country." But he remained silent about Villard's comment on Russian images of U.S. policy (Taft to Villard, Nov. 29, 1947).

tific research. It amounted to a new alliance between the services and big business.[53]

The cold war abroad was producing severe domestic repercussions—in fact, an anti-Communist hysteria was growing at home. Like a later generation of revisionists, Villard tied up the birth of the domestic anti-Red mania to Truman's need to drum up support for the cold war. Villard was most critical of J. Parnell Thomas' investigation of communism in Hollywood, and his series of congressional hearings that led to the imprisonment of ten Hollywood screenwriters. The House Un-American Activities Committee had an obvious bias, a zest for sensationalism, and an eager desire for publicity. The committee was a Star Chamber, and its hearings were undignified circuses that produced hearsay but not evidence. The committee sought publicity; its hearings were of no legal value.

The "sensational inquiries" of the committee were adding to "the alarming anti-Red hysteria that is sweeping the country and taking us dangerously close to war." HUAC was only helping convince Americans that "another holocaust is inevitable," and blinding them "to the one-sidedness of the Truman attitudes, to the un-American character of such deliberate attacks upon Russia as now mark the speeches of Secretary Marshall."[54] Villard found it most difficult to comprehend how some conservatives with whom he shared many views could support the committee's work.[55]

As 1947 ended, Villard's prognosis darkened. He now saw a

53. Villard, "The American Drift Towards Militarism," June 20, 1947—written for *Peace News,* a British publication, Villard MSS.

54. Villard article for *Peace News,* Nov. 12, 1947, Villard MSS.

55. When *Human Events* published a pro-HUAC article, Villard retorted that the writer's "hatred of the Communists" had caused her to "lose her balance." He found it hard to understand how Frank Hanighen and John Chamberlain could "be so favorable to the Un-American Activities Committee"; see also Villard to Frank Hanighen, Oct. 18, 1948. Hanighen answered that HUAC was "handling its investigation and hearings in about the average way," and was performing "a necessary task of exposure while the Department of Justice is shirking its duties and the Executive is obviously trying to conceal the real situation" (Hanighen to Villard, Oct. 27, 1948).

"danger of a third World War merely because the men in power when the war ended were so utterly stupid or wicked."[56] When the Marshall Plan was announced, Villard was utterly skeptical:

> Aren't we in a lovely situation in regard to the Marshall "Plan"? The Republicans are really up against it. If they don't vote for it and it fails, as fail it will, as our Greek intervention is on the rocks, then they will be the traitors who caused the failure of the plan and the triumph of Stalin. Every step the Government takes is now actuated solely by our fear of Russia. The Secretary of War who a little while ago declared war on Russia all by himself, now announces that if the plan doesn't go through we will have to spend more than it calls for in armaments in addition to the 11 billions we are again going to vote for this year—80 per cent of the budget goes for war past and future! Of course if our military bluff succeeds, our militarists will be on the top of the world, saying that they did it. Somehow I can't believe that the Russians can be deterred from any policy by military threats.[57]

As if to emphasize that opposition to the cold war consensus came from both Left and Right, Villard added: "Oh, for one newspaper in the East that would just tell the truth and show up these people, as the Chicago *Tribune* so often does from its background of complete reaction and unbounded hatred of the British."[58]

When the Communist coup in Czechoslovakia displaced the government of Jan Masaryk, Villard did not think further disruptions in American-Soviet relations necessary. He remarked sarcastically that it might be "divine retribution" for Czech wickedness toward the Sudeten Germans before the onset of World War II. Villard also felt that "Wallace is right; our Government is heading straight for war and we shall be lucky if the disaster does not happen in time to re-elect Truman."[59] One could no longer deny that the United States had "become an aggressor nation." Now the United States was even "calling upon

56. Villard to Margaret Ermarth, Dec. 17, 1947.
57. Villard to Charles A. Beard, Jan. 15, 1948.
58. Ibid.
59. Villard to Richard Koch, March 11, 1948.

anti-Nazi German Generals to unite with us in planning for the protection of Europe." Villard recalled that he had once predicted that German troops would be cheered as they marched down Fifth Avenue. Now the United States sought their aid as it searched for new allies to aid its attempt to fight all over the world.[60]

Villard so distrusted Harry S. Truman that he thought it likely the President would encourage war to ensure his re-election. Military minds dominated diplomacy, and America was being militarized while the people remained ignorant. The Congress, terrorized by fear of communism, was voting huge military budgets.[61] It would not change things if the Senate went Democratic, because there was "unanimity now on what seemed to be the worst policy, UMT, arming Europe . . . and threatening Russia."[62]

Truman's election victory was a stunning jolt for Villard and his friends. The conservative journalist and World War II revisionist George Morgenstern explained that "Dewey offered nothing . . . and the chumps are voting themselves rubber dollar prosperity (and presumably, another war and socialism) at the expense of their neighbors." Chiang's collapse in China, he believed, meant that FDR's war aims had failed. Instead of a Japanese puppet regime controlling Manchuria, the territory was "now in control of Russia's China auxiliaries."[63]

For Socialist party leader and presidential candidate Norman Thomas, "one of the worst features of the re-election of Mr. Truman is that it gives free play to the militarists who have controlled him so far." Thomas saw billions being spent for rearmament in Western Europe, and he agreed that if the U.S. tried to undertake "the insane policy of trying to conquer the victorious Chinese Communists we shall be in war over our necks

60. Villard to Peter Grimm, March 30, 1948.
61. Villard to Liddell Hart, May 17, 1948.
62. Villard to Irving Dillard, Oct. 23, 1948. He added that on Germany Henry A. Wallace, whose Progressive party platform he subscribed to "in the main," was as "bad as the worst." Villard's opposition to harsh treatment for Germany united him with the pro-German but anti-Soviet right wing.
63. George Morgenstern to Villard, Nov. 8, 1948.

and the military influence will permeate every phase of American life."[64]

Villard's analysis was similar to Thomas'. Truman took orders from Admiral William Leahy, General Dwight Eisenhower, and General Omar Bradley, and his Cabinet was composed of militarists. Villard foresaw a major effort to make us take Chiang's place in fighting the Chinese Communists, and he agreed with Thomas that the West European alliance would cost billions.[65] He told Morgenstern that Truman had won not because of foreign policy but because of high prices and a housing shortage that he had successfully blamed on the Republicans. Dewey had waged a weak campaign and had failed to provide any meaningful alternative to Democratic failures.[66]

The reign of the militarists commenced for Villard with the Truman administration's sponsorship of the North Atlantic Treaty Organization. NATO was a major digression from America's liberal tradition. Villard was most upset when a group to which he belonged, the Post World War Council, met on February 15, 1949, and failed to condemn it strongly.[67]

But the cold war was getting hotter daily. In June of 1948, after General Lucius Clay had introduced new currency into West Berlin, the Soviet Union responded to the provocation by arguing that Berlin no longer had to be maintained as a capital of all Germany. They developed a total blockade on all ground and water traffic to Berlin. The Western powers retaliated by issuing a counterblockade on the movement of goods from East to West Germany.

Arguing that if Berlin fell, communism would triumph in Europe, Truman announced that "we are going to stay, period." War seemed imminent, as Clay proposed shooting his way through the Russian blockade, but a better way was found. Truman began an air transport, round-the-clock mission into Berlin that supplied 13,000 tons of goods per day. The tactic

64. Norman Thomas to Villard, Nov. 9, 1948.
65. Villard to Liddell Hart, Nov. 12, 1948.
66. Villard to Morgenstern, Nov. 16, 1948.
67. Villard to Norman Thomas, Feb. 17, 1949.

eventually succeeded. On May 12, 1949, the Russians lifted the blockade. They had come to the conclusion, as General Clay had thought they would, that the counterblockade was hurting them more than the West. They conceded that they were unable to halt the development of a separate West German government.

Villard welcomed the news from Berlin as "a tremendous American victory." But he despaired that it came as "the result of the display of great force and a near war," because that would encourage Dean Acheson and Truman to base future U.S. policy on armed might.[68] As for NATO, Villard thought it had been pushed "through Congress like wildfire, in violation of our most sacred American traditions." The Soviet Union could truthfully argue that they had scared the United States into discarding the most basic American principles, as well as sacrificing an untold amount of the American people's wealth.[69]

When Truman signed the pact on April 4, Villard remarked that he "could not put the signing of the North Atlantic Pact on my television last evening, for to me it marks the final blow to our beloved Republic, and the establishment of a complete military State." Yet Villard saw some grounds for hope. NATO gave critics bigger targets to attack, and he was certain that if the people learned the facts, they would rise up in opposition.[70]

Villard viewed Russian intransigence as a response to an aggressive American posture. The way in which the cold war developed had much to do with American power and its deployment throughout the world. Oswald Garrison Villard was now an old and sick man, but he continued to urge his younger associates to speak out against the danger of war abroad and reaction at home. He died on October 1, 1949, before the outbreak of the Korean war and the deepening crisis that produced McCarthyism. Death spared him the sorrow and despair these events would undoubtedly have caused him.

Villard was no pristine reactionary. He was a consistent defender of the old American tradition of individual liberty and

68. Villard to DeLancy Howe, May 5, 1949.
69. Villard to Liddell Hart, March 22, 1949.
70. Villard to Irving Dillard, April 5, 1949.

avoidance of military alliances. His roots were in an America that no longer existed, but an America whose principles and precepts meant an unswerving opposition to the empire that America had become. "This isn't the country that you and I loved and worked for," Villard wrote his old friend Horace Ainsworth Eaton. "It has become a complete military state." The military now had all it desired. America of yesteryear had been destroyed. Its demise was not due to Russian aggression. For that "we are largely indebted to Harry Truman."[71]

Villard was not a well-known figure among the critics of the cold war in the late 1940s. From the time he had been removed from the *Nation* his audience had dwindled and his influence had become small. He wrote only for little magazines, and his political contacts were limited to members of the conservative Right.

The postwar liberals were, anyhow, fervent supporters of a new American empire. Villard felt more kinship with principled conservatives who had opposed FDR's version of internationalism. "Undoubtedly," he wrote a correspondent, "there is something in what you say about a basic kinship between my liberal ideas and those upheld by certain honest and fearless conservatives. At least I find that I can get on with such much better of late years than ever before, but that in turn has led to my being charged by the 'totalitarian liberals' with having betrayed my principles and gone conservative in my old age. Of course the unforgivable sin is that I have dared to criticize Roosevelt and the war policies."[72]

Because Villard was welcomed in the homes of some conservatives he was cast into oblivion by his old liberal, internationalist friends. Those who came in contact with him contented themselves with the accusation that he was simply an "isolationist" or a "conservative." That was enough to dismiss taking him seriously. The response revealed more about the difficulties cold-war advocates had in dealing with their opponents than it did about any shift to the Right by Villard, who insisted that he had not altered his views. He was and had been a liberal opponent of war

71. Villard to Eaton, May 23, 1949.
72. Villard to Richard Koch, Sept. 12, 1946.

and empire. He could not accept a wanton interventionism. He could not go along with the tide. He was permanently isolated and in personal despair. The country was denied a vigorous debate on the issues of the cold war and American militarism and interventionism.

Senator Robert A. Taft (THE BETTMANN ARCHIVE)

Robert A. Taft:
A Noninterventionist Faces War

UNTIL RECENTLY Senator Robert A. Taft has had the reputation of being a dogmatic "isolationist," who during the 1950s, in one writer's words, expressed "the public's ambivalent isolationist-aggressive state of emotion."[1] The language of other Taft critics may have been more judicious, but it was often hostile. Taft may have convinced some Americans to reassess the role of the United States in the world, John P. Armstrong wrote, but in an over-all sense he was poorly informed. Taft's major contribution, Armstrong argued, was to get Americans "constantly to rethink their positions, if only to refute him."[2]

This stereotyped view of Taft has recently been challenged. Radical historians such as Henry W. Berger and Barton J. Bernstein began the much needed re-evaluation.[3] *Mr. Republican*, by James Patterson, is an evocative and brilliantly written biography of Taft.[4] It is not surprising that Taft has received so

1. John W. Spanier, *The Truman-MacArthur Controversy and the Korean War* (Cambridge, Mass.: Harvard Univ. Press, 1965), p. 156.

2. John P. Armstrong, "The Enigma of Senator Taft and American Foreign Policy," *Review of Politics* (April 1955), pp. 130–131.

3. Henry W. Berger, "A Conservative Critique of Containment: Senator Taft on the Early Cold War Program," in David Horowitz, ed. *Containment and Revolution* (Boston: Beacon Press, 1967), pp. 132–139; Henry W. Berger, "Senator Robert A. Taft Dissents from Military Escalation," in Thomas G. Paterson, ed. *Cold War Critics* (Chicago: Quadrangle Books, 1971), pp. 167–204; Barton J. Bernstein, "Election of 1952," in Arthur M. Schlesinger, Jr., ed. *The Coming to Power* (New York: Chelsea House, 1971–72), pp. 385–436.

4. James T. Patterson, *Mr. Republican: A Biography of Robert A. Taft* (Boston: Houghton Mifflin, 1972). Readers of the Patterson volume will immediately discern my debt to his biography. Patterson, the first author to gain permission to use the Taft papers, used and commented on the same materials discussed herein. I am generally in agreement with Patterson's balanced and sensitive account of Taft, and the differences in my approach are generally those of emphasis. The nature of the treatment I

much attention, for of all the prewar noninterventionists, Taft alone was a major politician, a popular political leader who was to become titular head of the Republican party.

A son of William Howard Taft, a former President and Chief Justice of the United States Supreme Court, Taft grew to maturity in the atmosphere of a solid Republican family. During World War I he began his political training when he served under Herbert Hoover in the wartime food program. At the war's end Taft won election to the Ohio legislature. By means of a solid legislative record and hard work he rapidly rose to prominence. In 1938 he was elected to the U.S. Senate. Although he was an opponent of Franklin D. Roosevelt's domestic New Deal, Taft was flexible enough to offer support to relief spending, broadening of social security to include old-age pensions, and unemployment insurance to agricultural workers, as well as backing federal guarantees for collective bargaining and firmly supporting labor's right to strike.

Taft was most interested in domestic politics, but his own rise to leadership coincided with the rapid momentum toward war in Europe. He regarded the possibility of war with fear and apprehension. Like many other Americans, he favored the maintenance of neutrality. It was in the context of the political leadership he was to assume in the noninterventionist cause that he developed and made known his ideas on foreign policy.

On his second day as a senator Taft entered the debate by releasing a statement of his position: "Every American is determined to secure adequate defense, but the logical conclusion from the President's statement that we must be prepared to defend not our homes alone but various ideals including good faith among nations, would seem to be another war with American troops again sent across the ocean. Our armament program should be based on defending the United States and not defending democracy throughout the world."[5]

---

make of Taft in the 1950's, however, differs from that taken by Patterson. Readers of both books will be able to notice the way in which this volume differs from Patterson's.

5. Taft statement, Jan. 4, 1939, Robert A. Taft MSS., Box 1251, Library of Congress, Wash., D.C.

Unlike so many of his contemporaries, Taft did not seem motivated by a messianic impulse. A long memorandum presented his general philosophy as well as his position on particular changes in the Neutrality Act. Congratulating the President "on his clear statement that his whole efforts will be directed towards keeping the United States out of War as long as it remains in his power to do so," Taft devoted his energy to ensuring that Roosevelt stuck to his announced goal. As far as Taft was concerned, "the only way we can stay out is to be determined that we will stay out." This meant that the Neutrality Act had to be kept on the books.

A new world war, Taft argued, would not necessarily promote democracy. The first had only "set up more extreme dictatorships than the world had seen for many days." The United States might now enter the war to save England and France "and find that, when the war ended, their governments were Communist and Fascist." War could prove destructive to the very fabric of American democracy, as Congress would "be flooded by a large number of measures designed to have the government take over business and regulate every detail of private and commercial life." It would mean the virtual end of local self-government, the creation of "an absolute arbitrary government in Washington," and a plebiscite to see who would gain control.

If the United States kept out of war, Taft continued, it did not mean that German victories would occur elsewhere in the world. But he went a step further. Even if Germany did win, and "terrible" as such a victory might be, Taft claimed that Hitler's triumph in Europe would "not lead to a German attack on the United States." The United States could be adequately protected by a strong Caribbean defense and an adequate navy and air force. As for the argument that "our foreign trade might be destroyed by a Germany controlling a large section of the world"— an argument offered by many administration supporters—Taft responded with the simple assertion that trade would still continue. And even if it did not, he asserted that the American people "would probably rather give up that trade than go to war abroad." This belief perhaps was easy for Taft to come by. An Ohioan who represented the interests of Midwestern business,

Taft cared little for the concern about export markets voiced by larger Eastern interests.

Neutrality for Taft meant avoidance of those incidents that had brought the United States into World War I. That war, he thought, had taken place because of submarine warfare. Thus Taft backed sections of the Neutrality Act which prohibited "the entrance of American ships into war zones." Yet—and this is important—Taft supported the administration effort to have the ban on shipments of arms, ammunition, and implements of war repealed, "on condition that they be operated only on a cash and carry basis." There was nothing unneutral, he argued, "in the shipment of munitions of war to a nation which comes and gets them." What was crucial was that neutrality should not be implemented so that one nation would be favored over another so as to "impose embargoes against aggressors, or against those whom we dislike." That would lead toward war or at least toward propaganda for one side. It would thus encourage "those who are trying to stir up participation in war." Taft found it preposterous that the United States alone "should charge aggression and cover the world like a knight errant, protecting its friends and its ideals of good faith."[6]

Taft's first response to presidential rumors about changing the Neutrality Act was an attack on Roosevelt for stirring up prejudices against one or another nation. His statement brought an angry response from journalist Walter Lippmann, which made little impression on Taft. Lippmann, Taft wrote a friend, had only "a very limited influence among the intellectuals." The Republican party in New York was itself "out of touch with the people" and was affected by the fact that FDR's policies were "more popular in the East than in the West." "I cannot avoid taking a position on foreign policy," Taft informed David S. Ingalls, "and that position will be very critical of the President. The idea that he ought not to be attacked on foreign policy is pure bunk."[7]

From the perspective of the 1970s Taft's view seems thoughtful and reflective of a widespread feeling that executive power has

6. Taft statement, n.d. (Sept. 1939), ibid., Box 1250.
7. Taft to Ingalls, June 21, 1939, ibid., Box 78.

become too concentrated. But when he was voicing this view, Hitler had just taken over the Sudetenland and moved against the remaining parts of democratic Czechoslovakia. An attitude that would become a staple of New Left dissent was not appreciated by the interventionist supporters of Franklin Roosevelt back in 1939.

Taft admitted that he entertained "serious doubts about the question of shipping munitions abroad in wartime." Yet he intended to vote for the amendment of the Neutrality Act "to carry out that result." He then felt "sufficiently strong against Mr. Hitler" to be "willing to go as far as a real neutrality permits." The main consideration is that such a step, he believed, would not lead Hitler to provoke war. Taft doubted whether Germany would be able to "properly take exception to such a course."[8]

Taft's support to this moderate revision of the Neutrality Act revealed that he did not always stand eye to eye with Roosevelt's sharpest opponents. Anti-interventionists such as Gerald Nye of North Dakota and Burton K. Wheeler of Montana argued that revision would move the nation closer to war. Taft disagreed. It was absurd, he said, to prevent shipments of munitions while permitting belligerent nations to purchase strategic raw materials. The distinction between guns and cotton, he stated, "is sentimental rather than real."[9] A cash-and-carry policy would ensure that U.S. ships would not be exposed to German subs.

The world, however, was to continue to move away from peace. Neutrality was an elusive goal. Hitler seized Denmark in April and began his assault on Norway. By May 10 he had marched through Belgium, and German tanks were on their way to France. These developments, however, did not change Taft's assessment that war was to be avoided. It was in St. Louis, according to his biographer, that Taft "burst out with the speech that proved most damaging to his campaign."[10]

The Nazis, Taft told his audience, were simply not a threat to the United States. "There is a good deal more danger of the

8. Taft to Frederick J. Libby, May 1, 1939, Amos Pinchot MSS., Box 66, Library of Congress, Wash., D.C.

9. Taft statement, Sept. 1939, Taft MSS., Box 1150.

10. Patterson, *Mr. Republican,* p. 217.

infiltration of totalitarian ideas from the New Deal circle in Washington than there will ever be from any activities of the communists or the Nazi bund." Accusing Roosevelt of trying to "stir up the emotions of the people," Taft argued that American entrance in the war would be "more likely to destroy American democracy than to destroy German dictatorship." Taft acknowledged that Germany might possibly defeat Britain and then build a world in which "ruthless force" proved "triumphant over every principle of justice." Yet to Taft even "that alternative seems preferable to present participation in the European war."[11]

The enemy was war. Taft stood against the tide, even though popular pressure was developing on behalf of more aid to Britain. One result was that Taft was to lose whatever chance he might have had for the presidential nomination on the Republican ticket. The pro-intervention Eastern wing of the party did not trust him, and his St. Louis speech confirmed their skepticism.

Entrance into the war, Taft felt, would end "democratic government in the United States." Already, he claimed, "more power has been conferred on the Executive than has been conferred in most wars." Measures pending would make the American President "a complete dictator over the lives and property of all our citizens." If the line of defense became the English Channel, Taft predicted that the United States would "be engaged in war for the rest of our lives." Referring to the destroyers-for-bases deal, Taft added that they were given to Britain by the President "without congressional action." This violation of the Neutrality Act was not something to pass over lightly. It symbolized the reduction "to scraps of paper in truly Hitler fashion several treaties which are clearly binding on our government."[12]

Taft's strict constitutionalism allowed him to argue unabashedly that the New Deal had gone fascist. The destroyer deal proved that Roosevelt had "a complete lack of regard for the rights of Congress, and that if he has any reason to fear that his policies may not meet the views of Congress, he proposes to proceed in violation of the people's will." Taft feared that if Roosevelt sought to "regard his re-election as a mandate, he

11. *New York Times,* May 21, 1940, p. 16.
12. Taft to Phyllis Tinckler, Sept. 18, 1940, Taft MSS., Box 767.

might well regard it as a mandate to enter the war." Taft thought that Roosevelt might use his power "to involve the United States in war so that it may be impossible for Congress to refuse to declare war." Another tactic Roosevelt might use would be to "carry on an undeclared war." Like Charles A. Beard, Taft thought it was FDR's strategy to excite the populace about foreign quarrels as a device to get people's minds off domestic problems. "With war and a third term," Taft concluded, "the United States will move so fast towards the goal of national socialism that the dangers to our liberties will be far greater from our domestic enemies than from those who are thousands of miles across the ocean."[13]

Because he felt that many administration leaders wanted to move the nation into war, Taft voted against the appointment of Henry L. Stimson as Roosevelt's new Secretary of War. Fearing that Stimson would seek to create incidents in which Germany would be provoked to attack U.S. ships, Taft sharply interrogated Stimson when he appeared before the Senate Military Affairs Committee.[14] He also opposed the draft, calling for the creation of a volunteer army. But his main attack was on the proposed Lend-Lease aid to the Allies.

Instead of Lend-Lease, which would move the nation closer to war, Taft favored cash loans of $1.55 billion to Britain. Such loans would enable the British to hold out and defeat the Germans, but they would not give the President an excuse to provide convoys for British ships across the Atlantic. In spite of all this, Taft differed from the other noninterventionist critics of the President. The "charge that the bill contains dictatorial powers," Taft wrote Mrs. Albert S. Ingalls, "is rather overdone." He did agree, however, that the Lend-Lease Bill authorized the President "to take us into the midst of the war, and once we are there his powers will be unlimited. I really don't think it is too much to say that before we get through with that war the rights of private property in the United States will be to a large extent destroyed." Taft argued that his substitute bill would "give all the aid to

13. Taft, "The New Deal Goes Fascist," Oct. 31, 1940, speech at Cleveland, Ohio, ibid., Box 770.
14. Patterson, *Mr. Republican*, pp. 238–240.

England we can possibly give without entering the war ourselves."[15]

What Britain needed in the way of aid, Taft believed, was superior air power. "There is not very much that Congress can do about defense," he wrote his brother, "except appropriate the money. . . . Nothing will end this war except an overwhelming delivery of airplanes from this country to England."[16] Taft's arguments did not convince the majority of the Senate. The administration argued that Lend-Lease would have the effect of strengthening the Allies, so that they could do the job on their own. The Lend-Lease Bill was labeled with the patriotic number 1776. It passed, 60 to 31. As Taft had predicted, it was only a short time before the law led to an informal shooting war in the Atlantic between Germany and the United States.

For Taft, at the end of 1940 the sole issue was "whether we go to war or not." He was still "willing to extend aid to Great Britain to the extent that it does not involve us in war"; but he was certain that "convoying of ships would be war itself, and would probably put Hitler in a position where he could not help declaring war." He complained that the "exact limits of international law seem to have lost their importance." Yet, as a politician, he noted that he could not stand "on a complete refusal of financial aid to Great Britain." Such a step would put peace advocates "in an indefensible position, in which we will be accused of putting dollars ahead of patriotism."[17]

Taft reiterated that a German defeat of Britain did not mean that Hitler would attempt to invade the United States. As for the new concern about the loss of South American markets in the wake of a German victory, he could not understand the concern. That market was worth only $300 million, or one-tenth of the total amount of United States exports. It also was but one half of one percent of total U.S. production. Taft failed to see how loss of such a minimal market could be grounds for war. Making war on a country because "some day that country may be a

15. Taft to Mrs. Albert S. (Jane) Ingalls, March 3, 1941, Taft MSS., Box 108.
16. Taft to Horace Taft, Dec. 28, 1940, ibid., Box 25.
17. Taft to Mrs. Monte Appel, Dec. 26, 1940, ibid., Box 106.

successful competitor for foreign trade is completely alien to the point of view of the American people." War, he told his Senate colleagues, "is worse even than a German victory." Unlike others, Taft felt war was a virtual horror, a mass "murder by machine," that could "wipe out in a few years the whole civilization which Europe has been building for a thousand years." He thought that if the United States did enter "in order to save the British Empire," it would mean perpetual war. The United States would begin to undertake "military operations on the Continent of Europe." That would mean engaging "forever in the European game of maintaining the balance of power in Europe." Given a strong navy and air force, Taft believed, no nation would ever attack the U.S. across the Atlantic Ocean.[18]

Administration actions after passage of the Lend-Lease Act confirmed Taft's worst fears. In April United States ships patrolled sea-lanes and warned British ships of the presence of German U-boats. In July the United States occupied Iceland. The draft was extended in August, and the famous Atlantic Charter was signed by Roosevelt and Winston Churchill. By September the convoying of ships was taking place. The *Greer,* a U.S. destroyer, was hit by German torpedoes. It retaliated by dropping depth bombs on the German sub. Roosevelt responded by publicly calling for a shoot-on-sight policy, while failing to tell the public that the *Greer* had been engaged in tracking the sub on behalf of the British.

Taft's response to what he perceived as administration duplicity was firm. Pointing to the mounting evidence that many within and without the administration actively favored war, Taft criticized the hypocrisy involved in hiding the drift toward intervention "behind a demand for convoys . . . [which were] an effective means of getting us into the war, rather than any concern about the arrival of our munitions." Destruction of munitions often took place by bombing raids on harbor installations, and the convoys could not prevent that. Producing more airplanes for Britain would be a much more valuable form of aid.

18. Taft, "Aid to Britain—Short of War," March 1, 1941, ibid., Box 1256.

Once the logic of convoys was accepted, Taft believed, it would make equal sense to send the army in to handle use of the munitions. "Step by step," Taft asserted, "the advocates of war have led the country closer and closer to the precipice, always maintaining that at heart they are really for peace. Now the mask is off."

Taft analyzed the assumptions behind the administration arguments. To crush Hitler, he asserted, would cost $50 million per year and would lead to bankruptcy. The eighty million German people, moreover, would still remain the strongest body on the continent. The problem was that the United States was moving toward imperialism.

> If we wish to protect the small democracies, we will have to maintain a police force perpetually in Germany and throughout Europe. Secretary Stimson, Dorothy Thompson, and Henry Luce seem to contemplate an Anglo-American alliance perpetually ruling the world. Frankly, the American people don't want to rule the world, and we are not equipped to do it. Such imperialism is wholly foreign to our ideals of democracy and freedom. It is not our manifest destiny or our national destiny. We may think we are better than other peoples, more competent to rule, but will they think so? Will they welcome an Anglo-American benevolent despotism any more eagerly than a German despotism? The inevitable result of what the war party is urging on this country is an American Empire, doing what the British have done for the past 200 years.

Was the United States meant to "assume the task of maintaining forever a balance of power in Europe" and to join "a partnership the avowed purpose of which is to rule the world?" To this question, Taft answered with a resounding no.[19]

In June, Nazi Germany broke its nonaggression pact with the Soviet Union. The German invasion of Russia led to an abrupt shift in the Soviet position. The USSR, and hence Western Communists, now called for a military alliance of the world's antifascist powers. The Communists, who had been demanding

19. Taft, "Shall the United States Enter the European War?" address of May 17, 1941 (*Congressional Record,* May 19, 1941), Taft MSS., Boxes 760 and 1256.

nonintervention one day before the invasion, overnight became advocates of antifascist unity. The Soviet shift, however, was only one more reason Taft advanced that the United States should maintain neutrality.

Rejecting "a belief in our divine appointment to reform the world," Taft used Russia's new advocacy of antifascist war as proof that the conflict was not about democracy. "How can anyone," he asked, "swallow the idea that Russia is battling for democratic principles? . . . Except for the Russian pact with Germany, there would have been no invasion of Poland." Now the United States, in the name of democracy, was about to "make a Communist alliance with the most ruthless dictator in the world."

As for ideology, Taft would not choose between fascism and communism. However, the "victory of communism in the world outside of America would be far more dangerous to the United States from an ideological standpoint than the victory of fascism." Americans would never adopt Nazism. But masquerading "under the guise of democracy," communism was a "false philosophy which appeals to many." Hence the new alliance with Russia was proof that it was utterly futile "to bluster about the kind of freedoms we will impose everywhere in the world."[20]

Most of the time Taft attacked administration actions that he judged unjustified. The U.S. occupation of Iceland was not only unconstitutional but was meant to involve the United States in war without the consent or participation of Congress. It was a blatant repudiation of "the promise not to send American boys to Europe." If occupation of Iceland was part of the defense of the United States, Taft argued, "then any act the President cares to order is defense. If he can send troops to Iceland on the ground, he can certainly send troops to Ireland . . . to Scotland or England . . . to Portugal." To invoke Lend-Lease aid to justify the occupation was farcical, since the Act expressly forbade sending in troops to effect policy.[21]

20. Taft, "Russia and the Four Freedoms," radio address over CBS, June 25, 1941 (*Congressional Record,* June 26, 1941), Taft MSS., Box 768.
21. Taft, "Shall the President Make War Without the Approval of Congress?" radio speech on NBC Blue Network, July 15, 1941, ibid., Box 563.

On this point Taft was backed by Hoover. Noting that American and British troops were under joint command, Hoover wrote that "either they have to clear the British wholly out of Iceland or they ought to get the American troops out." Taft made his protest, he answered Hoover, "largely to slow up the next move, which I believe to be an occupation of Ireland." He pledged to confer with other Republicans about the possibility of getting legislation to limit appropriations for military operations solely to the western hemisphere.[22]

Taft and his supporters felt that while the popular will was with the noninterventionists, the Eastern establishment and the media were on the other side. In a state such as Minnesota, lawyer Monte Appel told him, the populace was "overwhelmingly opposed to our involvement in this war." Citing a figure of 80–90 percent opposed to the war, Appel informed Taft that the "minority for war" was led by a group he dubbed "society"—just about "everybody of wealth, position and influence." Both the papers controlled by John Cowles and those by the Ridder family were interventionist, "so much so that they deliberately, from day to day, suppress and pervert the news." Yet he stressed that the "overwhelming proportion of our people are against war despite a prolonged propaganda campaign by our so-called metropolitan dailies." It was true that Republican Harold Stassen was interventionist. But Appel informed Taft of Stassen's close ties with Thomas Lamont of J. P. Morgan and Company. "Stassen believes," he explained, "that it is essential that he have the support of Lamont and the Eastern financial interests if he is to be nominated for President in 1944."[23]

Like Appel, Taft was convinced that in defending nonintervention he was protecting the interests of the people against the desires of the elite Eastern financial interests. He moved closer to the anti-interventionist mass movement, led by the America First Committee. Responding to the name "isolationist" given him, Taft told supporters, "If isolation means isolation from European war, I am an isolationist." The occupation of Iceland, he

22. Herbert Hoover to Taft, July 14, 1941, and Taft to Hoover, July 16, 1941, ibid., Box 1179.
23. Monte Appel to Taft, June 9, 1941, ibid., Box 106.

charged, had led to the *Greer* incident. And that "was so intended by the President." Accusing war advocates of looking "forward to domination of the world by the United States and Great Britain," Taft again stressed that such a policy implied "continued policing of the continent of Europe." For such "a policy of imperialism," he argued, "this country is not adapted." Either the policy would collapse or the United States would turn itself "into a militaristic and totalitarian nation as Rome turned from a Republic to an Empire."[24]

Taft fought alongside other anti-interventionists to prevent any new appropriation for Lend-Lease. He also opposed the arming of merchant ships and the abolition of forbidden combat zones. Freedom of the seas, he stressed, "has never included the un-molested right to send ships with contraband to a country engaged in war." Roosevelt had now ordered the navy to fire on sight at any German ship it spotted if that ship was sighted in waters considered part of the defense zone. The zone now included "the entire Atlantic Ocean from here to Iceland," and Taft feared that FDR would extend the zone "right up to the shores of Europe."[25]

The incident with the *Kearny* increased the sharpness of Taft's attacks. The U.S.S. *Kearny* "was engaged in convoying, not American ships, but British and neutral ships, from this country. But the President did not so advise the American people." It was one thing for the President to make a clear argument for intervention and present his case to Congress. But he was not doing that. "If the President can declare or create an undeclared naval war beyond our power to act upon," Taft pointed out, "the Constitution might just as well be abolished." While he spoke of peace, the President had "already done what he could to plunge the Nation into a shooting war." Taft denied that the President had any legitimate authority to "prowl the ocean in quest of offensive warfare." Like Beard, Taft argued that no differences existed between the conditions in Europe during the 1940 presidential campaign and those of late 1941. To the contrary, he

24. Taft, address to the Ohio Federation of Republican Women's Organizations, Sept. 22, 1941, ibid., Box 767.
25. Taft broadcast for WGAR, Oct. 17, 1941, ibid., Box 1258.

argued, "conditions today do not justify war as much as did conditions at that time." In 1940 Britain was being bombed regularly and France had fallen to the Nazis. Yet Roosevelt pledged that the United States would stay out of the European war. "No man," Taft emphasized, "who gave his pledge that we should keep out of war, who gave his pledge . . . in November 1940 can today vote for the pending resolution without repudiating that pledge."[26]

What Taft and his supporters particularly objected to was the administration's secretiveness. Congressional consideration or even discussion was circumvented. Herbert Hoover informed Taft that American ships had recently been transferred to Panama. While they could have been given to Britain under the terms of Lend-Lease, they had been shipped to Panama in order to evade the Neutrality Act. They could then be sent directly into hostile ports with contraband. Some of the ships were even armed. This would have been impossible had they legally been listed as American ships.[27]

The key issue was presidential power. "I do not agree," Taft informed Joseph Newton Pew, Jr., "that under our Constitution the Executive can bring about a state of war without usurpation. He may have the power to get us into war, but he certainly has not the right. The mere fact that his power cannot be disputed in war does not mean that it is constitutional." Taft wanted to fight for the principle that Congress should not "admit rights which do not exist" and which, if granted, would mean an end to constitutional rule. "I recognize as you do that we will probably be in the war through Executive action," Taft noted sadly, "but I don't propose to acquiesce in any policy leading directly to war unless it is approved by Congress."[28]

This meant the necessity of fighting interventionist elements within his own party. Taft opposed the efforts of Wendell Willkie "to read out of the Party everyone who disagrees with him." He pledged to "oppose any extension of that policy by the President

26. Taft, "Repeal of Neutrality Act Means War," speech to the U.S. Senate, Oct. 28, 1941, ibid., Box 1258.
27. Hoover to Taft, Nov. 3, 1941, ibid., Box 767.
28. Taft to Pew, Nov. 11, 1941, ibid., Box 110.

in the direction of war when Congress has not declared war." As for the effort of some to send an expeditionary force to Europe to crush Hitler, Taft noted that the logic of such a step would be clear once neutrality was repealed. Taft thought that in November of 1941 even Roosevelt opposed such a step, "but he is like a boy playing with tin soldiers, and I have no doubt he will follow Iceland and Dutch Guiana with Dakar and Egypt and perhaps Persia."[29]

Taft expected war as a result of unconstitutional executive fiat. In the very last statement he was to make before Pearl Harbor Taft commented on the maiden article of political analysis offered by young Arthur M. Schlesinger, Jr. Schlesinger's argument, as well as the contents of Taft's rebuttal, suggested and prefigured the division between cold-war liberals and critics of U.S. foreign policy that was to occur during the 1950s. Schlesinger argued that isolationism produced a schism in the Republican party analogous to that created by the issue of slavery, which forced dissolution of the Whig party before the Civil War. Unless the Republicans gave full support to Wendell Willkie, Schlesinger maintained, they would meet the same fate as befell the Whigs, with "Willkie leading the 'Conscience Republicans' into a union with the New Deal Democrats behind some progressive candidate in 1944, in opposition to the Know Nothing and appeasement elements of both parties united behind someone like Lindbergh." For Schlesinger, neutrality was as impossible and reactionary as it had been back in 1858. New Dealer to the core, he singled out the business community as the force responsible for the isolationist position. Once business elements refused to commit themselves against slavery; now they failed to take "an aggressive policy toward Hitler."[30]

Taft's answer revealed much about him as well as his distance from mainstream contemporary liberalism. Schlesinger charged that Republicans had "harassed, sabotaged, and obstructed the attempts of the Administration to work for the destruction of Nazism." Taft countered that they only opposed measures that

29. Taft to Harry Sandager, Nov. 25, 1941, ibid., Box 110.
30. Arthur M. Schlesinger, Jr., "Can Willkie Save His Party?" *Nation,* Dec. 6, 1941, pp. 561–564.

would lead to sending an expeditionary force of ten million men to Europe. Republicans did not believe, Taft retorted, "that Hitler presents such a threat to the trade or safety of the United States as requires the sacrifice of several million American boys on the battlefields of the world." Taft went on to challenge Schlesinger's contention that the noninterventionist position could be attributed to business or conservatism:

> The most conservative members of the party—the Wall Street bankers, the society group, nine-tenths of the plutocratic newspapers, and most of the party's financial contributors—are the ones who favor intervention in Europe. Mr. Schlesinger's statement that the business community in general had tended to favor appeasing Hitler is simply untrue. I have received thousands of letters on both sides of the question, and I should say without question that it is the average man and woman—the farmer, the workman, except for a few pro-British labor leaders, and the small business man—who are opposed to war. The war party is made up of the business community of the cities, the newspaper and magazine writers, the radio and movie commentators, the Communists, and the university intelligentsia.

Taft was attacking the mobilization of public opinion carried out by the liberal press as well as by the corporate policy-making bodies. If the Republicans were dodging the issue of war, it was because they were being "held back principally by the big business interests of the East, fearful among other fears of Hitler's destruction of our foreign trade." The responsibility of the Republicans was not to outdo FDR with an interventionist stand but to come out solidly against war, "as the Whig Party should have come out definitely against slavery." Predicting that if differences on foreign policy continued, the Republicans would have to meet the issue, Taft concluded: "Obviously, it should not follow the Whig policy of appeasement. It should be opposed to risking the lives of five million American boys in an imperialistic war for the domination of Europe, Asia and Africa, and the supposed 'manifest destiny' of America."[31]

31. Taft statement in a forum, "The Future of the Republican Party," *Nation*, Dec. 13, 1941, pp. 611–612.

In a view that he might have shared with a confirmed Bolshevik, Robert A. Taft saw World War II as an imperialist war being fought for control of a large portion of the earth. But unfortunately for Taft, the Japanese attack on Pearl Harbor ended the debate before his article appeared.

Pearl Harbor came as a surprise to Taft. He had always stated that Nazi Germany would not attack the United States. When an interventionist paper editorialized that "when Pearl Harbor came, the Senate still echoed with Senator Taft's assurance that we were in no danger of attack," Taft showed marked anger. "I never made any statement about the possibility of attack by Japan," Taft explained, "because, like many other American people, I felt completely ignorant regarding the situation in the Far East. I did say that I thought it was impossible for Hitler to invade the United States successfully at that time and he was, therefore, unlikely to attempt to do so."[32]

Pearl Harbor did not change Taft's mind about the just nature of his position prior to the attack. Two weeks later he argued that perhaps a negotiated peace could still prevent the sending of U.S. troops abroad. A nation with a strong army and navy, he asserted as late as July 1942, should be able to remain at peace. While he admitted that the attack at Pearl Harbor had forced the United States to fight, he wondered whether Roosevelt's "policy of bluff" had indeed driven Japan to the attack.[33]

Taft informed a correspondent that Roosevelt "got us into a war without having the slightest idea of how he was going to carry it on." To Taft the "negligence at Hawaii" was "more than equaled by the complete lack of a plan for defending the Philippine Islands."[34] While he supported the necessity to fight the war, he was not happy about it. Writing Herbert Hoover, he expressed hope that the "working out of [America's] idealism may sink in on the American people before we finally have to send ten million men to Europe." Like the Chief, Taft hoped that the "Philippine fiasco" revealed that "the Pacific Ocean is still

32. Taft to editor of the Dayton *Daily News,* Sept. 17, 1945, Taft MSS., Box 31.
33. Patterson, *Mr. Republican,* p. 248.
34. Taft to Mrs. Lloyd Bowers, Feb. 6, 1942, Taft MSS., Box 27.

5,000 miles wide, and that we may be able to be completely safe in America without being able to conquer the world."[35]

It was heresy to raise the question of usurpation by the executive of the congressional prerogative to declare war at a time when the country permitted such executive prerogative in the belief that Hitler was a real threat. Taft focused on the lies used by the administration to provoke an incident, as well as on the dangers of a moral crusade that might end with an attempt to dominate the world.

Because he felt that his prewar position had not been invalidated by events, Taft faced a continuing fight against those who sought to defeat political leaders who had opposed the drift toward intervention. Freedom House, the Communist *Daily Worker* and the liberal *New Republic,* he complained, were all trying to defeat congressmen who had opposed participation in the war before Pearl Harbor. If their goal was accomplished, the independence of Congress would be destroyed. Such former non-interventionists had "opposed sincerely and conscientiously the entrance of the United States into the World War." If they had been able to achieve permanent peace, it would have indeed been preferable to war. "It would have avoided the necessity," Taft added, "of suspending the freedoms of the American way of life and submitting temporarily to Fascist controls over every human activity."[36]

More important, Taft believed that a fight had to be carried on against waging war in such a fashion that America would move toward empire. "If we march to Berlin and Tokyo, we will necessarily have assumed obligations to establish a world order which will prevent the recurrence of the tragedy of war." It was impossible to predict what that world order would be. But Taft stressed that there were "a good many plans, such as . . . a policing of the entire world by the Anglo-Saxon race, which do not seem to me to be practical." Republicans had to understand that they could not "out-intervention Roosevelt." Their strategy, Taft suggested, should be to attack mistakes in the conduct of the

35. Taft to Hoover, Jan. 3, 1942, ibid., Box 1179.
36. Summary of Taft's remarks on "Wake Up, America" radio program, July 5, 1942, ibid., Box 1259.

war and use of the war by Democrats as a "cloak for New Deal measures."[37]

What Taft feared, he informed George N. Peek, was a "violent fight in this country on the international question after the war." Without a Republican Congress, the administration would undoubtedly "lead us into all the foolish ideas of the Atlantic Charter against the wishes of a great majority of the people." Peek was upset that some public figures were arguing that the United States "must adopt imperialism." War against other political and economic systems was conducted under the cover of internationalism, when in reality it was a drive for a new world order. Taft agreed, and he noted as well that this necessitated "getting rid of Mr. Willkie as a leader of the Republican Party." Calling for a principled fight on behalf of a new point of view, Taft suggested that if the eastern Republicans did not go along with them by 1944, there might be "a realignment of the parties."[38]

Taft was willing to have some form of world organization established by the war's end. What he saw as doubtful was "how far the United States should go in protecting that setup by force." He was "willing to undertake some obligations," Taft said, but he did not want "to police Europe, or become involved in every little boundary dispute that there may be among the bitterly prejudiced and badly mixed races of Central Europe."[39] Perhaps America had to assume greater obligations in the postwar epoch, but policy could not be forced on the nation by "a few Utopian thinkers, whose interest appears to be more in foreign peoples than in the welfare of our own." Most objectionable to Taft was the tendency of the Roosevelt administration to commit the United States to an "international WPA." He opposed Cordell Hull's efforts to build an international free-trade system in which all nations would have "access on equal terms to the trade of the world."[40] He was more than willing to "cooperate in the post-war world,"

37. Taft to M. S. Sherman, editor, Hartford *Courant,* May 6, 1942, ibid., Box 103.

38. Taft to George Peek, May 2, 1942; Peek to Scott W. Lucas, May 16, 1942; Taft to Peek, May 16, 1942, ibid., Box 104.

39. Taft to Marrs McLean, June 23, 1942, ibid., Box 110.

40. Taft to Herbert Hoover, July 14, 1942, ibid., Box 1179.

he informed a friend, "but on the whole I would rather give the country back to the Indians than give it to the Europeans and the South Americans and the Russians and the Chinese."[41]

When Taft decided to set down his ideas in detail, he chose as the occasion a commencement speech prepared for Grove City College. Here for the first time he revealed why he opposed Henry Luce's famous plan for an American Century. Asking the graduating class to consider the purposes for which the nation was fighting, Taft declared a major premise of the war to be that "might in this world will not make right." The United States was not at war to establish FDR's Four Freedoms throughout the world, he stressed, nor to realize the purposes of the Atlantic Charter.

Agreeing that certain nations did not grant freedom of religion or expression, Taft denied that the United States should "interfere with the internal government of every country" because it failed to grant these desirable freedoms. Many nations fighting alongside the United States were dictatorships. These included Brazil, Cuba, and China. Metaxas, the Greek leader, even prohibited in Greece "the reading of the *Republic* of Plato." If the United States was to interfere in their affairs, it would mean a "permanent army" of over eleven million armed citizens, and that would mean the necessary suspension of freedom within the United States.

A crusade was dangerous, Taft continued, because if one believed "that the United States can properly go to war to impose our ideas of freedom on the rest of the world, then it seems we must admit that the Soviets have a right to crusade to impose Communism on the rest of the world because they believe Communism to be the final solution of the world's problems. We would even have to admit that Hitler . . . had a right to crusade to impose his ideas of national socialism on the world." For Taft a crusade was "by its very nature an aggressive act." To uphold crusades would mean the danger of "perpetual war."

Taft had supported the League of Nations back in 1920. Now the time was ripe to discuss newly proposed concepts for world organization. One plan proposed continuing "more or less inde-

41. Taft to Agnes Scandrett, April 14, 1943, ibid., Box 104.

finitely the post-war control of the world by the United Nations."
Such a plan was that being circulated by Henry Luce in his much
heralded American Century series of editorials. As Taft described
it:

> We are to dominate the world as England is said to have
> dominated it during the nineteenth century, but . . . the domi-
> nation will be much more effective. We are to be the senior
> partner in the control. Russia and China will be left to their con-
> tinental interests, while, with the British as our helpers, we will
> look after the oceans and the rest of the world. . . .
>
> . . . it is completely contrary to the ideals of the American
> people and the theory that we are fighting for liberty . . . It is
> based on the theory that we know better what is good for the
> world than the world itself. It assumes that we are always right
> and anyone who disagrees with us is wrong. It reminds me of the
> idealism of the bureaucrats in Washington who want to regulate the
> lives of every American along the lines that the bureaucrats think
> are best for them. . . . Certainly however benevolent we might be,
> other people simply do not like to be dominated, and we would be
> in the same position of suppressing rebellions by force in which the
> British found themselves during the nineteenth century.

Taft saw through the illusory hopes of the liberals, who
assumed that American benevolence always produced a better
world. Unlike these social liberals, whose inspiration was Secretary of Commerce Henry A. Wallace, Taft denied that American
policies were uplifting the peoples of the underdeveloped world.
He had visited Puerto Rico. The United States had been there
"for forty-five years without relieving poverty or improving anyone's condition." If the United States could not "make a success
of ruling a small island of two million people," Taft asked, "how
are we going to manage several billion people in the rest of the
world?"[42]

Speaking to the prestigious American Bar Association in 1943,

42. Taft address at the Grove City College commencement, May 22,
1943, ibid., Box 546. For the contrasting program of Henry A. Wallace
and the "social liberals" see Norman D. Markowitz, *The Rise and Fall of
the People's Century: Henry A. Wallace and American Liberalism, 1941–
1948* (New York: The Free Press, 1973), pp. 36–80. Taft rejected Wallace's so-called Century of the Common Man, which, Taft argued, still
had the United States trying to "dominate the world."

Taft began by talking about the nature of a new, postwar international organization. It was important to recognize from the outset that the United States could not "try to boss the boots off the world if we expect to avoid war in the future." A firm system of international law had to be established, with "an affirmative statement of the principles on which the nations of the world may live together in peace." The World Court would interpret the law. For it to work, there had to be created "a public opinion educated to peace and to the principles of law on which it is founded."

At present, Taft told his audience, there were three alternative plans being offered to the public. World Federalism, in the guise of a World Federal Union, Taft rejected as totally irrational. The idea that the major Allies would "submit themselves to an international state and have their seaports and airports run by an international bureaucrat" he found preposterous. The state would have to depend upon an international police force, controlled by an executive power selected by a combination of member nations. "If you can see Winston Churchill liquidating the British fleet, or Joe Stalin dismissing the Russian Army, or either of them turning over their forces to President Whoozis of Worlditania," Taft told the lawyers, "you are more clairvoyant than I."

But the real danger was that "the former interventionist forces in the East" seemed to be moving toward Walter Lippmann's plan for a British-Russian-American alliance. Taft thought the idea might appeal "to the nationalistic sentiment of those Americans who picture America dominating the alliance and the world" as well as to "the do-gooders who regard it as the manifest destiny of America to confer the benefits of the New Deal on every Hottentot." The problem was that "fundamentally this is imperialism." Relying upon the use of armed force, such a plan would require bases all over the world. It would lead to "vast national armaments in all parts of the world; every nation or at any rate every alliance of nations must be able to control the seas, which means, control the world. It has long been recognized that militarism . . . is a cause of war." Armaments by necessity created "a profession of militarists."

Lippmann's policy, Taft argued, meant "an alliance against

someone." It would arouse world antagonism and lead to attempts at building counteralliances. "Once the world is lined up in two opposing camps," Taft noted, "another world war is only a question of time." Such a military alliance based upon control of sea- and air-lanes was "bound to produce imperialism." Taft informed his audience why he rejected that path:

> Our fingers will be in every pie. Our military forces will work with our commercial forces to obtain as much of world trade as we can lay our hands on. We will occupy all the strong strategic points in the world and try to maintain a force so preponderant that none shall dare attack us. How long can nations restrain themselves from using such force with just a little of the aggressiveness of Germany and Japan? Look at the history of the British Empire, how a trading post in India extended itself into a rule over 300,000,000 people . . . how the desire for Chinese trade led to the colonization of Hong Kong. Potential power over other nations, however benevolent its purpose, leads inevitably to imperialism.

Taft believed that Americans were "not fitted to a role of imperialism and would fail in any attempt at world domination." And if Americans did succeed at imperialism "abroad, it would be likely to change our whole attitude at home." The nation might then move toward "totalitarianism."[43]

Taft did not retreat from the implications of his analysis. The New Deal solution, he noted some time later, was that "American money and American charity shall solve every problem," particularly through the supply of American money distributed to weaker nations. Along with this would come the development of new corporate cartels to "control world trade in various raw materials." The only plan Washington had, he asserted, was to indiscriminately lend money "with the idea that it will create a tremendous demand for our exportable goods." This meant inflation and accumulated debt, plus a "grand form of international WPA hidden behind the jargon of reciprocal exchange and international cooperation."

An Anglo-American-Russian alliance to rule the world was,

43. Taft, "American Foreign Policy," address to the American Bar Association at Chicago, Aug. 26, 1943, Taft MSS., Box 552.

Taft charged, American imperialism. Taft doubted that Americans wished it. Hence he opposed plans for universal military training. War, he argued, would create a "condition in which America shall become an armed camp and be diverted from the progress" for which World War II was being fought.[44]

Taft favored regional plans, and he believed that territorial and economic rivalries had to be settled before the United States became part of a new league of nations. While he sometimes gave evidence of extreme feelings of nationalism, Taft diverged from the mainstream of liberalism by refusing to impart what James Patterson has aptly called "broad humanitarian motives to American war aims." Thus he was "cool to the idealistic 'one world' of Wendell Willkie, the power politics of Walter Lippmann, the American Century of Henry Luce," as well as, we might add, the People's Century of Henry A. Wallace.[45]

Despite his wariness about the potential of United States interventionism, Taft did support the Republican party's Mackinac Declaration, in which the party approved participation by the United States in a postwar organization that would prevent military aggression. He supported the Connally resolution, which demanded U.S. Senate approval for participation in a new league of free nations. He vacillated when it came to supporting major postwar administration proposals. He attacked the form of postwar planning suggested at the 1944 Bretton Woods Conference. Instead of massive investments abroad channeled through the International Monetary Fund, Taft favored the smaller movement of dollars through the purely American-controlled Export-Import Bank.

Like other former noninterventionists, Taft was wary of the new United Nations Organization. Commenting on the charter framed at Dumbarton Oaks in 1944, Taft questioned whether it was "calculated to insure peace rather than to provoke war." He did not approve of the provisions for a General Assembly, Security Council, and an International Court of Justice. These were

44. Ibid., "Are Administrative Foreign Policies Making More Difficult the Formation of a Post-War Peace Organization of Nations?" Taft address to the War Veterans' Republican Club of Ohio, Cleveland, May 6, 1944.

45. Patterson, *Mr. Republican,* pp. 290–291.

so structured that "a few nations will dominate the whole organization." Precisely because a veto power was to be placed in the hands of a few large nations, Taft had few illusions about the potential of the new UNO. The veto meant that "if the great powers agree, they may crush any small nation which ventures to disagree with them, and do so under the authority of the international organization." Yet it was not a military alliance, because no great power was obliged to come to the aid of any other member nation. Informal agreement, however, might lead to a practical combination of some powers and to the arbitrary use of power. Other nations, Taft felt, would be "bound to fret under the great powers' rule." The permission to maintain "vast military forces," moreover, would "certainly encourage militarism and imperialism." Despite these factors, Taft gave the United Nations his support. It did provide, he maintained, for a "continuous consulting body" in which the weaker nations were taking part, and it was "infinitely preferable to a direct military alliance."

Viewing the UN from a legalistic standpoint, Taft saw as its greatest failure the emphasis on use of force and the omission of a "rule of law and order." It was just a modern Briand Pact, renouncing war without having reached any prior agreement on a code of international law that all nations were obliged to accept. The Security Council provisions were not adequate. There was "no recognition by the great powers that there is any international law to which they should be subject."

Concerning the latter point, Taft's anticommunism was evident. A system of international law had not been developed because Russia "has not the slightest intention of submitting [its] disputes for such a decision." Taft believed that when any nation threatened peace, disputes should be referred to the International Court, not to the Security Council. In his view, the public had neglected the function of law and had forgotten that force was only a means of making law effective. "If we can establish an international law and a Court to apply it," Taft surmised, "the moral force of those decisions may well dominate in time public opinion of the world, so that no nation dare defy it." Perhaps this statement was Taft's most naïve opinion, a reflection of his illusions about the role and impact of law on the international community of nations.

Nevertheless Taft did not share with the social liberals their extreme optimism concerning the UN. The Roosevelt administration, he argued, "has grossly misrepresented the hope of permanent peace arising out of this organization." Like Oswald Garrison Villard, Taft made a rather harsh judgment about the prospects of the UN:

> We are not abolishing the causes of war. We are not abolishing militarism. We are enthroning it in a higher seat. We are not abolishing imperialism. We are not abolishing political sorespots, for we are recognizing the domination of Russia over Finland, Esthonia, Latvia, Lithuania, and to a large extent over Poland and the Balkans. We are recognizing the domination of England over India and of the Dutch over the East Indies, without any agreement on their part that they will work toward self-government. We are leaving unsettled the problem of whether Russia will dominate Manchuria . . . Any structure which departs so far from the freedom of peoples that desire freedom and the right of peoples to run their own affairs is handicapped from the start. The American people ought to realize this when they enter into this international organization, for otherwise they are doomed to a disillusionment which may lead them to withdraw from all international cooperation.[46]

Was Taft naïve, as his biographer asserts? It certainly was true that Taft was "cautious, nationalistic," as well as "anti-Communist." And he did hold to a strange faith in the power of international law as a major solution to the world's problems.[47] Yet in retrospect it is reasonable to view Taft's skepticism about the UN as more than justified. Unlike many other political leaders, Taft questioned the viability of an international organization based upon consensus among the large and powerful nation states.

It was Robert A. Taft's unique contribution to have maintained a critical position in an era when criticism of United States foreign policy had been all but abandoned. The euphoria of

46. Taft, "Notes on the Dumbarton Oaks Proposal," May 1945, Taft MSS., Box 546.
47. Patterson, *Mr. Republican*, p. 297.

waging an antifascist war caused political liberals to suspend critical judgment. To challenge the actions of the Roosevelt administration was not only suspect; it opened one up to being labeled an appeaser or a protofascist. The American Left, with the exception of small and isolated Trotskyist groups, and such rare independent voices as that of the writer Dwight Macdonald, had also joined the Roosevelt camp as part of the great war against fascism.

In this context Robert A. Taft's outspoken views reflected a rare political courage and acumen. Almost alone among political leaders, he had called attention to the negative effects of concentrated executive power, and he had condemned the usurpation of an independent congressional role by the executive. But Taft had gone beyond such constitutional concerns. He had warned his fellow citizens against creating a Pax Americana at the war's end, and he spoke of the possibility of a new imperialism breeding what later would be called the military-industrial complex. When few others had dared to use such an expression, Taft had told his audiences that the danger existed that an American imperialism might move to dominate the world.

Such spoken views almost assured that Taft would be anathema to the liberals and that his views would be easily distorted by opponents. It was Taft's strength, as perhaps it was also his political weakness, that he did not sound the messianic note so common among the voices of the political interventionists. Whether that group favored Luce's American Century or Wallace's People's Century, both Luce and Wallace saw a better world emerging as the result of a purely American world role. The United States, if it only followed a wise policy, would somehow meet the needs of all the world's peoples.

Much later this view would be synthesized in Hubert Humphrey's statement that Americans should act to remake Southeast Asia, because "there is a tremendous new opening here for realizing the dream of a great society in Asia, not just here at home." Back in the 1930s Robert A. Taft had already learned that American expansionism had not been able to create a great society at home, and that it was dubious whether it could transfer its society abroad.

Senator Robert A. Taft arrives in Chicago for the 1952 Republican Convention.
(INTERNATIONAL NEWS PHOTOS)

Robert A. Taft and the Emergence of the Cold War

TWENTY YEARS after Taft's death historians and journalists have turned back to inquire once more whether a study of his views might shed some light on the interventionist policies developing during the cold-war years. A positive assessment of Taft's policies was presented first by historian Henry W. Berger. Taft, Berger argued, made a "critique of the Truman foreign policy" that was "quite perceptive." Rather than viewing Taft as an isolationist, as did Arthur M. Schlesinger, Jr., and Selig Adler, Berger saw him as a "conservative nationalist at odds with the struggling attempts of liberal American policy-makers to fashion a program in the postwar years."[1]

Quoting excerpts from a famous Taft speech opposing NATO and the claim of presidential authority to send troops to Europe, columnist Nicholas von Hoffman wrote that "a full generation later" it "turns out that Taft was right, right on every question all the way from inflation to the terrible demoralization of troops." "And yet," Hoffman continued, "in the face of all these years of facts and experience Acheson comes out of nowhere to say 'asinine' and Nixon calls it 'isolationism.' " Hoffman contended that Taft's views were neither. They were "a way to defend the country without destroying it, a way to be part of the world without running it."[2]

1. Arthur M. Schlesinger, Jr., "The New Isolationism," *Atlantic* (May 1952), p. 34; Selig Adler, *The Isolationist Impulse: Its Twentieth Century Reaction* (New York: Abelard-Schuman, 1957), pp. 401–404; Henry W. Berger, "Senator Robert A. Taft Dissents from Military Escalation," in Thomas G. Paterson, ed. *Cold War Critics* (Chicago: Quadrangle Books, 1971), pp. 194–195.

2. Nicholas von Hoffman, "Warnings Out of the Woodwork," *Washington Post,* May 19, 1971, editorial page.

As the cold war developed, critical opposition was centered among the small and isolated bands of the Right and Left in American politics. This point was acknowledged during the period by Joseph M. Jones, a Truman administration adviser who had played a critical role in the development of both the Truman Doctrine and the Marshall Plan. Referring to opponents of cold-war foreign policy, Jones wrote:

> Most of the outright opposition came from the extreme Left and the extreme Right of the political spectrum; from a certain school of "liberals" who had long been strongly critical of the administration's stiffening policy toward the Soviet Union, and from the "isolationists," who had been consistent opponents of all foreign-policy measures that projected the United States actively into World Affairs. Thus Henry A. Wallace, Fiorello La Guardia, Senators Claude Pepper and Glen H. Taylor found themselves in the same bed with Colonel Robert McCormick, John O'Donnell, Representatives Harold Knutson and Everett M. Dirksen; and the Marshall Field papers (*P.M.* and the *Chicago Sun*), the *Chicago Daily News,* the *Nation,* the *New Republic,* and the *Christian Century* found themselves in the same corner with the McCormick-Patterson press. The opposition of the Left emphasized that American aid to the existing Greek and Turkish governments would not promote freedom but would protect anti-democratic and reactionary regimes; and that the proposed action by-passed the United Nations and endangered its future. The opposition of the Right emphasized that the President's policy would probably, if not inevitably, lead to war; and that the American economy could not stand the strains of trying to stop Communism with dollars. But both Right and Left used the full range of arguments in a bitter attack. "Power politics," "militarism," "intervention," were charged against the administration. "You can't fight Communism with dollars," "the new policy means the end of One World," "the Moscow Conference will be undermined," "we should not bail out the British Empire"—these were among the arguments used.[3]

For Jones the two extremes were balanced by the responsible mainstream, whose leaders understood that the United States

3. Joseph M. Jones, *The Fifteen Weeks* (New York: Viking, 1955), p. 177.

could not shirk meeting its international responsibilities. Yet he had put his finger on a critical insight—an agreement between a part of the Left and Right on the opposition to interventionist policies.

Taft's response to postwar developments can be discerned from viewing his attitude toward the major policies of the Truman administration—the Truman Doctrine, NATO, the Marshall Plan, and the Korean war. It reveals both the strengths and the limitations of his critique of the cold war.

Taft's anticommunism had been long established. Victory of communism outside of America, he had stated in 1941, was "far more dangerous to the United States . . . than the victory of fascism." But he had made it clear that his reference was "not to a military danger but to an ideological danger."[4] By 1946, however, what was soon to be called the cold war was on in earnest. It may have started on March 5 when Winston Churchill, with President Harry S. Truman sitting beside him, asked Americans at Fulton, Missouri, to understand that "God had willed" the United States to possess atomic bombs. To take advantage of the "breathing space" afforded by that weapon, Churchill asked for a "fraternal association of the English-speaking peoples" operating under UN principles—but outside the UN apparatus— to build a new world order. This had to be accomplished, Churchill had argued, because "from Stettin in the Baltic to Trieste in the Adriatic an iron curtain has descended across the Continent," in which "police governments" now ruled Eastern Europe. The Soviets did not want war, Churchill stated, but they did desire "the fruits of war and the indefinite expansion of their power and doctrines."[5]

Churchill's speech, with Truman's implicit endorsement, sparked a flurry of anti-Soviet sentiment. Taft agreed with Churchill and Truman that there was a "clear issue between Russia

4. Taft to George F. Stanley, Sept. 8, 1944, Robert A. Taft MSS., Box 31, Library of Congress, Wash., D.C.

5. *New York Times,* March 6, 1946, p. 4. See also Walter LaFeber, *America, Russia and the Cold War, 1945–1971* (New York: Wiley, 1972), pp. 30–31.

and the English-speaking peoples on form of government." Like the administration, Taft felt that Russia's "totalitarian state makes a policy of aggression more likely." But unlike the cold-warriors, Taft was "determined . . . to avoid a war with Russia if it can possibly be done."[6]

This placed Taft somewhere between the administration position and that of its most severe critic, Secretary of Commerce Henry A. Wallace. Wallace had already opposed Secretary of State James Byrnes's move to obtain a U.S. air base in Iceland, and he had strong criticisms of Bernard Baruch's proposals for the control of atomic energy. Wallace summarized his approach in a speech delivered on September 12 at Madison Square Garden in New York City.

A political understanding with Soviet Russia, according to the Secretary, required a guarantee of Soviet security needs in Eastern Europe. Wallace indirectly attacked Churchill by asking that the United States give its assurance that "our primary objective is neither saving the British Empire nor purchasing oil in the Near East with the lives of American soldiers." The heart of Wallace's speech called for putting the competition between Russia and the United States on a friendly basis, so that "the Russians should stop conniving against us in certain areas just as we should stop scheming against them in other parts of the world." The United States "should recognize that we have no more business in the political affairs of Eastern Europe than Russia has in the political affairs of Latin America."[7]

Wallace's speech produced an immediate demand that he be dismissed from his Cabinet position. Byrnes and Arthur Vandenberg argued that the speech was undercutting their attempt to carry out a "get tough" policy with the Russians in negotiations then under way in Paris. After a few days of delay President Truman requested Wallace's resignation on September 20.

6. Taft to William M. Davy, March 18, 1946, Taft MSS., Box 784.
7. Henry A. Wallace, "The Way to Peace," Sept. 12, 1946, in John Morton Blum, ed. *The Price of Vision: The Diary of Henry A. Wallace, 1942–1946* (Boston: Houghton Mifflin, 1973), pp. 660–669. See also Ronald Radosh and Leonard Liggio, "Henry A. Wallace and the Open Door," in Paterson, ed. *Cold War Critics*, pp. 86–87.

Taft's position may have been similar in some respects to Wallace's. But he accused Wallace of "advocating a milder policy towards communism and a less friendly attitude towards England" than did Byrnes and Vandenberg. He also endorsed Byrnes's demand that Wallace be dismissed. Wallace's speech, Taft asserted, "is a direct attack on the Byrnes policies. By supporting Mr. Wallace's remarks the President had betrayed his Secretary of State who . . . has been resisting every effort of Russia to extend its influence throughout the world." The Democratic party, Taft said in a fit of premature McCarthyism, was "divided between Communism and Americanism."[8]

This anti-Communist defense of State Department policy was most likely based on Taft's close association with Arthur Vandenberg. Taft's major analysis, however, seemed to indicate that his own thinking lay in a quite different direction. On October 5, 1946, Taft delivered a speech on the nature of justice which, as his biographer notes, "came as close as any of his lifetime to setting out his fundamental convictions."[9]

In this speech, delivered at Kenyon College in Ohio, Taft criticized the dependence of the new United Nations Organization on force instead of on accepted principles of international law. His citation of the war-crimes trials conducted at Nuremberg—which he branded a regrettable use of arbitrary power against individual rights—received most of the attention. The trials, Taft stated, "violate that fundamental principle of American law that a man cannot be tried under an *ex post facto* statute." A trial of "the vanquished by the victors," he continued, "cannot be impartial no matter how it is hedged about with the forms of justice." Taft questioned whether the hanging of the Nazi leaders would work to "discourage the making of aggressive war, for no one makes

8. Taft, press release of Sept. 13, 1946, Taft MSS., Box 1267. Taft's remark that Truman had supported Wallace's speech was based on the President's Sept. 12 press conference, at which he had stated that "I approve the whole speech." On Sept. 14, however, Truman clumsily tried to claim that he had approved only Wallace's right to make a speech, and had not endorsed it as "a statement of the foreign policy of this country."

9. James T. Patterson, *Mr. Republican: A Biography of Robert A. Taft* (Boston: Houghton Mifflin, 1972), p. 326.

aggressive war unless he expects to win." He saw in the trials "the spirit of vengeance, and vengeance is seldom justice. The hanging of the eleven men convicted will be a blot on the American record which we shall long regret."[10]

It was this portion of the speech that led Taft's opponents, such as Senate majority leader Alben Barkley, to proclaim that Taft "never experienced a crescendo of heart about the soup kitchens of 1932, but his heart bled anguishedly for the criminals at Nuremberg."[11] Taft, however, was not presenting an argument on behalf of the Nazi leaders. He had no objection, he wrote columnist Westbrook Pegler, to having the Allied governments, "even without a trial, shutting these men up for the rest of their lives as a matter of policy and on the ground that if free they might stir up another war." His objection was merely to "use of the forms of justice to carry out a pre-determined policy."[12]

With the attention of the public focused on Taft's remarks about Nuremberg, contemporary observers may have missed Taft's doubts about the ability of the English-speaking peoples to lead the world to a condition of lawfulness. In "recent foreign policy," he had stated in the same address, Americans had been "affected by principles of expediency and supposed necessity, and abandoned largely the principle of justice." The United States had "drifted into the acceptance of the idea that the world is to be ruled by the power and policy of the great nations and a police force established by them rather than by international law."

The Truman administration, Taft maintained, had lost sight of the basic fact that the policeman was incidental to the law, that without adherence to international law a world policeman could become a tyrant or a creator of anarchy. Taft noted that an amendment he favored, one that directed the U.S. delegate to the United Nations not to vote for action against any other nation

10. Taft, "Equal Justice Under Law: The Heritage of the English-Speaking Peoples and Their Responsibility," conference at Kenyon College, Gambier, Ohio, Oct. 4–6, 1946, Taft MSS., Box 210.
11. Quoted in Patterson, *Mr. Republican,* p. 327.
12. Taft to Westbrook Pegler, Oct. 14, 1946, Taft MSS.

unless it accorded with international law, had been rejected by Congress. This showed "the extent to which" the administration had "accepted the philosophy of force as the controlling factor in international action." This development was not accidental. "For years," Taft said, "we have been accepting at home the theory that the people are too dumb to understand and that a benevolent executive must be given power to describe policy and administer policy according to his own prejudices in each individual case. Such a policy in the world, as at home, can lead only to tyranny or to anarchy."

During the war, Taft argued, Americans took the position that "no nation had the right to remain neutral." Suggesting that this attitude had been transformed to the postwar period, he concluded: "Our whole attitude in the world, for a year after V.E. Day, including the use of the Atomic bomb at Hiroshima and Nagasaki, seems to me a departure from the principles of fair and equal treatment which has made America respected throughout the world before this second World War. Today we are cordially hated in many countries."[13]

Yet this same speech revealed the ambiguity that was to weaken the force of Taft's criticism throughout the cold-war years. He moved on to praise and offer support to the hard-line policy of Byrnes and Vandenberg, men who Taft claimed had "reversed our policy in many of the respects I have referred to." These same men, however, were the architects and supporters of Truman administration policy that Taft purported to be critical of, a policy based on what Taft called "the general prevalence of the doctrine of force and expediency." Because Taft backed the Byrnes approach, he opposed suggestions that President Truman should fly to Moscow to confer directly with Stalin. "Such a move on the part of President Truman," he stated, "would be interpreted by the Russians as indicating an intention of changing our policy and agreeing to those Russian policies which Secretary Byrnes has been resisting." Taft preferred to have Stalin travel to the United States, since "in negotiations, you are always at a

13. Taft, "Equal Justice Under Law," conference at Kenyon College.

disadvantage if you insist on going to see the other man in his home."[14]

Taft was sufficiently critical, however, to offer a negative response to the announcement of the Truman Doctrine. In February 1947, after the British ambassador had informed Washington that his government could no longer provide aid for Greece and Turkey, the United States government acted to take up the burden and to replace the vacuum left by British imperialism. If Greece fell to the Communists, Dean Acheson informed the President, all of Europe would soon succumb to Communist aggression. Acheson believed that it was imperative for the United States to come up with a program of financial and military aid.

On February 27 Truman summoned congressional leaders to inform them of his decision. Taft, considered by the administration to be a leader of "isolationist" forces, was significantly excluded from the meeting. But Truman took care to invite Arthur Vandenberg, the former "isolationist," who had now become the symbol of bipartisanship in foreign policy. Truman wanted $250 million for Greece and $150 million for Turkey. He needed the backing of Vandenberg, who was chairman of the Senate Foreign Relations Committee and who would use his influence to get reluctant congressmen to back the request. On March 10, this time with Taft present, Truman held a second meeting with congressional leaders. Vandenberg came from the meeting expressing complete agreement with Truman's call. On March 12 the President addressed a joint session of Congress to ask immediate aid for Greece and Turkey. "I believe," he told Congress, "that it must be the policy of the United States to support free peoples who are resisting attempted subjugation by armed minorities or by outside pressures."

Truman's statement, Stephen Ambrose has noted, "defined American policy for the next twenty years. Whenever and wherever an anti-communist government was threatened, by indigenous insurgents, foreign invasion, or even diplomatic pressure

14. Taft to Philip Leserman and Kingston Fletcher, Oct. 15, 1946, Taft MSS., Box 778.

. . . the United States would supply political, economic and most of all military aid. The Truman Doctrine came close to shutting the door against any revolution, since the terms 'free peoples' and 'anti-communist' were assumed to be synonymous. All the Greek government, or any dictatorship, had to do to get American aid was to claim that its opponents were communist."[15] A struggle in Greece between Left and Right had been transformed by Truman into a conflict between freedom and slavery. The United States was meant to play the role of policeman on the side of the angels.

Truman's new policy would have the United States interfere in the affairs of people outside the hemisphere in time of peace. Leaving the meeting of March 10, Taft was skeptical. The policy, he told the press, seemed to "accept . . . dividing the world into zones of political influence, communist and anti-communist." Moreover, if the United States held "a special position in Greece and Turkey, we can hardly longer reasonably object to the Russians' continuing their domination in Poland, Yugoslavia, Rumania, and Bulgaria." Taft did not "want war with Russia," he emphasized. "Whether our intervention in Greece tends to make such a war more probable or less probable depends upon many circumstances regarding which I am not yet fully advised and, therefore, I do not care to make a decision at the present time. I want to know what our top military people think of the possibility that Russia will go to war if we carry out this program, just as we might be prompted to go to war if Russia tried to force a communist government on Cuba."[16]

The Truman administration continued to build up pressure to gain congressional support. Truman spoke and acted as if the Greek situation was a postwar Pearl Harbor. The powerful Vandenberg defined the crisis as part of a "world-wide ideological clash between Eastern Communism and Western Democracy." Taft did not budge. When Vandenberg asked for sugges-

15. Stephen E. Ambrose, *Rise to Globalism* (Baltimore, Md.: Penguin Books, 1971), p. 150.
16. *New York Times,* March 13 and 16, 1947.

tions to be presented to the President, Taft offered a list of critical questions:

Did U.S. military authorities, Taft asked, "feel that Soviet Russia's military strength is such that they are likely to declare war against the United States"? Should Russia do so, would Greece be able to "resist an invasion"? Where was the "evidence that a government dominated by Greek Communists could spread communism in other parts of the Mediterranean," or spread "confusion and disorder . . . throughout the entire Middle East"? Where was the evidence that American "national security" was involved? What form of organization would direct U.S. policy? Would U.S. commissions remain "after Greece is restored to a normal economic condition"? Whether the loan was granted or not, why did not the U.S. simply "file a complaint" with the UN? Finally, Taft noted that Truman stated "we are entering Greece to protect the government against the terrorist activities of a minority of armed men led by Communists." Taft wanted to know whether the U.S. would "permit elections to be held," and whether the U.S. would "retire from Greece in case a duly elected majority of the Greek people . . . request our retirement."[17]

The administration paid little attention to his doubts, but Taft gathered support from some other Republicans. Fiorello La Guardia wrote him that he also considered the Truman Doctrine a "gross blunder," pointing out that the $400 million allocated was to be used for weaponry, not food.[18]

Taft responded that he did not "like this Greek-Turkish proposition, but I do recognize that perhaps we had better maintain the status quo until we can reach some peace settlement with Russia. I don't like to appear to be backing down." He would have preferred that the loan to Britain should not have been granted without stipulation that "the British would go on supporting Greece."[19] While Taft disapproved of the aid for Greece and Turkey, he felt that he had to vote for it "because I don't want to

17. Taft to Arthur Vandenberg, March 18, 1947, Taft MSS., Box 790.
18. Ibid., Fiorello La Guardia to Taft, April 18, 1947.
19. Ibid., Taft to La Guardia, April 18, 1947.

discredit the President during his negotiations with Russia in the making of peace treaties."[20] "I intend to vote for the Greek and Turkish loans," he announced on April 10, "for the reason that the President's announcements have committed the United States to this policy in the eyes of the world, and to repudiate it now would destroy his prestige in the negotiations with the Russian government on the success of which ultimate peace depends." Taft viewed such aid as temporary. He noted that he did not regard it as "a commitment to any similar policy in any other section of the world." He believed that the United States would "withdraw as soon as normal economic conditions are restored."[21]

Taft's vote in support of the Truman Doctrine must be regarded as a surrender of critical judgment. He had endorsed a policy that was the opposite of a limited and temporary commitment, a program that, in truth, symbolized the perpetual program of anti-Communist interventionism that was to dominate the decade. Perhaps because of his loyalty to Vandenberg, as well as his own anticommunism, Taft stepped back from making the deductions of the critical questions he had raised. As a result, his biographer notes, Taft did not become a "thoughtful spokesman about the proper American course in the Cold War." It was easier for him "to submit to the judgment of Vandenberg than to lead his party along the path of obstructionism."[22]

Yet there were elements within the Republican party that were developing a firm criticism of the Truman Doctrine. Taft might have acted to support Representative George H. Bender, Republican from Ohio. The major Taftite in the House, and later Taft's successor in the Senate, Bender tried his best to offer alternatives to waging the cold war. His evaluation of the Truman Doctrine was more forthright than Taft's:

> I believe that the White House program is a reaffirmation of the nineteenth century belief in power politics. It is a refinement of the policy first adopted after the Treaty of Versailles in 1919

20. Ibid., Taft to Joseph R. O'Connell, April 5, 1947.
21. *New York Times,* April 11, 1947, p. 1.
22. Patterson, *Mr. Republican,* p. 372.

designed to encircle Russia and establish a "Cordon Sanitaire" around the Soviet Union. It is a program which points to a new policy of interventionism in Europe as a corollary to our Monroe Doctrine in South America. Let there be no mistake about the far-reaching implications of this plan. Once we have taken the historic step of sending financial aid, military experts and loans to Greece and Turkey, we shall be irrevocably committed to a course of action from which it will be impossible to withdraw. More and larger demands will follow. Greater needs will arise throughout the many areas of friction in the world.[23]

Bender also opposed funds for the Voice of America, military collaboration with "the petty and not so petty dictators of South America," and the Truman administration's "military control at home." All these measures, he asserted, were "part of the whole Truman doctrine of drawing off the resources of the United States in support of every reactionary government in the world."[24]

Bender tried to move Taft toward a position of committed opposition. "I do not see any way," the congressman informed Taft, "to keep foreign policy out of the 1948 campaign." Bender thought that Truman was "further out on the limb on foreign policy than on any other issue." Citing Taft's opposition to arming "of the South American dictatorships" and the accusations made against Taft because of his opposition to universal military training, Bender urged him to recognize that the "whole Truman policy is one of military aggression pure and simple and cannot but create more conflict rather than less."

"It seems to me," Bender told Taft frankly, "that it is wrong to let Vandenberg continue to push us into the arms of the Democrats under the guise of this phony bi-partisan foreign policy." Bender warned Taft that the Democrats expected to "drag us back here in the Fall to vote another five or ten billions a year for Harry to squander here and there around the world." He urged Taft to create a "Taft Plan for American foreign affairs" stipulating that all international disputes be handled through the United Nations, and that economic relationships be placed on a "solid

23. *Congressional Record,* March 28, 1947, 2831–32.
24. *Congressional Record,* June 6, 1947, 6562–63.

business basis" without regard "to those damnable idealogical [sic] bugaboos." Bender accused Truman of killing the United Nations and of tying the United States "every day to the British either in a military or economic way." The starting point for the Taft plan, he suggested, should be a powerful UN rather than an Anglo-American alliance, personified by the Marshall Plan.

As for Communist ideology, Bender argued that business had to be done "with large hunks of the world which have adopted some type of economy other than ours." Either the United States would "live at peace with them" or it would go to war. If the first alternative was chosen, Bender saw no reason why business could not take place, "particularly since they furnish a market for every type of American industrial product." Bender saw foreign policy "over-riding everything else by November 1948" because of the "mad foreign policy of military alliances which Truman has let the military sell him." Bender wanted the Republicans to present Truman with a strong frontal attack. He felt that this could be done only if Taft was to take "the offensive and give affirmative direction through a Taft Plan." Bender argued that they could win the Republican convention for such a policy, but only if Taft agreed to "sock Truman . . . on this foreign policy business." There was "no good reason," he emphasized, "to let Vandenberg make suckers out of the Party and swing votes for Dewey."[25]

Taft did not join Bender in waging a frontal attack on the Truman foreign policy. Because he still wished to be able to concentrate on domestic affairs, and because he had close ties to Vandenberg, he chose to support major Truman policies. On June 5 General George C. Marshall announced the second phase of the administration policy—large-scale economic aid to Western Europe. Taft questioned whether the assumptions behind the Marshall Plan were sound. "I am afraid," he informed Herbert Hoover, "that the manner in which the Marshall Plan was presented invites the foreign nations to gang up and make unreasonable demands. Instead of making them come to us and imposing conditions on our assistance, we always seem to be begging them

25. Bender to Taft, July 14, 1947, Taft MSS., Box 548.

to let us help them as if it were to our financial or economic advantage to do so." Europe, Taft implied, could be restored to health more quickly if it restored its own production. The only advantage he affirmed was the "long-range desire to see peace and prosperity in the world."[26] Taft agreed that "we should help the nations whose economy was destroyed by the war to get on their own feet." An "international WPA," however, "would fail to solve the problem."[27]

Taft also denied that Marshall Plan aid was needed to prevent a Russian military threat to European security. The United States still had the strongest navy and army, as well as possession of the atomic bomb. To defeat Russia in military battle would require sending an army of five million men to Europe, "and even then it is doubtful what we could accomplish." He believed, however, that "the Russians know enough about the situation so they do not want war within any reasonable period of years." Their desire was to spread communism on an ideological basis. Taft agreed that the European nations had to be helped "to the extent that it will really be of aid to them in combatting communism." But it had to be left to the French people "ultimately" to "decide whether France will be communist." The United States could only "help restore normal economic conditions so that the atmosphere will be less favorable to communism." Dollars alone, Taft warned, could not do the job—"too lavish a distribution of dollars may well do more harm than good." Taft favored aid to maintain only "a minimum standard of subsistence."[28]

The Secretary of State's plan, Taft argued, was "useless unless we change our policy in Germany and our policy in China." Marshall, he charged, was uninterested in saving China from communism, while advocating spending "billions for Western Europe." His goal would fail, Taft predicted, "as long as he continues in Germany to destroy the industrial plants which alone can make Germany self-supporting."[29] Marshall's policy

26. Taft to Hoover, Aug. 13, 1947, Hoover MSS., Hoover Institution of War and Peace, Stanford University; Palo Alto, California.

27. *New York Times,* Sept. 26, 1947.

28. Taft to Fred W. Kinley, Oct. 20, 1947, Taft MSS., Box 175.

29. Taft address on NBC radio, Nov. 17, 1947, ibid., Box 263.

was a plan "permitting Marshall to do what he wishes." Taft hoped Americans would "get free from the idea that we are bound to cooperate in everything." He charged that "the Administration foreign policy has brought the world to a state of complete bankruptcy."[30]

Taft enlarged on his position in a statement prepared on the topic of foreign affairs. The United States was concerned with the economic welfare of other nations only because world prosperity meant less of a chance for attacks on America's security. The Truman administration had pursued an "inept and futile" policy toward communism. Lend-Lease aid had been granted without any agreements obtained on postwar behavior. At Yalta and Potsdam the United States had "recognized the right of the Russian army to occupy the Balkans, Berlin and Vienna." At Potsdam, Truman and Marshall had "abandoned all the principles of the Atlantic Charter" and had approved the Morgenthau Plan [to partition Germany], which had "wrecked the economy of Europe."

Marshall had admitted that "China was completely wrecked by civil war," yet he opposed "the policy of extending vigorous military aid, which alone could bring an end to civil war." To Taft the Far East was "ultimately even more important to our future peace than is Europe." The problem was that the administration was "pinning all of its anti-Communist hopes on the Marshall Plan." Taft supported aid to Western Europe, but he insisted it be "confined to specific needs and to fields where we can see that it will actually accomplish the purposes we want to achieve." Only West European governments on their own could act to develop a stable currency "and create the incentive to produce and export. All we can do is remove bottlenecks and prime the pump."[31]

Taft went on to emphasize the possibility of a new American imperialism emerging from the administration's policy toward Western Europe. Americans were too "much inclined to overestimate the effect of American dollars," he pointed out. "A credit of American dollars encouraging unsound policies and giving the

30. Taft to Ferdinand Lathrop Mayer, Nov. 19, 1947, ibid., Box 189.
31. Taft, "Foreign Affairs," n.d., Taft MSS., Box 205.

basis for the charge that we are trying to dominate their country may easily assist communism rather than prevent it."[32] Taft introduced an amendment that would reduce the amount provided for European Recovery Plan aid from $5.3 billion to $4 billion.

Debate on the aid bill took place from March 1 through 13, 1948. A few days earlier, on February 25, the Communists had seized power in Czechoslovakia by a coup. This event strengthened administration efforts to gather support for the Marshall Plan. General Lucius Clay had wired Truman to suggest that war with Russia was likely in a matter of weeks. On March 17 Truman addressed the House of Representatives, stressing the "increasing threat" to the very "survival of freedom." Proclaiming that the Marshall Plan was "not enough," because Europe needed protection against both internal and external "aggression," Truman asked Congress for universal military training, resumption of Selective Service, and rapid passage of the Marshall Plan.[33]

Vandenberg, as well as Truman, was arguing that the Czech coup indicated how close war might be. Taft refused to join the chorus. The reason he supported the Marshall Plan, he told the Senate, was precisely because it was "not aimed at opposing any communistic military attack." Taft, moreover, argued that "the tone of the President's statement that his confidence in ultimate world peace has been shaken is unfortunate." Taft rejected the administration's attempt to use the Czech coup to gain passage of the Marshall Plan. "I myself," he continued, "know of no particular indication of Russian intentions to undertake military aggression beyond the sphere of influence which was originally assigned to the Russians. The situation in Czechoslovakia is indeed a tragic one; but the Russian influence has been predominant in Czechoslovakia since the end of the war. The Communists are merely consolidating their position . . . but there has been no military aggression since the end of the war."[34]

32. *Congressional Record,* Nov. 20, 1947, 4253.
33. Cited in LaFeber, *America, Russia and the Cold War,* p. 64.
34. *Congressional Record,* March 12, 1948, 2641–2644.

Taft's desire to avoid war, and his view that the conflict with Russia was primarily an ideological one, pushed him more toward the Bender position of opposition. Taft was not willing to accept administration propaganda that tried to substantiate the existence of a Soviet desire for military conquest. He felt that it was "most discouraging to have the President so disposed to believe that Russian governments always desire to conquer the world." He agreed with lawyer Grenville Clark that there had to be "a new approach" taken toward the Russians, although he did feel that the Russians refused to discuss "any of the proposals except those which expand Russian power." Taft was unsure of the Russians' intentions, but he did not believe "that they are foolish enough to want another war."[35]

Henry A. Wallace, the exponent of an alternative path within the Democratic party's ranks, declared that Taft's foreign policy was "the most liable to keep peace during the next four years." Wallace, like other opponents of UMT, had put Taft on his "list of preferences" because of the senator's opposition to that measure in particular.[36]

Wallace would shortly declare his presidential candidacy on a third-party ticket. But others continued to hope that Taft would assume responsibility for uniting the anti-Truman and the anti-cold-war leadership. Yale anthropologist George P. Murdock thought he detected "a terrific undercurrent of opposition to the Marshall Plan throughout the country." He could not find a "single farmer, small businessman, or mechanic who is not outspokenly opposed." Murdock hoped that these people would be able to "find a political channel of expression," but that could only occur if the Republicans nominated "someone who is opposed to the Plan or at least reasonably skeptical about it." This meant a movement away from bipartisanship. Murdock was a "lifelong Democrat with political views perhaps slightly to the left of center," but he could not "support Mr. Truman this year."

35. Taft to Clark, March 31, 1948, Taft MSS., Box 797.
36. Wallace statements of Dec. 11 and 12, 1947, cited in Curtis D. Macdougall, *Gideon's Army*, I (New York: Marzani and Munsell, 1965), p. 239.

He promised that if Taft became the Republican presidential nominee, he "would gladly vote and work for [him]."[37]

Murdock was not the only person on the Left to support a Taft candidacy. Socialist party leader Norman Thomas wrote Taft that he also had opposed Franklin Roosevelt and James Byrnes when they were "helping to create the conditions which now almost ruin the world." And like Taft, Socialist Thomas felt that the United States could no longer "afford to go crusading around the world." Thomas was disturbed by the reimposition of the draft, which, he felt, might indoctrinate "our people to accept the peacetime military conscription which has led to war." Thomas noted that although he opposed Taft, as "you would expect a Socialist to oppose a Republican," he respected him for his "forthrightness on all issues."[38]

Truman's policy had led many others to urge Taft to assume leadership with an alternate program. Conservative editor Felix Morley saw Truman's speech on the draft as "a confession of bankruptcy." He predicted an electoral drift away from the Democrats. It was only a question of "whether Wallace or the GOP nominee will get the benefit." New Dealers who had "no respect whatsoever for Wallace," Morley informed Taft, were "all hoping that you will get the nomination." Thomas E. Dewey was going about me-tooing Truman's anticommunism, a losing game. That was "Truman's only card now," Morley remarked, "and the aspirant can't play it as well as the man in power." The

37. Murdock to Taft, Feb. 8, 1948, Taft MSS., Box 545.
38. Norman Thomas to Taft, March 15, 1948, ibid., Box 797. Enclosed in the correspondence is a copy of the Socialist party's analysis of Truman's speech to Congress of March 17. The Socialists saw it as "an aggravation of world crisis, not a solution of it." They accused Truman of trying to "exploit an international crisis" for political advantage in an election year, and went on to note their opposition to "Henry Wallace's faith in appeasement." The Socialist party also claimed that Truman had "invited our present troubles by continuing at Potsdam the Yalta policy of appeasing Stalin." This approach revealed a basic agreement between the Socialist party and conservative analysts such as John T. Flynn and Taft. Now, the Socialist Party continued, Truman seemed "to believe that he can terrify Stalin by seeking power to create mass armies which under no circumstances can ever equal the Russian in size."

senator was "the only man in the run who [had] not been roped in by UMT; who [had] sounded warnings about Russia without any 'warmongering,' " and who was "universally respected for his courage and integrity." But the only way Taft would be able to challenge a popular belief that he was not a good vote-getter, Morley argued, would be for him "to move in actively on the field of foreign policy." The major issue in the 1948 campaign would be whether the U.S. was "going to drift into another war." Morley hoped Taft would respond with "a series of major speeches . . . in the field of foreign policy" which would concentrate "on the necessity of saving ideals which are as much menaced by domestic stupidity as by any threat of external aggression." Morley thought the "honest and courageous course" would turn out as well to be "the best course politically" and would "set up an irresistible current" demanding Taft's nomination.[39]

Taft appreciated Morley's suggestions, but he pointed to what he called "difficulties." He did not have the facts Truman had, and he feared that this would result in his making "some mistake which [could] easily be shown up." Moreover, Taft noted that "a man who is against war when everyone else is for it becomes very unpopular indeed." Taft's negative response indicates the way in which political concerns kept him from assuming leadership. "I have had more criticism for my very mild appeals to look the whole situation over before acting," he wrote, "than I have had for anything else I have done." Yet Taft agreed that he "must do everything possible to discourage war excitement and hold us back from any action which will bring war about." He did not, however, see how he could "be against full preparedness."[40]

Taft's stance, mild as it was, was enough to lead some critics to charge him with softness toward communism. Liberal columnist Marquis Childs informed *Washington Post* readers that Truman's message to Congress "should convince the tough-minded men who make up the Politburo . . . that the United

39. Ibid., Morley to Taft, March 18, 1948.
40. Ibid., Taft to Morley, March 23, 1948.

States will not permit the conquest of western Europe by communist tyranny." Referring to "dissenters from this view," such as Henry A. Wallace, Childs noted that at the "opposite pole" of the political spectrum stood "old-time isolationists" for whom Taft spoke. Taft, Childs wrote, "said he could see no threat to this country that might bring war. The best answer to that was the cartoon showing the Taft head in the sand and the Taft rear rather plainly exposed to the world." Childs believed that Taft's new position was "the same kind of isolationism that Taft expressed in the years before Pearl Harbor . . . to the effect that Japan had no aggressive intentions."

Child's column drew Taft's anger. He had not stated that no threat existed that might bring war but "that there was nothing that [he knew] of which indicated any change in the Russian policy of the past year regarding an aggressive use of their military forces to take over new territory." The Russians had only been "conducting a steady campaign of consolidating through support of communist forces within each country the position which we gave them at Yalta." If there were circumstances which had changed the Russian policy toward waging aggressive war, Taft answered that "Truman and Marshall ought to tell us what they are." If there were none, Taft found there was a "reasonable chance of maintaining peace." Because he favored an ideological battle, he had voted for the Voice of America, the Marshall Plan, aid to Greece and Turkey, and had supported supplying arms to China. On a final note of pique Taft informed Childs that he could not "quite tell from your column whether you think we should go to war at once."[41]

Childs agreed that Taft had indeed "supported measures for peacetime resistance to Soviet aggression." But Taft's weak support was not sufficient for militantly liberal interventionists. Taft's proposed amendment to cut down Marshall Plan aid to $4 billion, Childs wrote, would have meant "such a serious handicap as to have made the program unworkable." Childs denied that he wanted war with Russia; he supported a policy based

41. Ibid., Taft to Childs, March 25, 1948. Enclosed with the correspondence is the undated Childs column.

upon peace through strength. "If we take the essential measures to make America strong," he retorted, "we shall be able to prevent war with the Soviet Union."[42]

The drift of events, combined with the attacks on Taft from the liberal camp, seemed at times to be bringing him closer to the more aggressive opposition advocated by Bender and Morley. What he privately called "the rather alarmist attitude adopted by the government" in response to the Czech coup pushed Taft farther away from Vandenberg. The problem was that when it came "to foreign policy," Taft explained, "it is almost impossible for Congress to have much effect on it. The power is all in the President's hands." All that members of Congress could do was comment after the fact. While Taft tried "to keep in accord with Vandenberg," he admitted that "he is very much inclined to follow the suggestions of the President and General Marshall and avoid any public criticism." Taft was inclined to agree that the Republicans should "take an affirmative position." Yet he stopped short of doing so, demanding "fairly unanimous agreement among the party leaders" if that was to be actually done.[43]

Taft's vote in favor of the peacetime draft had infuriated many of his followers. But he moved into a solitary opposition when the Truman administration introduced the North Atlantic Treaty Organization in 1949. Created with the participation of nine European nations, Iceland, and Canada, NATO was to provide a new system of military alliances and arms to deter the Soviet Union from an aggressive military course. Though Truman and his advisers had offered no hard evidence of a real Soviet military threat, the alliance required member nations to respond with use of force to an attack against any other member.

On the issue of NATO Taft went back to themes he had raised before the outbreak of World War II. The Republican party had to take the position that there could be "no greater tragedy than war." War was justified only if it became essential "to protect the liberty of our people." Yet it now seemed to Taft that the United

42. Ibid., Childs to Taft, April 9, 1948.
43. Ibid., Taft to Roy D. Moore, March 26, 1948.

States had "adopted a tendency to interfere in the affairs of other nations, to assume that we are a kind of demigod and Santa Claus to solve the problems of the world, and that attitude is more and more likely to involve us in disputes where our liberty is not in fact concerned." Taft once again warned about the United States becoming an empire. "It is easy," he stated, "to skip into an attitude of imperialism where war becomes an instrument of public policy rather than its last resort."[44]

The vote on the NATO treaty was coming up in the Senate in early July. Taft declared he would vote for it if the treaty provided no obligation to offer arms. The administration returned vague assurances. Taft and Senators Kenneth Wherry (Republican, Nebraska) and Forrest C. Donell (Republican, Missouri) pointed out that a May 1949 State Department publication had noted that military aid would be a "vital corollary" of NATO. This above all pushed Taft into opposing the alliance. It meant a rupture with Vandenberg. "My friend from Ohio," the bipartisan Republican leader confided to his diary, "has given me a first class headache tonight."[45]

In scores of articles and speeches Taft explained why he had joined the thirteen other negative senatorial votes many times. He had wanted to vote for NATO, and had favored a warning meant to stop Russia from ever trying to attack Western Europe. "But the Atlantic Pact," Taft noted, "goes much further. It obligates us to go to war if at any time during the next twenty years anyone makes an armed attack on any of the twelve nations." It would also allow the President to take the nation into war without consent of Congress. It was "part of a much larger program by which we undertake to arm all those nations against Russia." NATO had become "an offensive and defensive military alliance against Russia." Such an alliance was "more likely to produce war than peace."

44. Text of Taft speech, "The Future of the Republican Party," Jan. 28, 1949, delivered at Niles, Ohio, *Congressional Record,* Jan. 31, 1949, A 455.
45. Arthur Vandenberg, Jr., ed. *The Private Papers of Senator Vandenberg* (Boston: Houghton Mifflin, 1952), p. 498. See Patterson, *Mr. Republican,* pp. 437–438; cf. Henry W. Berger, "Senator Robert A. Taft Dissents from Military Escalation," p. 184.

It would also have the effect, Taft continued, of "stimulating the Russians to increase still further their development of war forces." A new arms race would result. Taft asked Americans to try to see how the Russians might respond to the existence of NATO. Arming "all the nations around Russia from Norway on the North to Turkey on the South," he suggested, might lead Russia to "decide that the arming of Western Europe . . . looks to an attack upon Russia." From the Russian standpoint, he acknowledged, such a view was not "unreasonable." And since the arming would take years to complete, the danger existed that the "arms policy is more likely to incite war than to deter it." Referring to the fact that nations right on Russia's own borders were to be armed, Taft inquired: "How would we feel if Russia undertook to arm a country on our border, Mexico, for instance?"

Unlike the administration, Taft felt that the United States already had enough armed strength to deter an attack. Fifteen billion dollars per year on defense, the atomic bomb, and a powerful air force were sufficient to deter attack. But NATO was a project whose cost was "incalculable," since the sixty divisions needed by Europe for safety against Russia would cost $24 billion per year. That, Taft noted, "would cost more each year than the housing, education and limited health plans combined." Taft was obliged to refuse to "give the President . . . unlimited power to go out and arm the world in time of peace."[46]

NATO might be called defensive, but the line between defense and offense, Taft noted, is indeed shadowy. In addition, the pact violated the UN charter. "A prior undertaking by the most powerful nation in the world to arm half the world against the other," he wrote, violates the UN charter and its entire spirit. "It makes a farce of further efforts to secure international peace through law and justice. It makes permanent the division of the world into two armed camps."[47]

Taft began to criticize the globalist interventionism of the Truman administration in such strong terms that he seemed

46. Taft radio address on the Drew Pearson hour, July 24, 1949, Taft MSS., Box 552.
47. Taft, "Washington Report," July 20, 1949.

almost to be echoing the position of the most severe critics on the Left.

> Think of the tremendous power which this proposal gives the President to involve us in any war throughout the world, including civil wars where we may favor one faction against the other. . . . I am opposed to the whole idea of giving the President power to arm the world against Russia or anyone else, or even to arm Western Europe, except where there is a real threat of aggression. We are stimulating an armament race. We are trying to restore a military balance of power on the European continent. Such policies in the past have always led to war rather than to peace.[48]

And President Truman, he charged, was falling back on the old generalities, trying to smear NATO's opponents "with the opprobrious epithet of isolationists."[49] Apparently "those [administration supporters] who make the charge," Taft stated, "feel that anyone who varies from the pattern established by our State Department is to be cast into outer darkness." To these people State Department policy had "become a party line and they jump back and forth just as quickly as did the communists when Stalin favored or opposed Hitler." Taft was not about to accept a State Department party line. He denied that he considered a war with Russia inevitable or even likely; indeed, he was "inclined to the opposite point of view." The Russians, on the contrary, "have shown no sign of impending military aggression. In four years they have not moved beyond the line of occupation given them in substance at Yalta."[50]

48. Taft, "Washington Report," Aug. 3, 1949; cf. Ronald Radosh and Leonard P. Liggio, "Henry A. Wallace and the Open Door," p. 104. Wallace argued that NATO proved the failure of the Marshall Plan, which was supposed to preclude the need for any military programs in Europe. He concluded, in terms similar to those used by Taft, "Any fair appraisal of [NATO's] consequences demonstrates that it can lead only to national insolvency, the surrender of our traditional freedoms, war, a possible military disaster, and the certain sacrifice not only of life and treasure but of the very system of government which it is supposed to preserve."

49. Taft, "Washington Report," Aug. 31, 1949.

50. Taft, "American Foreign Policy in Its Relation to the United Nations," n.d. (1950), ibid., Box 270.

Considering the general mood and the events, Taft's persistence took great political courage. The years 1948 and 1949 marked the height of the cold war—Czechoslovakia, the Berlin blockade, fear of Soviet espionage rings. In this context, Taft's biographer points out, "NATO seemed to many people the only way to prevent a return to the appeasement of the 1930's. Taft could have bent to the popular mood by voting for the pact, then saved his fire to fight the military assistance bill that followed two months later. That he did not, that he insisted instead on drawing attention to the long-range possibilities of such a pact, that he even raised the heretical notion that the United States was imperialistic, attested to his integrity, his sense of responsibility, and even his gift for prophecy."[51]

It is not surprising that Taft's colleague in the Senate Arthur Vandenberg expressed his candid feeling that he would "feel much more comfortable for the country if he [Taft] and I did not seem to be drawing farther apart in respect to 'foreign affairs.' I hope," he confided to Taft's brother, "we can find common ground upon which to reverse this trend."[52] But Taft shared no common ground with the policy makers. Mocking John Foster Dulles' statement that "it would be foolish for us to send arms to the continent if Russia were about to invade it," Taft rejoined that it would be "foolish for us to send arms if Russia is not about to invade it." A Russian attack, to Taft, would be "the only justification for arming Germany." Taft had gone so far as to declare the arming of western Europe "just as offensive as it is defensive," and he reminded his fellow senators that "the Russians are not going to be deceived."[53]

While the world's attention was centered on Europe, Mao Tsetung led the Chinese Communists to victory; Chiang Kai-shek's government collapsed, and its leaders and army fled to Formosa. Taft wanted the U.S. Navy to be put into action to defend that island. In Europe, Taft argued, the United States had risked war with Russia to maintain its position in Berlin. It had moved to

51. Patterson, *Mr. Republican*, p. 437.
52. Vandenberg to Charles P. Taft II, Nov. 11, 1949, ibid., p. 439.
53. *Congressional Record*, Sept. 22, 1949, 13,400.

send billions to arm Western Europe without any evidence that the Russians contemplated military attack. There was no more evidence "that Russia will go to war with us because we interfere with a crossing to Formosa." Taft seemed to back action to prevent Communist take-over of Formosa because he felt certain that it would not lead to war. He did not favor a commitment to Chiang's Nationalists "in any prolonged war against the Chinese Communists." It could be determined later "whether we ever wish to recognize the Chinese Communists and what the ultimate disposition of Formosa shall be."

Nor did Taft "desire . . . an aggressive war to recover land the Communists have occupied." As for Truman's statement that the United States did not desire to become involved in civil conflict, Taft noted that Truman had "involved [Americans] in the civil conflict in Greece, in Korea and elsewhere." Others were calling for aid to the French in Indochina, "although it is infinitely less practical and more expensive and difficult than the maintenance of an independent Formosa."[54] Taft favored elections which, he thought, would end with the Formosan people probably voting "to set up an independent Republic of Formosa." The United States would then have the "means to force the Nationalists' surrender of Formosa."[55]

Mao's revolution ended all attempts of the United States to intervene in China. But the situation in Korea was a different matter. On June 25, North Korean troops crossed the 38th parallel into South Korea, and Truman immediately moved to gain passage of a UN resolution condemning the North Koreans for armed aggression. The resolution demanded an end to hostilities and a northern withdrawal behind the 38th parallel. "The resolution," Stephen Ambrose has pointed out, "was a brilliant stroke, for without any investigation at all it established war guilt and put the United Nations behind the official American version. Its sweeping nature tended to commit the United Nations in advance to any step the United States might wish to take in

54. Taft statement on Formosa, n.d. (1950), Taft MSS., Box 257.
55. Taft, " 'Hang On' to Formosa," *Vital Speeches,* Feb. 1, 1950, pp. 236–237. The magazine prints Taft's speech of Jan. 11, 1950.

Korea and . . . it gave the United States the benefit of United Nations cover for military action in Korea."[56]

Within twenty-four hours after passage of the UN resolution Truman had acted to give fresh military aid to the French in Indochina and aid to the Philippines. He had sent the Seventh Fleet to stand guard by Formosa and had ordered the air force into action in Korea. Two days later, on June 30, the President ordered U.S. combat troops into action.

At first Taft offered the administration his support. "Without question," he told the Senate, "the attack of the North Koreans is an outrageous act of aggression against a friendly independent nation." The attack, he also admitted, was "in all probability . . . instigated by Soviet Russia." Noting that he had in the past tried to help develop a firmer anti-Communist policy in the Far East, he now concluded that the "time had to come, sooner or later, when we would give definite notice to the Communists that a move beyond a declared line would result in war."

Once he had established his support to the principle, Taft took up a moderate line of criticism. The United States should have sent in its forces a year earlier and given notice that they would respond to any attempt to subjugate the South. "In short," he charged, "this entirely unfortunate crisis has been produced first by the outrageous, aggressive attitude of Soviet Russia, and second, by the bungling and inconsistent foreign policy of the administration."

As Taft reasoned, the United States had already agreed to divide Korea along the 38th parallel. The United States had made it clear that it was not prepared to give Nationalist China military assistance—a fact that he thought had led the Communists to assume it would not use troops to defend Nationalist Korea. The U.S. had not intervened to protect Formosa, yet "intervention in Korea from a military standpoint is a good deal more foolish an adventure than intervention on Formosa." Taft accused Dean Acheson of pursuing a policy of appeasement in the Far East. He referred to the Secretary's statement of January 12, 1950, that Korea was not considered part of the American defense perim-

56. Ambrose, *Rise to Globalism*, p. 197.

eter in the Pacific. "With such a reaffirmation of our Far Eastern policy," Taft asked, "is it any wonder the Korean Communists took us at the word given by our Secretary of State?" Had an alternate policy been followed it would have been "far easier to defend Formosa without becoming involved in war than it is to defend Korea or Indochina without becoming involved in war."

Finally Taft raised the difficult issue of the war's legality. Truman had brought "that war about without consulting Congress and without congressional approval." Taft supported the policy, but not the methods. "If the President can intervene in Korea without Congressional approval," he noted, "he can go to war in Malaya or Indonesia or Iran or South America." There was simply no legitimate "authority to use armed forces in support of the United Nations in the absence of some previous action by Congress dealing with the subject." The Korean war was "a complete usurpation by the President of the authority to use the Armed Forces of this country." If it were not protested by the Senate, Taft concluded forcefully, "we would have finally terminated for all time the right of Congress to declare war."[57]

But as the war stalemated, Taft began to advocate decisive action. "Now that we are in this war," he wrote to one correspondent, "it seems to me that we should go all out in every respect and make it clear that the United States cannot be so defied."[58] But at the same time he had doubts that led him in the opposite direction. When columnist Dorothy Thompson wrote him that advocating "using the A-bomb in Korea furnishes the Russians with the greatest psychological weapon they could desire," Taft wrote back that he again had the feeling that the United States was "in real danger of becoming an imperialistic nation. The line between imperialism and idealism becomes very confused in the minds of those who operate the system. Certainly, the present occupant of the White House cannot draw the line."[59]

57. Taft, "The Korean Crisis," speech to the U.S. Senate, June 28, 1950, Taft MSS., Box 251.
58. Taft to James J. Barry, Aug. 3, 1950, ibid., Box 241.
59. Thompson to Taft, July 13, 1950, and Taft to Thompson, July 25, 1950, ibid., Box 819.

Taft told Dorothy Thompson that he was trying to develop a Republican position that could offer a criticism of the fundamental errors that had brought the country to its present mess. But that was where the problem lay. Taft was proposing a policy that would have led to U.S. action at an even earlier date; it was a proposal that confused his critique of interventionist tendencies within the United States. He seemed to want it both ways, and his position satisfied very few.

By mid-August it appeared that General Douglas MacArthur's troops might be able to destroy the North Korean units. The administration then shifted its goals. It was no longer sufficient to push the North Korean troops behind the 38th parallel; it was necessary to move beyond containment toward liberation. By October 25, American troops had reached the Yalu River at Chosan. At that point, for the first time in the war, Chinese "volunteer" units massed on the border. When MacArthur launched a major offensive on November 24, the Chinese responded with a massive intrusion. MacArthur's strategic position was quickly reversed.

Taft's assessment of the situation, which was filled with contradictions, now led him to reconciliation with Vandenberg. In his campaign for the Senate he had contended "that the policies at Yalta and Potsdam built Russia up unnecessarily to a position of power in Central Europe and in China which was wholly unnecessary." Taft now told Vandenberg that "the policy of appeasement was checked in Europe only when you came into the picture at San Francisco and then in Germany, but that the same pro-Communist policy continued in Asia and led to a Communist victory in China and to the Korean war." Saying that he wished to discuss foreign policy with him, Taft informed Vandenberg that he had "no great conflict of principle" with him, "but only one of degree."[60]

Taft backtracked from an insistence that there was no Russian military threat. Before World War II he had "never felt that the Nazis were any threat to us, particularly after they became involved in a war with Russia." Now, he argued, the situation

60. Taft to Vandenberg, Nov. 11, 1950, Taft MSS., Box 811.

was different. President Truman had announced on September 22, 1949, that the Soviets had exploded an atomic bomb. "With greatly extended air power and the atomic bomb, it is possible for the Russians to attack us." He defended the interest in European reconstruction, agreeing that Russian control of Germany and France would give them too much power. In a dramatic comment on his own earlier position, he wrote John Foster Dulles that "we can hardly be isolationists any more."[61]

Still, he wanted to avoid spending $40 billion per year, which would mean "a completely controlled economy for at least five years to come." Defense of Europe must be practical. He hoped that "we are not turning this country into a garrison state simply for the purpose of scaring Russia." He now raised a new point of difference with the Truman administration. Taft doubted the need to base policy on a large land army. Defense and "deterring of Russia," he believed, "rests far more on an all-powerful air force."[62]

In Korea the military situation continued to go badly for MacArthur's troops. Chinese units had isolated them onto three separate bridgeheads. On November 30 Truman created a storm when he announced that if military action against China was authorized by the United Nations, MacArthur might be given the power to use the atomic bomb at his own discretion. The use of the bomb, he added, had always been under active consideration. Taft rejected this saber rattling, although his objections seemed almost primarily tactical. "With regard to the atomic bomb," he wrote, "I think it would be a tragic error to use it against China, and I don't believe it would be successful in a land war operating over a 200-mile front. If we use it and it fails, we would be inviting Russian aggression in Europe."[63]

The turn of events in both Europe and Asia lead to what became known as the Great Debate on Foreign Policy. On December 20, 1950, former President Herbert Hoover proposed that the United States recognize its limitations and acknowledge

61. Ibid., Taft to Dulles, Nov. 16, 1950.
62. Ibid., Taft to Titus Lloyd Crasto, Nov. 24, 1950.
63. Taft to Basil Brewer, Dec. 6, 1950, ibid., Box 815.

that it could not keep a foothold on both the European and Asiatic mainlands. Americans had to make the "Western Hemisphere the Gibraltar of Western Civilization." The oceans could still serve as an adequate defense. The New World would be protected by its naval and air force units. Hoover opposed reinforcing NATO unless the European allies shared the burden of defense. Insisting that any land war "against this Communist land mass" in Asia would be "a war without victory, a war without a successful terminal," Hoover predicted that such a war "would be the graveyard of millions of American boys and would end in the exhaustion" of the American Gibraltar.[64]

In a speech delivered during the same week, former Ambassador to Britain Joseph P. Kennedy also warned of the threat of a new land war in Europe or Asia. Arguing that the United States was incapable of preventing areas of the world from going Communist, Kennedy insisted it was not the business of the United States to support French colonial policy in Indochina or Syngman Rhee in Korea. Kennedy advocated an American withdrawal from Korea, Berlin, and Europe. Acknowledging that such a policy would "be criticized as appeasement," Kennedy maintained that the United States could not be sucked into making commitments that endangered American security. He favored conserving life for American ends, not wasting "them in the freezing hills of Korea or on the battle-scarred plains of Western Germany."[65]

Truman now made known his intention to send more troops to Europe to fulfill America's NATO commitment. He did not seek congressional approval, claiming that as Commander in Chief of the Armed Forces he had the authority to send troops anywhere in the world. Conservative New York congressman Frederic R. Coudert, Jr., of New York City's fashionable "silk-stocking district," introduced a resolution on January 3 declaring it to be the sense of Congress that "no additional military forces" be sent

64. Herbert Hoover, "Our National Policies in This Crisis," *Vital Speeches,* Jan. 1, 1951, pp. 165–167.
65. Joseph P. Kennedy, "Present Policy Is Politically and Morally Bankrupt," ibid., pp. 170–173.

abroad "without the prior authorization of the Congress in each instance." It also provided that no funds appropriated for the armed forces could be used to send troops abroad, only to help them return from Korea.[66]

Two days after Coudert introduced his resolution Taft joined the debate with a major Senate speech. He offered statistics to prove that available air and naval power gave the U.S. all the protection it needed. Challenging those who sought to compete with the millions of Russian troops stationed in Germany, Taft again urged that the United States depend on air power. If it did not, a future war would be fought on the land where the U.S. would be "at the greatest possible disadvantage in a war with Russia."

Taft pointed to administration duplicity. When Dean Acheson had sought congressional approval for NATO, he had stated that the U.S. would not be expected to send substantial numbers of troops to Europe. Now Taft feared a land war with Russia was being contemplated, even though it would be "an invasion along the lines which Napoleon and Hitler found to be impossible. It implies that the nations which signed this pact expect us to send American troops to defend their frontiers." He was blunt: "The President has no power to agree to send Americans to fight in Europe in a war between the members of the Atlantic Pact and Soviet Russia."

Further, Russia could attack during the three years the troop buildup would be taking place. If they did not intend to attack, new armed forces were not needed, "at least in such coordinated form and in such close proximity to Russia as to seem to threaten an attack on them." He agreed on the need to fight communism, but concluded that "we should not be a military aggressor or give the impression of military aggression or incite a war which might otherwise never occur."[67]

When Kenneth Wherry, a Nebraska conservative Republican, introduced a Senate resolution that "no American troops shall be

66. Quoted in Arthur M. Schlesinger, Jr., *The Imperial Presidency* (Boston: Houghton Mifflin, 1973), pp. 135–136.
67. Taft, "The Basis of an American Foreign Policy," speech to the Senate, Jan. 5, 1951, Taft MSS., Box 554.

sent to Europe for the purposes of the Atlantic Pact without the approval of Congress," Taft gave it his backing. Appearing before a joint session of the Senate Foreign Relations Committee and the Armed Services Committee, Taft reminded his colleagues that Germany was in ruins "because Hitler thought he could beat the world." The same could happen, Taft implied, if the United States overextended itself.[68]

Taft's concern about how excessive presidential power might affect America domestically led some on the Left to encourage him. Socialist party leader Norman Thomas wrote again, asking that Taft take further leadership in opposing the permanent draft.[69] Taft wrote Thomas that he opposed sending more troops to Europe, because such a step would contribute to a third world war. And he agreed that Truman "seems to be in the hands of the Military when it comes to action." He saw no reason "for the President and the Secretary of State and everybody else calling the Russians names on every occasion. I realize that they are impossible to deal with, but I really do not believe that they intend to start a third world war."[70] As long "as there is no direct invasion of Russia or a satellite country by American or UN troops," he later explained, "I do not think the Russians are going to start a third world war."[71]

Taft was once again taking an active course. Liberal supporters of the administration were aghast. Historian Henry Steele Commager wrote that although the Taft-Coudert program might be expedient, its principles had "no support in law or history," and Arthur M. Schlesinger, Jr., called Taft's statements "demonstrably irresponsible."[72] There was very little critical thinking.

68. "Testimony of Senator Taft Before the Foreign Relations Committee and the Armed Services Committee of the Senate," Feb. 26, 1951, ibid., Box 559.

69. Thomas to Taft, March 1, 1951, ibid., Box 874. Thomas told Taft that exponents of both free enterprise and democratic socialism held similar assumptions about the evil state that UMT would create.

70. Taft to Thomas, March 13, 1951, ibid., Box 874.

71. Ibid., Taft to James B. Parker, April 30, 1951.

72. Schlesinger, *The Imperial Presidency,* p. 139. Mr. Schlesinger now "freely concedes that Senator Taft had a much more substantial point than he supposed twenty years ago." He notes that by "the early 1970s liberal

The major Democratic party opponent of the cold war, Henry Wallace, rejoined the political center. Wallace, who had gone so far as to run for the Presidency on an isolated third-party ticket in 1948, now announced that "when my country is at war and the United Nations sanctions that war, I am on the side of my country and the U.N. . . . I cannot agree with those who want to start a propaganda drive to pull the U.N. troops out of Korea."[73]

Taft finally voted to send four army divisions to Europe, rather than the six originally proposed by the administration. He also favored the assumption of the defense of Britain, Japan, the Philippines, Indonesia, and even Spain, since he felt that air and sea forces could protect these regions. Taft's liberal critics can easily exclaim, as they do, on how contradictory it was for Taft to argue that troops were a provocation to the Russians, only to accept them in smaller numbers. Taft's biographer may be correct when he claims that Taft was actually "closer to the bi-partisan consensus on foreign policy than many people realized." But if he was, that was hardly comforting to the liberal interventionists.[74]

The nature of liberal opposition to Taft's policy on Korea and NATO is instructive. The *Nation* was particularly upset that it was the "first tendency of the professional critics of the Administration . . . to question the constitutionality of the President's move." The *Nation* saved a lot of its ammunition for Taft, who had begun to "lay down the first major line of attack." His friend and colleague Senator Wherry, an editorial noted, "now asks by what authority we are establishing a quarantine around Formosa, since we had no directive to do so from the Security Council." As for themselves, the editors of the weekly were pleased; Truman's intervention had undercut Senator Joseph McCarthy's arguments that the Democrats had sold out Asia to the Communists. "Mc-

---

Democrats assumed positions once cherished by conservative Republicans —another warning against stating relative issues in absolute terms" (pp. 286, 311–312).

73. *Time,* July 24, 1950, p. 13.
74. Patterson, *Mr. Republican,* p. 482.

Carthyism," it was explained, "will have a hollow sound when applied to the government that stood up to the Russians." Having disposed of the Wisconsin senator, the *Nation* went him one better. "Many top Republicans," it stated, "are now following a line almost indistinguishable from that of the Communists. The *Daily Worker* agrees fully with the *Chicago Tribune*'s contention that the President's statement 'is an illegal declaration of war.' " And like Senator Taft, it noted, the leftist congressman Vito Marcantonio was worried that " 'the power of Congress to declare war has been usurped from us.' " Far from examining the validity of the issue, the *Nation* preferred a little red-baiting of its own. "McCarthy could make much of that," it concluded, "but he won't."[75]

Hoover's speech on the Great Debate led the journal to pull out more stops. World communism, it announced, "has captured for its purposes Herbert Hoover and a good section of the Republican Party of the United States." The line Hoover, Taft, and Wherry "are laying down for their country should set the bells ringing in the Kremlin as nothing has since the triumph of Stalingrad. Actually the line taken by Pravda is that the former President did not carry isolationism far enough."

According to the *Nation,* Hoover's doctrine meant that beyond a limited sphere, "the Russians would be free . . . to grab what they could get, including . . . the industrial power of the Ruhr, Belgium, and France." The Hoover doctrine meant that America was divided, and that if the Western European nations put "their confidence in us they may be abandoned to the mercies of the Russians if the Republicans win the election two years from now." Calling the Hoover-Taft approach sinister, the *Nation* described Hoover's speech as a "rallying cry for all the discredited forces of isolationism, to all men who since Pearl Harbor have covertly nursed their infantile illusions of a hemispheric 'Gibraltar' without having the courage to give them voice." The opposition Republicans, it argued, were "quite prepared to give the Russians nothing less than the rest of Asia and

75. Editorial, *Nation,* July 8, 1950, p. 25.

the whole continent of Europe on the ground that the countries affected don't seem up to stopping the Russians by their own strength." Defending Dean Acheson, the *Nation* chastised the Republicans for sabotaging the Secretary and for showing "a world in crisis the face of American disunity."[76]

The more influential *New Republic* challenged Taft's estimate of Russian behavior. Although it conceded that "war now is probably not in the interest of Stalin," it thought that the Soviet dictator might indeed decide that "1951 may seem as good a time as any to attack." By its estimate, the Hoover-Taft scenario included making a deal with the Russians. Stalin would attack in the name of preventing German rearmament. He would seize the Ruhr, reach the English Channel, and, from an unassailable position, would appeal to the "narrow self-interest of the U.S. and offer a 20-year peace."

Stalin would offer this deal to Truman, but he "might refuse it." Taft and Hoover would not. Truman's "opposition who saw nothing alarming in Hitler's conquest of Europe would clearly grab at the bait. Stalin, after raising the ante, as he did with Hitler, and sweeping over Asia, would move on until the Stalinist caucus in the *Tribune* tower would bring out in triumph the first Communist edition of the *Chicago Tribune*."[77]

The *New Republic,* therefore, was condemning the "isolationist" Republicans for being willing to negotiate with the Russians. The Truman administration deserved total support because of its unstinting hard line, whereas the isolationists blamed the Korean war not on Stalin, but on Truman; "just as Roosevelt, not Hitler, caused the Second World War."[78] In Congress, the *New Republic* complained, "Republican isolationists were getting ready to shape the Hoover doctrine into an instrument of sabotage against the Atlantic Alliance." Calling its readers' attention to Representative Coudert's resolution, it charged that both Coudert and Taft were engaging in an "often repudiated" legalism. "Presidential power to send the armed forces overseas has

76. "Hoover's Folly," *Nation,* Dec. 30, 1950, p. 688.
77. "Can We Save World Peace?" *New Republic,* Jan. 1, 1950, p. 5.
78. *New Republic,* Nov. 20, 1950, p. 7.

been solidly established by history"; and the editorial equated the opponents of Truman's cold-war policies with the prewar isolationists. "There has historically been a working affinity between the isolationists and the legalists—the former attacked Roosevelt's 1941 destroyer deal as warmongering, the latter as dictatorship. There are signs that this coalition is again tightening." Using Coudert's resolution, they proclaimed, "Sen. Robert Taft . . . [has] presented the full GOP case—based on Hoover, the value of the dollar and a benign image of the Politburo."[79]

Taft was similarly opposed by the Republican maverick Senator Wayne Morse of Oregon. Morse was sure that if Russia continued "down the road of aggression against freedom," the United States would "once again, although at terrible cost . . . crush totalitarianism and preserve freedom, no matter how high the cost." Morse disputed Taft's opinion that the Soviets were not about to start a war: "Elementary common sense should tell us that we have to be prepared for the fact that Russia may move into Europe any day from now on, whenever it suits her convenience." Quoting Taft's speech of January 5, Morse charged that his "minimizing of the Russian threat has disheartened the free nations and given aid and comfort to those who would destroy us." Morse accused Taft of endorsing "the pious Soviet claims of their abhorrence of war and their devotion to peace," of seeming to "support the Russian allegations of warmongering on our part."

Senator Morse then invoked the domino theory. The United States was not only an intended victim of Soviet aggression "but indeed its absolutely inevitable target . . . If Russia can knock us out, the rest of the world would fall like a ripe apple in her outstretched hand." The Korean war was proof of the dynamics of the Russian drive for world mastery. Russia, he said, had "pushed her North Korean satellite into a military campaign which clearly involved the risk of a general war."

As for Taft's opposition to NATO, Morse noted that his statements were exactly "what the Russians themselves have been saying in season and out and in every language in which the

79. *New Republic,* Jan. 15, 1951, p. 7.

Voice of Moscow broadcasts its lying propaganda." The Truman Doctrine, the Marshall Plan, and NATO were, for Morse, all necessary measures simply meant to build a "barrier of strong, economically stable states in the path of Russian aggression." Moscow opposed them not because of legitimate security fears but because "the stronger the free world becomes the less likely those nations are to become victims of Communist . . . subversion."[80]

If the liberal critics scolded Taft for lack of firmness against potential Soviet aggression, they would soon have occasion to attack him on Korean policy. Once Chinese troops had entered the Korean war, Taft became alarmed. He now felt that Chiang Kai-shek should be allowed to use his soldiers and planes against the Chinese Communists on the mainland. "What is required is that we release him from his restraint and let him go ahead as he was going before the Korean invasion." Taft criticized the administration's decision to adopt a cease-fire proposal for Korea, which he termed "a permanent betrayal of Chiang Kai-shek."[81]

Publicly, Taft continued to stress that he sought only to avoid a land war on the continent of Asia or Europe. But if its allies had "run out" on the U.S. in Korea, he felt that the United States had "no alternative except gradually to withdraw from Korea to a defensible position in Japan, Okinawa, and Formosa." After the troops were withdrawn, Chiang could be unleashed, promoting a diversion that would occupy the Chinese Communists in the south of China and prevent "the threatened offensive against Indo-China, Burma and Siam." U.S. soldiers would not be committed. Taft's policy depended upon his belief that China would not see fit to declare war, inviting U.S. bombing and an economic blockade.[82]

While Taft was presenting these arguments the military situation in Korea shifted once again. From January through March MacArthur's troops drove both the Chinese and North Koreans

80. Wayne Morse, "A Reply to Senator Taft's Foreign Policy Proposals," speech to the Senate, Jan. 15, 1951, Taft MSS., Box 1320.
81. Taft to L. H. McCamic, Jan. 17, 1951, ibid., Box 874.
82. Taft, "Military Aspects of our Foreign Policy," address before the Executives Club of Chicago, Jan. 26, 1951, ibid., Box 548.

back behind the 38th parallel. Taft took the occasion to remind Americans that he still considered the war totally illegal, reiterating the point perhaps with even more force than originally. He raised the issue of Theodore Roosevelt's acquisition of the Panama Canal, which he condemned as blatantly illegal. He cited Abraham Lincoln's opposition to the Mexican War of 1840, comparing it to his analysis of the Korean war. Taft added that when Truman involved the United States in Korea, "the American people . . . never had the slightest voice in determining whether that war should be undertaken." The sending in of U.S. troops was an action that "violated all the precedents which have been established as to the limitations of the President's power to make war." It was clear to Taft that Truman's action "was an absolute usurpation of authority by the President."[83]

No sooner had Taft uttered these words than the military situation again changed drastically. General MacArthur sabotaged efforts to obtain a cease-fire by crossing the 38th parallel and demanding what amounted to an unconditional surrender from the Chinese. On April 5 Representative Joseph Martin, Jr., read to the House a message from MacArthur. He was demanding the reunification of Korea, the unleashing of Chiang, and a decision to fight communism in Asia rather than in Europe. The die was cast. Truman, fearing an all-out war in Europe, dismissed MacArthur from his command.

MacArthur's views had great appeal for many Americans. While British Prime Minister Clement Attlee was urging the Americans to negotiate, MacArthur wanted to fight. Liberals attacked the General for being simplistic, but their own views were based upon simpleminded assumptions. MacArthur's suggested policy, after all, was itself based upon the administration's descriptions of a worldwide Communist menace. MacArthur's policy had the advantage of feeding off the frustration inherent in the containment program, since the Truman policy was not leading to success.[84]

83. Taft, "The President Has No Right to Involve the United States in a Foreign War," speech to the Senate, March 29, 1951, ibid., Box 554.
84. Ambrose, *Rise to Globalism,* p. 212.

Taft was quick to support MacArthur. The President had a right to dismiss the General, but it was Truman's own policies, he argued, that had invited the war prior to June 1950. Finally the administration had shifted policy and fought the North Koreans, a policy he had supported. Yet now it stopped short at fighting the Chinese. The war could be ended, Taft argued, by three courses—appeasement, the Truman policy of stalemate, or the use of Chiang's troops in Korea and southern China, as well as the bombing of Chinese communication lines.[85]

Thus Taft supported "logistical aid . . . transportation, airplanes, arms." But he "would not send an American soldier to the mainland of China." The U.S. government "invited the invasion of Korea by the weakness of its policy," exemplified in Acheson's January 1950 statement that "we would not intervene in Korea under any circumstances." Taft would have warned the North Koreans that any attack on the South would mean engagement of U.S. troops. Taft pointed to his support in principle of Truman's eventual intervention. What he had opposed was the "weak reed" of using the United Nations as a cover. But Taft now opposed British plans for a new cease-fire and negotiation as "appeasement."

According to Taft, Truman had started the war and had defended his entrance as a measure that prevented the outbreak of World War III. Yet he now failed to invoke the same argument when it came to repelling the Chinese aggression. Taft favored the measures suggested by MacArthur; Truman refused to implement any of these. Taft even favored bombing beyond the Yalu, and discussion of whether or not to undertake a complete blockade of China. In Asia, he argued, the United States should "follow a general policy of containment of communism."[86]

Taft's position was contradictory. He was arguing that the United States "should never have moved into Korea" and at the same time he was asking for aggressive application of the containment policy he disapproved in Europe. Why, his critics

85. *New York Times,* April 13, 1951, p. 4.
86. Taft, "American Policy in the Far East: How Do We End the Korean War?" speech to the Senate, April 27, 1951, Taft MSS., Box 554.

wondered, might it not also lead to war in Asia? How could he be so sure that the Russians would not respond with force?

The United States, Taft pointed out, had moved into Korea without any preparation for dealing with China. We could not punish the Chinese, since the effort would require one million American troops, and we could not risk any such enterprise as long as Russia was in the background. The only course was to support MacArthur and use "every possible means to drive the Chinese Communists from Korea." A cease-fire at the 38th parallel and withdrawal of U.S. troops would result "in Korea becoming 100 per cent Communist," and, he suggested, would bring a Communist victory in Japan.[87]

Taft's support of an effort to achieve military victory allowed his critics to avoid confronting the other parts of his critical analysis. Thinking only about his advocacy of the MacArthur program, few noticed his admonitions about usurpation of executive power. Taft's pitfall, columnist Walter Lippmann reported, was that he had failed to understand that what Chiang wanted was "much more fighting by Americans in the Far East." That would produce all-out war with China rather than a localized one in Korea. Because Taft backed only limited war and opposed ground action by U.S. troops, he had "allowed himself to believe that Chiang's army [could] take over and be a substitute for our ground troops." Lippmann believed that Chiang wanted a general war with China to secure Formosa and plan for a Nationalist return to the mainland. For him the only question was "whether to enlarge the Korean war into a general war."[88]

Taft really had no answers for Lippmann. As far as he was concerned, there was simply "no valid argument against the release of Chiang Kai-shek to conduct raids, or a war, in South China." Such a strategy might lead to creation of a successful anti-Communist government in parts of southern China or Chinese withdrawal from Korea.[89] The United States should not

87. Taft to Thomas Murphy, June 16, 1951, and Taft to Dr. H. L. Chandler, June 25, 1951, ibid., Box 874.
88. Lippmann, "Today and Tomorrow," April 16, 1951, ibid., Box 878.
89. Taft, address to Republicans of Indiana, June 23, 1951, ibid., Box 874.

make peace until it was "safely guaranteed a complete Korean republic covering all of Korea." Otherwise the whole effort would have been a failure. If a truce were to be made on the 38th parallel, the U.S. would "have to maintain a large army in South Korea" until that nation was rehabilitated and a strong South Korean army was built up. Taft preferred "an aggressive war" to drive the Chinese out and set up a "complete Korean republic."[90]

Taft was ignoring his own repeated advice to exercise restraint and caution. The senator, who had argued so persistently against overextending American power, and who had insisted that the fight with communism was ideological rather than military, was now asking for an open-ended aggressive war of terrible risk. He did not acknowledge that Lippmann might be correct about Chiang. Taft thought that the Chinese Communists were more militaristic than the Russians. "Undoubtedly," Mao Tse-tung is "a sincere Communist," Taft reasoned, "perhaps even more aggressive in his military intentions than is Stalin." Taft was grateful that there was doubt as to whether Mao would take orders from Stalin, but he felt it was clear "that we must treat him as a determined Communist fully sympathetic with the idea of a Communist domination of the world."[91]

It is misleading, however, to overemphasize Taft's decision to opt for the MacArthur course. For he was essentially accurate in his judgment that the original decision to move for unification of all Korea was the Truman administration's civilian policy—not MacArthur's military one—though the administration had originally claimed that Korea was not to be part of the U.S. defense perimeter. For Taft the result of Korea was clear:

> We are just where we were three years ago, except that a hundred thousand American boys have been killed or wounded, the country we went to defend has been levelled to the ground and hundreds of thousands of its citizens killed, and . . . we have spent billions of dollars of our taxpayers' money. Altogether, no directors of foreign policy have ever made the stupid mistakes

90. Ibid., Taft to George W. Curtis, July 13, 1951.
91. Taft to Mrs. Alexandra de Goguel, Aug. 7, 1951, ibid., Box 848.

in judgment which have been made by those who still control our foreign policy. Furthermore, the President and his advisers claim the right to take the United States into war without approval by Congress, which makes their continuation in power exceedingly dangerous.[92]

Under pressure Taft seemed to reveal some doubts concerning the MacArthur proposals he had endorsed. If the United States was to actually move to bomb China, he admitted on one occasion, it might be "more likely to bring the Russians in." He then argued that bombing should be "held in reserve for the present."[93]

Taft's contradictory statements allowed his liberal opponents to effectively challenge him. If war with North Korea was dangerous because it might lead to war with Russia, Senator Brien McMahon of Connecticut asked, why was it not an equal or greater danger to bomb targets in Manchuria, which had a common border with Russia? Taft's only answer was that Truman had originally taken a risk, and then had decided to try to keep the conflict in Korea "a little mild war." The fact was that Russia had not come in, and he believed that MacArthur's course too would not result in "any third world war with Russia."[94]

Perhaps because it was a Republican Eisenhower administration that eventually moved to make peace along the lines Taft had once condemned as appeasement that he gradually modified his stand. "I am in favor of concluding an armistice in Korea," he explained in 1952, "providing it can be done with honor." He admitted that it might be an unstable armistice and that the chance of renewal of war remained as long as Korea was divided. But the increase of Russian air power was not sufficient to prevent the United States from "conducting a successful war to push back the Communists into Manchuria, as could have been done when General MacArthur proposed it some ten months

92. Taft to Chase Kimball, Nov. 15, 1951, ibid., Box 876.
93. Ibid., "How Can We Best Defend America?" text of Univ. of Chicago Round Table forum, with Taft, Malcolm Sharp, and Hanson Baldwin, on NBC, April 18, 1951.
94. Text of the "American Forum of the Air," May 20, 1951, Vol. XIV, No. 20, with Taft, Brian McMahon, and Theodore Granik, ibid., Box 1281.

ago." A "stalemate peace," he now concluded, was "better than a stalemate war."[95] Taft maintained that had he been President, he would have submitted to Congress the question of what course to pursue after U.S. troops had crossed the 38th parallel. When he was asked whether his Korean proposals had shown him to have been inconsistent, Taft acknowledged, "No doubt I have."[96]

Oddly, Taft also seemed to move away from support of Hoover's Fortress America. "Some Republicans," he wrote, "apparently would throw our whole weight into Europe and neglect the rest of the world." Hoover, on the other hand, would "do nothing whatever in Europe." He was inclined to agree with Hoover's "general thesis, but it seems to me that we have to do what we can in Europe." Taft now felt only that an all-out effort "would go far beyond our economic capacity," would lead to neglect of sea- and air-lanes, and would "be more likely to lead to war than to prevent it."[97]

Taft even seemed to offer new support for NATO troop commitments. "As far as the European project is concerned," he stated, "I'm quite willing to finish that project out . . . We have made the Atlantic Pact. I am in favor of carrying out our obligations whatever they might be." This meant support to completing "this project of arming the European nations."[98] Previous worries about provoking the Soviets by arming Germany "do not seem to have been borne out up to this time." When Europe was strong enough on its own, U.S. troops could be "withdrawn from the continent of Europe."[99]

Yet despite Taft's attempts at accommodation with the interventionist policy makers, his general approach and inconsistencies still met with disdain and lack of trust. In two articles for the *Reporter*, McGeorge Bundy, Associate Professor of Government at Harvard, and later a key Kennedy administration ad-

95. Taft to Fred Line, April 29, 1953, ibid., Box 1064.
96. "Meet the Press," transcript, Jan. 20, 1952, ibid., Box 1294.
97. Ibid., Taft to Robert E. Dant, April 6, 1951.
98. "Meet the Press," transcript, Jan. 20, 1952, ibid., Box 1284.
99. Taft, *A Foreign Policy for Americans* (New York: Doubleday, 1952), chap. 6.

viser, criticized Taft for opposing encirclement of the Soviet Union by a new military alliance.[100]

Bundy was not satisfied that Taft had moved closer to the center in some respects. Acknowledging that Taft was no longer an isolationist, since "he considers the Russians more dangerous than the Germans," Bundy noted that Taft still felt that "we would try to do too much at too great a cost." Pointing to Taft's concept of our conflict with Russia as primarily ideological, Bundy cited Taft's attempts to whittle down existing military programs. Taft's policies, Bundy complained, "do not aim to *deal* with power, or even to use power (for Senator Taft is strongly opposed to the notion of preventive war); they aim rather to create a situation in which power is irrelevant and in which the American people can securely proceed to the better realization of the American dream. This, I think, is the basic pattern of thought from which Senator Taft advances to the tough problems of the present world."

Bundy acknowledged that Taft was aware that the world was in "the throes of a great struggle for power between the Kremlin and the field," but he was wary because Taft "does not like it." Taft's aversion to the struggle led him toward "notions which may make it less pressing and demanding and expensive." Bundy rejected Taft's belief that "the central struggle is for the minds of men, and not for control of resources and peoples." Such a perspective meant that the United States "should not take the lead in organizing the defense of Europe." This was evident as well in Taft's "scarcely concealed mistrust of almost all military men." Most of all, there was the senator's failure to endorse what Bundy saw as "the central requirement of American policy . . . American political leadership in a partnership with other free nations." He concluded that Taft held a "wide and dangerous misunderstanding" of world politics, and he predicted that it would be "a sad and dangerous day if the Senator ever becomes President." In Bundy's opinion, Taft was an incurable and simple

100. McGeorge Bundy, " 'Appeasement,' 'Provocation,' and 'Policy,' " *Reporter,* Jan. 9, 1951, pp. 14–16.

isolationist: "He is in the tradition of Americans who wish the rest of the world did not exist. It does."[101]

Whatever the ambiguities and inconsistencies in Taft's approach—and there were many—his critics were perturbed because his over-all approach would not countenance the waging of a successful holy crusade against communism. Bundy saw Taft as the "Reluctant Dragon," unable to wage permanent war against the Soviet menace. It was no surprise that he welcomed the nomination of Dwight Eisenhower at the 1952 Republican convention.[102] Republicans Richard M. Nixon, William F. Knowland of California, and Barry Goldwater of Arizona—all of whom were close to the China lobby—also voted against Taft at the convention.

Because he favored limiting military spending, because he raised the issue of control over presidential authority to dispatch troops abroad, and because he questioned the long-term value of defense pacts such as NATO, Taft was far removed from the mainstream of liberalism. Perhaps because his brief attempts at accommodation to his critics' views did not pay off, and he was unable to gain support for the Republican nomination, he reverted toward the end of his career to a critical perspective that bordered on opposition.

Taft understood the use of moral leadership, but he also understood that some who used terms such as "American Century" really wanted "to force on . . . foreign peoples through the use of American money, and even perhaps American arms, the policies which moral leadership is able to advance only through the sound strength of its principles." In Taft's view the Atlantic Pact commitments were "unnecessarily extensive." Calling his audience's attention to subsequent calls to bind Southeast Asia in a similar defense pact, he said: "I certainly do not think we should be obligated to send American troops to defend Indo-China or Burma or Thailand where they would become involved

101. McGeorge Bundy, "The Private World of Robert Taft," *Reporter,* Dec. 11, 1951, pp. 37–39.

102. McGeorge Bundy, "November 1952: Imperatives of Foreign Policy," *Foreign Affairs* (October 1952), pp. 2–4.

in a much more serious war than we have been forced into in Korea."[103]

He was beginning to sound once more like the old Robert Taft. Again Taft attacked the entire basis of the Truman program of containment:

> I do not question the necessity of a great increase in American military force. . . . But it is clear that our present program is not going to bring peace to the world. The constant building up of armament on both sides, the race for superior weapons and stronger military positions, is more likely to lead to war finally than to peace. The whole program of the containment of Russia is a negative program, designed only to prevent Russia from extending the power of communism through military aggression and propaganda. The best the program can produce, without war, is a stabilization of the present division of the world into two great armed camps. There can be no real peace as long as this condition exists. One small incident or another, one act of carelessness, or even one accident, may precipitate the tragedy of a third world war.[104]

This program was supported as well by many Republicans. He hinted at disapproval even when such policies were being pursued by the Eisenhower administration. Referring to "the program which we have to create a joint anti-Russian front in Europe," Taft noted that he had "never thought this was a wise thing to do." Yet, he admitted, he had "been pretty well overruled by opinion among both Democrats and Republicans." Taft now favored, in 1953, "arming the British and French to create centers of strength against the Russians," but he cautioned that he did not "think we can be successful [in defending] Europe in the long run."[105]

His last speech—which was delivered for him by his son on May 26, 1953—showed that he insisted upon remaining critical

103. Taft speech at the Univ. of North Carolina, Nov. 27–29, 1951, Taft MSS., Box 1283.
104. Ibid., Taft speech to the Women's Republican Club of Massachusetts, Dec. 11, 1951.
105. Taft to Robert Q. Bekins, Feb. 26, 1953, ibid., Box 1064.

of policy, even as the Eisenhower administration was negotiating a truce in Korea that would divide that nation at the 38th parallel. Taft's critical illness did not lead him to take a pause or to change his outlook. He favored negotiating a truce. If we failed, he would let England and the other allied powers know that "we are withdrawing from all further peace negotiations in Korea." Taft would have preferred "general peace negotiation with China," unification of Korea under the aegis of the South, and obtaining a pledge from the Chinese Communists against further expansion in Southeast Asia.

He still said we must stop Communist aggression "where it occurs and *where it is within our means to stop it*" (my italics). But, he stressed, "I have never felt that we should send American soldiers to the Continent of Asia, which . . . included China proper and Indo-China, simply because we are so outnumbered in fighting a land war . . . that it would bring about complete exhaustion even if we were able to win." As in 1947 in Europe, and 1950 in Asia, the United States was still "really trying to arm the world against Communist Russia." He raised the heretical question of whether "this policy of uniting the free world against Communism in time of peace [is] going to be a practical long-term policy." His answer was that it was not. "I have always felt," he concluded, "that we should not attempt to fight Russia on the ground on the continent of Europe any more than we should attempt to fight China on the continent of Asia."[106]

On his deathbed Taft was still attacking the bipartisan consensus built around the creation of military alliances. He implied that he would still favor use of air power, and it is true that his dependence on such a course only worked to weaken the core of his critique of cold-war policy. But at a moment in our history when the policy makers and crisis managers believed firmly in a policy of "uniting the free world against Communism," Taft had the foresight to know that such a course would prove costly and fruitless. At a time when advocators of an American Century urged negotiations from positions of strength, and piled arma-

106. *Vital Speeches,* June 15, 1953, pp. 530–531. Text of Taft's speech of May 26, 1953, delivered by his son to the National Conference of Christians and Jews, Cincinnati, Ohio.

ments on anti-Communist nations, Taft saw such measures as violations of the best elements of the American tradition.

Taft did not raise the question of whether or not that tradition was itself warped, or whether the urge to imperialism was ingrained within the system and could not be removed without fundamental structural change. But he called for restraint and liberty at a moment when these themes appeared as anachronistic cries from a past age. America of the 1950s had little use for such a voice. From the perspective of the 1970s Taft's views seem sober, wise, and realistic. Perhaps, as Henry A. Wallace had suggested, Taft might have been better equipped to guarantee the peace than those who acceded to the Presidency.

John T. Flynn (ACME)

John T. Flynn and the
Coming of World War II

A NOTED American social scientist described John T. Flynn as "perhaps the outstanding example" of an American who was "liberal or radical in economic matters," but who later on in life became a "domestic conservative." Another writer described him as "once a New Deal liberal, later a passionate spokesman for the extreme Right Wing."[1] To these commentators Flynn was another renegade New Dealer, a liberal who had cut away his roots and gone over to support the cause of FDR's most conservative opponents.

Flynn would have disagreed with such estimates. He saw himself as a consistent upholder of liberalism, an advocate whose hopes had been betrayed by the conservative drift of the New Deal. Born in October 1882 and raised as a devout Catholic in Bladensburg, Maryland, Flynn attended Catholic schools in that town and in New York City. Eventually he decided to study law at Georgetown University in Washington, D.C., but before long, he changed to the field of journalism. After years of struggle he landed a job with the New York *Globe* in 1920. It was on that paper that he began to make a mark as a writer in the area of financial analysis, particularly in the exposure of fraudulent transactions on the stock market. Soon his articles began appearing in *Collier's,* the *American Magazine, Forum,* and *Harper's.* By 1929, at age forty-seven, Flynn was beginning what would become a long, distinguished and politically volatile career.

In addition to magazine and newspaper articles Flynn published a series of books on economic issues, works that merited

1. Seymour Martin Lipset, "The Sources of the 'Radical Right,'" in Daniel Bell, ed., *The Radical Right* (Garden City, N.Y.: Doubleday-Anchor, 1964), p. 334; Ralph Lord Roy, *Communism and the Churches* (New York: Harcourt, Brace, 1960), p. 230.

serious attention. Titles such as *Investment Trusts Gone Wrong!* (New York: New Republic, Inc., 1930), *Graft in Business* (New York: Vanguard, 1931), *God's Gold: The Story of Rockefeller and His Times* (New York: Harcourt, Brace, 1932), and *Security Speculation: Its Economic Effects* (New York: Harcourt, Brace, 1934) established Flynn as an economic thinker whose analysis of America's economic collapse had to be taken into account.

In all these works Flynn wrote as a liberal reformer seeking to find an answer to the curse of bigness in industry. Influenced by Louis D. Brandeis, the Boston corporation lawyer and former Supreme Court Justice whose own works had been the cornerstone of Woodrow Wilson's "New Freedom" years, Flynn thought that corporations could give the public what it desired at prices the populace could afford. Competition had to remain pure, and standards of fair play had to be established that could not be violated. Business concerns that obeyed the proper rules would prosper; those that failed to heed the new rules would collapse. Government had to act as supervisor to assure a functioning economic structure. Laws had to be passed that would give investors legal access to all pertinent facts about securities, bonds, and investments. The ultimate responsibility for investing wisely lay with the individual capitalist. But government had to act to curb monopolies, which took undue advantage of the individual as a consumer.[2]

A confirmed Democrat, Flynn supported Franklin D. Roosevelt in 1932. His fondest hope was that FDR would usher in an era of prosperity as well as advance the cause of domestic liberalism. For many years prior to Roosevelt's campaign Flynn had offered proposals meant to rectify domestic inequities. Stockholders functioned as an electorate within industry. To work properly, investment trusts of a semipublic nature had to be created. They were necessary if democracy in management was to be attained. Americans were developing a state, Flynn wrote,

2. The above summary is based upon the analysis and information provided in a thorough and important biography of John T. Flynn by Richard C. Frey, Jr., "John T. Flynn and the United States in Crisis, 1928–1950" (unpubl. diss., Univ. of Oregon, 1969), pp. 348–351. Much of the first part of this discussion is based on Frey's dissertation.

"in which we are producing a socialization of industry without socialism and an organization of society under private ownership without capitalism."[3]

Flynn objected to the lack of protection offered the individual investor, who faced the power of investment trusts. Within a dozen or twenty years, he feared, all the productive and distributive machinery of the nation would be owned by insurance companies, holding companies, or investment trusts. That form of ownership, he wrote *New Republic* publisher Bruce Bliven, would be the most corrupt and demoralizing type of ownership ever devised.[4]

To deal with the problem, Flynn favored the following: making investment trusts public units; the passage of laws against commercial bribery; laws to define management obligations and rights of ownership; the outlawing of holding companies; laws to prevent the practice of business graft; and revision of federal antitrust laws in order to prevent holding companies from ignoring them. Such a law would allow legitimate large productive firms to operate efficiently.[5]

The failure of the United States to emerge from the Great Depression taught Flynn the need for reform. If capitalism was to be preserved, he wrote, it had to function "as a social economy rather than a racket." Government had to enter the economy. It was the only neutral agency that represented all citizens, no matter what function they performed as individuals.[6] Although he advocated a philosophy of liberalism, Flynn noted that exponents of that viewpoint had to work against the old and anachronistic ideology of laissez-faire, believers in which were opposed to government making a proper response to society's desperate need for change.[7]

3. John T. Flynn, "Who Owns America?" *Harper's* (May 1926), p. 762.
4. Flynn to Bliven, Feb. 11, 1930, John T. Flynn MSS., Univ. of Oregon Library, Eugene, Ore. Unless otherwise indicated, citations of all correspondence, radio scripts, and speeches are from this collection.
5. Frey, "John T. Flynn," pp. 30–36.
6. Flynn to Dagobert D. Runes, Dec. 16, 1931; Flynn, "The Security Wage," *Forum and Century* (Oct. 1931), p. 249.
7. Flynn, "Why a Liberal Party?" *Forum and Century* (March 1932), pp. 158–163.

With the political defeat of Herbert Hoover, Flynn hoped that government would reform the capitalist system by enforcing competitive fair play. Then capitalism would be made socially responsible and obedient to public demand. Roosevelt would, hopefully, advocate new liberal economic and political reforms along the lines Flynn had been advocating for years. As a critic of unsound banking practices Flynn had begun to comment regularly on the financial practices of Wall Street as a columnist for the *New Republic*. In March 1933 the magazine published his first weekly column under what was to become its permanent heading, "Other People's Money." The title had been taken from Louis Brandeis' own book criticizing the money trust of years gone by. Flynn was pleased that Justice Felix Frankfurter, Brandeis' old friend and former student, had given him permission to use the title.

> I note that the New Republic is carrying my little department this week under the title of "Other People's Money" and this morning a copy of a new edition of the judge's book "Other People's Money" comes to my desk with a suggestion that I review it. Of course, I am delighted to have the opportunity, as I have had the little volume close by me for a good many years and feel it ought to be read by every young man and woman in America.[8]

Flynn favored investigation by the federal government of banking practices and manipulation of securities. As soon as Franklin D. Roosevelt became President, he acted to deal with the effect of wild speculation on the stock market. On March 4, 1933, FDR declared a national bank holiday in order to gain time for reviving the banking system and to prevent other banks from joining those that had failed. Flynn praised the President's action, but urged that he move more rapidly. He feared massive currency inflation if a concurrent credit expansion did not take place. "What is needed now," Flynn wrote, "is a plan . . . to produce income by producing work; to produce work by launching great public and private construction enterprises that will

8. Flynn to Frankfurter, May 3, 1933, quoted in Frey, "John T. Flynn," p. 55.

yield wages to those on jobs and in the material factories."
Billions had to be appropriated by government, even if it meant
abandoning the gold standard. The government had to undertake
building projects, and private industry had to finance loans to
clear slums.[9]

Flynn had the opportunity to be of direct influence as an
adviser to counsel Ferdinand Pecora, who carried out an investigation into banking, stock exchange, and security practices for
the Senate Banking and Currency Committee from January 1933
through 1934. One result of the widely followed Senate hearings
was the Securities and Exchange Act, which provided moderate
requirements for trading stock on margin, a practice that Flynn
had hoped would be entirely outlawed. It also established a Securities and Exchange Commission, which had the power to license
stock exchanges and regulate their practices.

Much of what the Democratic platform of 1932 had promised
appealed to Flynn. Like the Democrats, Flynn hoped for economic recovery. Capitalism had to be humanized, he realized,
and the system reordered to function in a stable manner. Poverty
amidst plenty existed because of a failure in the method of distribution of goods. The purchasing power of the public had to be
increased as soon as corporate and individual debts were liqui-
dated. Flynn favored an administrative receivership, which would
allow corporations to reorganize and reduce capitalization, rather
than the granting of loans to business through the discredited
Reconstruction Finance Corporation (RFC). Excessive profits
had to be eliminated, Flynn argued, and a federal income tax on
excess profits had to be passed. Most essential, he believed, was a
tax on employers out of which a social security system would be
financed.[10]

By late 1933, however, Flynn started to believe that the
administration was not acting firmly enough to reverse the Depression. Measures it was taking were actually steps in the wrong

9. Flynn, "The Bankers and the Crisis," *New Republic,* March 22,
1933, pp. 157–158.
10. Flynn, "The New Capitalism," *Collier's,* March 18, 1933, pp. 12–13,
52–53.

direction. The administration had given up on meaningful public works. As of mid-September it had spent only $9.9 million on them, while the RFC had doled out twice as much to pay off debts accumulated by failed banks and corporations.

Most of Flynn's hostility was reserved for the National Recovery Act (NRA). The early New Deal program was characterized by planning techniques that had antecedents in trade associations developed within industry during the Hoover years. Heads of large businesses wanted government control of prices, production, and trade practices. In an effort to break the Depression, industry itself was given the power to draw up codes of fair competition, which included regulations governing prices and production. NRA meant the suspension of the antitrust laws, as power over prices and production was delegated to trade associations, which became private economic governments. Large corporations came to dominate the code authorities, which used their power to stifle competition, cut back production, and reap huge profits from price-raising rather than from business expansion. But because labor was granted the right to organize and bargain collectively with representatives of its own choosing, under NRA Section 7-a, most liberals went along with it. They realized that FDR was using the methods of big business and wartime regimentation, but they rationalized their support because the President wanted more jobs and better working conditions as a result.

Flynn did not share the positive feelings toward NRA expressed by other liberals. Rather than acting as harbinger of a true planned society that had a national mechanism for control of production and distribution, NRA was returning America to a corporate self-rule in industry that emanated from the Harding era. The nation was being put on the road to guild fascism, Flynn proclaimed. The rights supposedly granted labor led many liberals to view NRA as a shift toward the Left.[11] Flynn argued

11. Flynn, "Other People's Money," *New Republic,* Nov. 22, 1933, p. 46; Dec. 6, 1933, p. 100. Hereafter the *New Republic* will be cited in footnotes as *NR.*

that it was the reverse: "I say this New Deal is a fake. . . . It has been sold to our people as a great liberal revolution. That is a fraud. It is nothing else than the scheme which the Chamber of Commerce of the United States has been fighting for for twelve years—the modification of the Sherman anti-trust law and turning over the control of industry to the tender mercy of the trade associations. Employers are compelled to combine. But laborers are not."[12]

The entire New Deal, Flynn was beginning to feel, was a failure. The government relied for economic strength on borrowed funds, rather than on new tax receipts. Roosevelt had betrayed liberalism and the fondest hopes of millions of his early supporters. He had failed to enforce the antitrust act, and had moved to cartelize industry along corporate lines. To mask his actions he would have his picture taken with planner Rexford Tugwell, which served as "proof to the world that the President [had] gone to the left. Hoover was called a fat Coolidge. Roosevelt is really a smiling Hoover."[13]

Flynn proposed formation of a new party, one that could gather support for a real plan based upon spending of money obtained through progressive taxation. FDR was serving the needs of large corporate business while playing the liberals for fools, because they continued to support his conservative measures. Flynn continued to hope that the liberals would defect for the New Deal camp and use FDR's failures to launch "a powerful third party upon modern radical economic issues."[14]

With no such alternative present, Flynn hoped that many voters would support Socialist party candidate Norman Thomas in 1936. At least a strong vote for the Socialist candidate in New York, he thought, could lead Roosevelt to lose his own home state.

While Flynn was dismayed with the failure of the New Deal, he was able to put in effort in one other area of importance. In

12. Flynn, "Consumer Under the New Deal," text of radio address, December 1933.
13. Flynn, "Other People's Money," *NR,* Feb. 27, 1935, pp. 74–75.
14. Flynn, "A Plan," *Common Sense,* April 1935, pp. 12–14.

September of 1934 Flynn served as a member of Senator Nye's three-man advisory council, which carried out research and preparatory work for the investigation of banking and munitions industry during World War I. His hope was that overseas conflict might be avoided if a system could be created to take the profit out of war. Flynn appeared formally before the committee, presenting a plan that would have the government pay for war out of taxes financed concurrently with the military action, rather than through borrowing of funds from financial sources. Flynn's plan was rigorous. Government would take 50 percent of the first 6 percent of a corporation's profit and 100 percent of the rest; it would limit individual incomes to $10,000 per year, and take all amounts over that; it would impose heavy taxes on all individual incomes of $10,000 to cover current expenses of waging war.[15]

By 1940 Flynn was able to sum up his major objections to FDR in a scathing little book, *Country Squire in the White House* (Doubleday Doran, 1940). In 122 brief pages Flynn accused Roosevelt of having betrayed the liberal 1932 Democratic platform. The administration was dominated by the corporatist NRA idea; by militarism, wasteful spending, a possible imperialist foreign policy, and potential threat of dictatorship. FDR was a product of the Hudson Valley aristocratic gentry. While that group was made up of benevolent and paternalistic people who desired to help the common man, their members did not have the necessary ability. Roosevelt himself was a weak and contradictory figure, more than likely to experiment with militaristic policies and incapable of restoring real prosperity. Deficit spending had become a popular but self-defeating policy, and the President's ability to dispense funds without congressional approval strengthened his position and gave him a large amount of power. The New Deal was at an impasse; war hysteria would be the only way out.

It is no wonder that after reading an attack by Flynn on the President and his aide Harry Hopkins, Roosevelt protested to the *Yale Review*'s editor, Wilbur L. Cross, that Flynn had become "a destructive rather than a constructive force." Flynn, the President urged, "should be barred hereafter from the columns of any

15. Frey, "John T. Flynn," pp. 118–141.

presentable daily paper, monthly magazine or national quarterly, such as the *Yale Review*."[16]

Roosevelt would have even more reason to hope for Flynn's isolation in the near future. In the midst of a developing sentiment for intervention abroad Flynn used his financial column in the *New Republic* to present the opposite case. Domestic economic developments, he argued, were propelling the nation toward war. Inquiring into what he called the mysteries of the steel industry, Flynn discovered that plants were operating on three shifts at full capacity, but were not producing structural steel, railroad ties, or equipment metal. He surmised that "a large margin of the steel mill business must be 'war order.'" Noting that the stock market was rising with growing munitions production, Flynn asked whether Americans were seeing "now the first phase of a little war-business boom similar to that which roused and delighted us in the winter of 1914–1915."[17]

As the economic needs of the nation produced their own thrust toward militarism, political and military developments threatened peace. In December 1937 the Japanese Navy sank an American ship, the *Panay*, on duty in the Yangtze River. Flynn argued that the Yangtze River patrol was "an act of unmixed impudence." China and other powers were not asked to patrol American rivers. If Roosevelt wished to avoid war with Japan, "why not take the Yangtze Patrol out of the Yangtze?" Roosevelt had stated on August 31 that all Americans had to leave China or remain at their own peril. Yet the President and his Secretary of State were the *provocateurs*. They had asked for billions of dollars to protect American interests. That, Flynn warned, was "how wars are made."[18]

Privately Flynn expressed even greater anger. He was shocked, he told Senator William E. Borah, at the way in which the administration used the *Panay* sinking to inflame public opinion and to gather support for a large arms buildup. Flynn com-

16. Roosevelt to Cross, July 7, 1939, in Elliott Roosevelt, ed. *F.D.R., His Personal Letters, 1928–1945,* II (New York: Duell, Sloan and Pearce, 1950), p. 904.
17. Flynn, "Other People's Money," *NR,* March 31, 1937, p. 239.
18. Flynn, "Other People's Money," *NR,* Jan. 5, 1938, p. 254.

mended Borah for being the only senator who called attention to the fact that the *Panay* had been sunk while convoying Standard Oil vessels. The President had warned Americans that they remained in China at their own risk. "Yet long after this warning," Flynn emphasized, "we find the Standard Oil, which elected to remain supposedly at its own peril, still operating on the Yangtze . . . at the peril of the people of the United States because its ships were being convoyed by an American gunboat."

The *Panay* incident revealed that the administration planned to develop a giant arms program as the major Keynesian device to create employment at home. To put it into effect, FDR would "have to keep on using war scares in order to keep public sentiment behind these expenditures." Flynn believed that a recovery program based on armaments meant the destruction of America's heritage. "We will not be able to stop it," he wrote Borah; "it will get all mixed up with our thinking." Like Charles Beard, Flynn believed that it would "thrust forward into the solution of our domestic problems foreign quarrels with which we should have nothing to do." Flynn hoped for a "strong voice to rally the opinion of the American people against . . . the most monstrous idea in this country today."[19]

Strong voices were already bending to the interventionists. Senator George W. Norris, whom Flynn regarded as "a model of integrity . . . and of true liberalism," had shocked anti-interventionists by supporting appropriations for a large navy, in view of the troubles in the Orient. This was particularly disturbing because Flynn regarded Norris as one of the few who had kept their heads "during the Great War when powerful nations were trampling on their weaker neighbors and when the whole world" had gone mad. Along with Robert M. La Follette of Wisconsin, Norris had stood with those "who held fast to their faith when this country declared war on Germany." His new statement

19. Flynn to Borah, Jan. 7, 1938. The *Panay* was on duty in Chinese waters as part of the general protection afforded U.S. corporations abroad. The incident did not become cause for a new harsh policy toward Japan. FDR accepted the official apology made by the Japanese government. The U.S. collected economic compensation offered by Japan, and the incident was formally closed on the diplomatic books.

produced in Flynn "a sense of spiritual depression." If people like Norris gave in, Flynn feared, "all is lost."[20]

Norris was not persuaded. Japan had become an outlaw nation, bent on a course of "murder and destruction." Norris now seemed to have developed a sense of mission to preserve civilization. The Axis alliance could "destroy the civilization of the world." An increased navy would give Japan pause and she would "not be moved by anything except a realization that other nations such as ours have the present power to stop her in her course." He agreed that militarism breeds war, but like others who saw America facing a hostile power, he now thought it "imperative on our part that we present an armed front."[21]

The apostasy of men like Norris encouraged Flynn to speak out even more forcefully. It was true, he informed the Foreign Policy Association, that Germany and Italy menaced England. But what they threatened was not her "democracy, but her empire. What they covet is not her soil, but her colonies, not her liberty but her markets." England desired to "save her empire and in doing this she seeks to range on her side the might of the world." It was foolish "for Americans to yield to it—to permit themselves to be drawn into a war to save England's empire under the illusion that they are saving her democracy."

Leaders of the West sought to protect their economies by "spending vast sums and creating employment with war industries," and they needed war scares to gain financial sacrifices from the populace and to keep industries producing at a rapid pace. For America to unite with Britain was a "guarantee of war." Flynn was trying to tell the American people that they had a militarist in the White House, and he publicly charged that Roosevelt was "deliberately planning to use a great armament program as a means of spending money to create employment."[22]

20. Flynn to Norris, Dec. 31, 1937. During World War I, Norris and Robert M. La Follette were two senators who steadfastly opposed America's entrance into the war. Both voted against Woodrow Wilson's declaration of war against Germany, which passed in the Senate by a vote of 82–6.

21. Norris to Flynn, Jan. 4, 1938.

22. Abstract of Flynn address before the Foreign Policy Association, Hotel Astor, New York, Jan. 8, 1938.

Flynn found administration requests for military appropriations to be a break with the nation's most hallowed traditions. It was absurd for Americans to worry about Europeans and Asians arming when the United States had more armaments and was thousands of miles away from their shores. The real reason for talk of a foreign menace was that FDR was unable to get the nation out of depression. The United States had slipped back to where it was in 1933, except that now it had a new $20 billion debt to make up.[23]

If the populace was stirred up about mythical foreign enemies, Flynn argued, "they might be willing to submit to further weird methods of spending money." Domestic issues would fall by the wayside as the nation united against the foreign threat. The American executive would have to develop war scares, just as had Mussolini and Hitler. Flynn cited an example of the manipulation of the media. Stories of Japanese insults to Americans were kept out of the papers until Roosevelt was about to appear in Congress to ask for a new military appropriation. The next "blast" might concern South America. The Japanese dealt badly with Americans in their country and in Chinese cities, but Americans and the British were in Asia as "invaders." After the Boxer Rebellion, Western armies ravaged Peking and committed savageries that were "a blot on civilization." Americans were not protecting the Chinese against the Japanese, but simply guarding the Chinese trade and its profits. Talk about human rights was "just a lot of bunk." Flynn appealed to the American people to resist being slaughtered "to keep our pitiful little trade in China alive."[24]

"Recovery Through War Scares" was the title of his first long attack in the *New Republic*. Repeating his charge that Roosevelt had "set out as the drummer of fear" and was "deliberately selling to our people the baleful notion that some enemy is about to assail us," Flynn asked whether liberal groups in America had become so "enfeebled by confusion and doubt that they will permit themselves to be marched off behind this fantastic banner." He became the first liberal columnist to point to the irony

23. Flynn speech on radio station WEVD, New York, Jan. 28, 1938.
24. Ibid.

involved in the American Communist party's newfound support of the doctrines of collective security and rearmament. "Its position," he wrote, "is logical and easy to understand. It has one great interest in Europe and that is the preservation of the Russian experiment," which meant that it wanted the West "on the side of Russia." That is why it favored "entangling this country in the politics of Europe" and "arming this country to take part in that struggle effectively." The irony was that the Communists had "lined up with the extreme right-wing internationalists of our Eastern border who would press in the same direction but for a different reason."

Flynn's reaction to Communist priorities gives an insight into why he later developed a strong anti-Communist position. From his perspective, the Communists had betrayed their earlier antiwar orientation and had lined up with interventionist-minded business elements. Earlier the Communist-initiated peace movement had organized antiwar mobilizations and had supported the Oxford Oath, in which young British men pledged not to take part in any war in which Britain might engage. But by 1937 they had abandoned this position for collective security against the fascists.

Many of the liberals and pro-Communists were jumping on the administration bandwagon. FDR was trying to create an arms program as the basis for economic recovery. The leadership for it was not coming from munitions makers; it was not they who were sending out alarms about a German trade invasion of South America, fascist penetration of Mexico, and the great strength of Axis infiltration. It was not the warcraft builders or economic royalists who were acting to protect trade and profits. Neither was it the Republican party as a whole, nor the traditional big-navy advocates. "It is being done," Flynn wrote, "by a Democratic administration supposedly in possession of its liberal wing."[25]

The so-called liberals had put America on the "armament bandwagon." Forces too powerful to be resisted were pushing America on the road to war. The administration had succeeded

25. Flynn, "Recovery Through War Scares," *NR,* Nov. 2, 1938, pp. 360–361.

210 / *Prophets on the Right*

in forging a united front on behalf of armaments. All parties and ideologies "from the tip of the right wing to the tip of the left [were] clamoring for war preparations." Lewis Mumford now demanded arms "along with old time Republican reactionaries." The tradition of American liberalism—an antiwar tradition—had disappeared. Liberals who once provided resistance now thought that if Hitler and Mussolini were destroyed democracy would be safe. Flynn disagreed. Democracy would be worse off, because nothing harmed its preservation more than war and vast military preparations.

Those who had opposed the drift toward war in 1937, he complained, now "sprang to the bait of preparedness as an avenue toward recovery." Democrats, Republicans, liberals, and radicals all favored it. Flynn was certain that unless the drift were stopped, war would conquer. Making war industry the basis of work would lead to people keeping on "inventing reasons for it."[26]

The nation, he wrote Senator Borah, was "being slowly and relentlessly conditioned for getting into a European war." Whether or not it was deliberate was of "no consequence." The effect would be the same. "England, which was willing to abandon a real democracy—Czechoslovakia—to her fate, now attempts frantically to rally the democracies when Poland, which is far more fascist than democratic, is threatened." American leaders were trying "to sell the American people a spurious idealism which will cost them another war and some more billions, a wrecked economic system and maybe the loss of our own democracy."[27]

Flynn dedicated himself to deflating myths that propped up the defense momentum. Particularly objectionable were the arguments for a western-hemisphere security belt and the propaganda about the Axis taking over Latin and South America. That whole "South American trade bugaboo about German penetration and barter," he argued, "has been a thoroughly dishonest one, got up for no better reason than to stimulate the fears of Americans as

26. Flynn, "The Armament Bandwagon," *NR*, March 8, 1939, pp. 121–122.
27. Flynn to Borah, April 3, 1939.

part of the propaganda for arming the country." It was simply more of the "busybody fever meant to feed spy scares" so that a "war psychosis" would develop.[28]

Armaments had become popular, Flynn charged, with conservative groups whose members had previously opposed Roosevelt and the New Deal. Now they supported the President on behalf of "spending money for national defense, despite the fact that it must be done with borrowed funds." Flynn outlined the reasons for the conservatives' reconciliation:

> If the conservative objectors to deficits do not like WPA, very well, he will give them what they like—battle ships, armies. He will create an industry for them: the armament industry, which henceforth is to become one of the props of our national economy. A short time ago the liberals were trying to invent some reasons for further support of government deficits. But now the President has found one which the Tory elements will applaud. It remains to be seen how the liberals will like, under the leadership of their new Messiah, what they have always denounced.[29]

The once-hated New Deal was now backed by business-minded conservatives who saw an answer to their problems in war production. War had broken out in Europe in September 1939, and now Flynn sought to convince Americans that the United States could maintain neutrality only if it avoided economic commitments with any of the belligerents. FDR wanted to repeal the arms embargo imposed by neutrality legislation and to sell weapons to the Allied belligerents on a cash-and-carry basis. Flynn saw this step as one that would deplete Allied credit reserves, a development that would force the United States to step in as supplier of credit. It would then be but a short time before America itself would be involved militarily in the war.

To help stop the drift toward war Flynn had formed the Keep America Out of War Congress—a noninterventionist group cofounded with Norman Thomas and other liberal, socialist, and labor leaders. A central body meant to create united antiwar action, the group was affiliated with the Women's International

28. Flynn, "Other People's Money," *NR,* Oct. 25, 1939, p. 339.
29. Flynn, "Other People's Money," *NR,* Nov. 1, 1939, pp. 367–368.

League for Peace and Freedom, the War Resisters League, and the National Council for the Prevention of War. He appeared before a meeting of the congress at Carnegie Hall on November 10, the eve of Armistice Day.

Although the audience was small, Flynn summed up the themes that had preoccupied him during the previous year. World War I had produced a world "worse than the old world with all its evils," a world with little democracy and a great amount of militarism. War had now become "the chief business of the world." The Neutrality Act was not neutral. Under the new cash-and-carry terms, arms could be sold to a belligerent if the U.S. agreed with its policies. Yet, he hoped, the law might still prevent an unneutral President from operating behind closed doors. Americans had cash-and-carry only because of the fight waged to support antiwar political leaders.

Flynn was not persuaded that Roosevelt sought to lead the nation into war. Rather, he believed that the President's policies would produce a situation that resulted in war, and it would then take "fifty years of research to find out how we got in." FDR simply sought a means out of depression via arms. War was not just a "device of munitions makers to make profit"; he rejected the naïve economic determinism of Senator Nye. War was a "stratagem of befuddled politicians" who hoped to make the economy work, and arms were the only type of deficit spending left to engage in. For this reason Roosevelt had engaged in deliberate attempts to frighten the people into believing that a threat existed, and America had now thrown a 300-mile belt around its hemisphere. While Germany had only annexed Poland, we had annexed "the Atlantic and Pacific Oceans." Proposals for a new $3 billion arms budget were an attempt to establish a vast arms industry supported by borrowed funds.[30]

In 1940 Flynn charged that secret preparations were being made "to fight in Asia against Japan," and liberals had helped make these plans. Under FDR, America had moved as steadily "as the most reactionary junker administration towards militarism." It was the "bland complaisance of almost all the pro-

30. Flynn speech before a Keep America out of War mass meeting, Nov. 10, 1939, Carnegie Hall, New York.

gressive groups" which made this possible. Now liberals and progressives had "allowed an old-fashioned Mark Hanna Republican program, including a runaway military and naval spree, to be put over on them under the label of liberalism."[31]

War scares also meant a repressive political mechanism that worked to curb expression of dissent. Roosevelt had acted to broaden the FBI into an agency that would ferret out and track down political dissidents. "I wonder if you have noticed the manner in which the FBI has become a part of the military and naval establishment of the United States," Flynn wrote Senator Bennett C. Clark of Maryland. J. Edgar Hoover was the same individual who "carried on J. Mitchell Palmer's atrocities after the last war." But Flynn did not attribute the FBI's new role directly to Hoover. "It is a part," he wrote, "of Roosevelt's deliberate plan to disturb the peace of mind of the American people with his spy scares and submarine scares." The President has "to terrify the people before they will authorize military expenditures."[32]

In so many ways the nation seemed to be moving toward a dictatorship based upon a corporate state, a development that would surely take place if war arrived. Already FDR had shown how centralized his power was when he secretly traded fifty destroyers with Britain in exchange for bases. That act was "an invasion of the rights of Congress so grave" that were Congress not already subdued because of its "servile submission to the executive," it would "meet this usurpation promptly with impeachment proceedings."[33]

With the 1940 nomination on the way, Flynn moved to oppose another term for Roosevelt. This election he would not give his support to a third-party candidate. For the first time Flynn saw hope for an alternative with the Republicans. The GOP was the only real hope for ousting Franklin Roosevelt. Strangely, Flynn found Robert A. Taft "frightfully inadequate" and "reactionary," even though Taft's response to the move toward war was similar to his own. When the Republican convention nominated

31. Flynn, "Other People's Money," *NR,* Jan. 22, 1940, p. 115.
32. Flynn to Senator Clark, Feb. 15, 1940.
33. Flynn, "Other People's Money," *NR,* July 22, 1940, p. 117.

Wendell Willkie, Flynn used the opportunity to give campaign talks in which he attacked FDR while barely mentioning the Republican candidate.[34]

During the last half of 1940 liberal opinion began to shift toward intervention. In April the liberal Kansas Republican newspaper editor William Allen White, along with Clark Eichelberger, set up a national group to get Congress to give aid to Britain and to strengthen U.S. defenses. Named the Committee to Defend America by Aiding the Allies, the group quickly became a major force for intervention. "By the end of the year," James J. Martin has commented, Flynn was "almost a solitary voice defending what had now become a minority viewpoint. The passage of five years had seen no change of heart so spectacular as the about-face performed by American liberals in general on the subject of arms manufacture and the growth of military institutions."[35]

That shift in position even began to affect the *New Republic*. The editors of the magazine had previously supported neutrality legislation and had rejected collective security. But the Nazi victories in Europe caused many of their principal supporters to move toward favoring aid to the Allies. In June contributing editors Lewis Mumford and Waldo Frank offered letters of resignation. They complained that the moral neutrality of the *New Republic* was similar to the lack of leadership of those European statesmen who allowed fascism to triumph in Europe.[36]

Given this kind of pressure, many readers of the *New Republic* were deeply offended by the tone of Flynn's remarks. In late 1940 Flynn offended his audience by suggesting that FDR was developing tendencies that approximated those of Hitler. In a review of a book by Gustav Stolper, who argued that Germany moved to fascism via social reform, Flynn wrote that "when we

34. Frey, "John T. Flynn," pp. 183–186.
35. James J. Martin, *American Liberalism and World Politics: 1939–1941,* II (New York: Devin-Adair, 1964), p. 777. Professor Martin's neglected volumes are a virtual compendium of information on the conflict between interventionists and noninterventionists during this period, particularly on the shift in liberal opinion regarding the issue of war and peace.
36. Frey, "John T. Flynn," pp. 188–189.

get through with this last phase of the New Deal, we shall have added the elements of militarism, the shifts of power to the executive and the militant chauvinism, basing our economy on a war industry promoted by an aggressive foreign policy."[37]

Flynn's column became so controversial that the editors prefaced it with the remark that they were publishing it for its own intrinsic worth and not because they agreed with it. They proceeded to reply to his column with their own comments, printed under the nasty heading, "Flynn Again."[38] Flynn did not comprehend the growing accusations made against him.

> One of the things I cannot understand is that a liberal writer who is saying now the same things he said five years ago and ten years ago, who is opposed to third terms for Presidents, to war-mongering and militarism and conscription and corrupt political machines and vast public debt, to shipping subsidies, to scrapping the anti-trust laws and the fostering of monopolies, to hidden taxes, should be accused of holding these views because of a personal feeling against the President. I held these views before Roosevelt was President and I have now lost my liberal credentials because I do not agree with the New York Times, the Herald-Tribune, Mr. Harry Stimson [sic], Mr. Franklin Roosevelt and Wendell Willkie about the war.[39]

It was clear that the *New Republic*'s editors could no longer tolerate Flynn. Editor Bruce Bliven wrote Flynn, "[you have] lost a good deal of your interest in the subject of your column," which was supposed to be Wall Street's economic policy. Bliven promised to continue to print Flynn's comments on finance and investments, but to run his other remarks only in the correspondence section of the magazine. "It is you who have changed," Bliven added, "and not the paper."[40]

Bliven ran the caption "Mr. Flynn on War Hysteria" over Flynn's November 11 column, rather than the usual title, "Other People's Money." A note also appeared that Flynn's regular column, which had appeared continually since May 1933, would

37. Flynn, "Other People's Money," *NR,* Sept. 9, 1940, p. 352.
38. *NR,* August 5, 1940, p. 173.
39. Flynn to Bruce Bliven, Sept. 12, 1940.
40. Bliven to Flynn, Nov. 4, 1940.

be discontinued with that issue. "Lacking sufficient material for a weekly column on the original subject," Bliven explained to his readers, "Mr. Flynn has ranged far afield and has frequently collided head-on with the views of the editors, to the annoyance of some readers, the pleasure of others and the bewilderment of many." The editors announced that they had asked Flynn to write articles on his original theme, and they hoped these would appear often.[41]

Flynn was angry and defensive when he received Bliven's note. He denied that he had changed his philosophy. It was the war and "the appalling betrayal of the American people by the President and the hysterical state of mind he has produced" which had caused "many divisions amongst old friends." The *New Republic,* Flynn charged, had failed to come to grips with the real problems of the economic system. Abandoning the position it had taken for many years, its editors had swallowed "hook, line and sinker the program of the war party."

It was "of the utmost importance" Flynn wrote, "that the foremost liberal weekly journal of opinion" in the United States, "which for years thundered against the collective securityites, the foreign policy of the Stimsons and Hulls, the warmakers and militarists, should almost overnight, not only abandon that tune and plunge headlong into the forefront of the war party but should suppress a columnist who remained at least one voice for its old opinions and announce to the world that no writer should appear in its columns who was in complete collision with its views."[42]

Flynn's dismissal, the Reverend John Haynes Holmes wrote, was "grievous news . . . With Villard flung from *The Nation,* and now you from the paper with which you have so long and so honorably been associated, to say nothing of Harry Elmer Barnes tossed off the Scripps-Howard papers, to what a low degraded estate has liberal journalism in this country fallen."[43]

The *New Republic* editors may have had another reason for

41. Flynn, "Mr. Flynn on War Hysteria," *NR,* Nov. 11, 1940, p. 660.
42. Flynn to Bruce Bliven, Jan. 8, 1941.
43. Holmes to Flynn, Dec. 11, 1940.

dropping Flynn's column. In August of 1940 he joined with Philip La Follette, former governor of Wisconsin, and General Robert E. Wood of Sears, Roebuck and Company, to build a new noninterventionist national group, the America First Committee. Flynn was a member of its national executive committee and chairman of the New York City chapter, and his participation in a group that included prominent right-wingers was an embarrassment to the prowar liberal intellectuals. Flynn has lost all respect for the liberal interventionist establishment. On the other hand, such writers as William Rose Benét were intimating that Adolf Hitler had created the isolationist movement in America. Men such as Benét, Lewis Mumford, and Herbert Agar, Flynn wrote a few years later, had "completely lost their reason. . . . two-thirds of the men who operate under the mask of liberalism are not liberals at all, but are merely bigoted advocates of some system of their own or intolerant enemies of some other system."[44]

Flynn was right in saying that many liberal internationalists shared the imperial vision of the empire builders. Some liberals, such as *Nation* editor Freda Kirchwey, found the unabashedly imperialist sentiments of Henry Luce repulsive, and denounced his pleas to establish the United States as the dominant power in the world. But other liberals responded favorably to Luce's famous "American Century" editorials, which appeared in March and April of 1941. The noted liberal intellectual Max Lerner, who was at that time close to the Marxist Left, delivered a long reply, "The People's Century."

Lerner saw much to praise in Luce's views. Luce's thesis, that the United States and Britain should combine "to establish . . . hegemony in the world, control the world sea lanes and world trade, send out technicians to develop the world and education to teach it and food cargoes to feed it and ideals to inspire it," had already been proposed, he noted, in *New Republic* editorials back in December 1940.

True, Henry Luce held individualistic social ideals based upon

44. Flynn to Ernest E. Wheeler, Aug. 10, 1942.

commitment to private ownership, which Lerner found repugnant. But he stressed that liberals could not merely dismiss Luce as an imperialist, and urged that they search for what they had in common. The *Time* editor, Lerner wrote, spoke "for a new capitalist-conscious group, most of them younger men, who do not fear the war but regard it as an opportunity." Lerner made it clear that he was more in sympathy with Luce than with the antiwar liberals. "I prefer him infinitely, though our purposes are as far removed as the four corners of the winds, to men like Burton Wheeler and John Flynn."[45]

In January 1941, a month in which Flynn set out to campaign actively on behalf of the noninterventionist goals of the America First Committee, Flynn announced that America "stands on the brink of war." Yet the world war was not about democracy; it was a war "between empires and about imperialism." Flynn did not think the character of the war had changed merely because England had been bombed. Describing Britain as "the biggest of all these imperialist grabbers," Flynn argued that she had declared war on Germany not because she loved Poland but because Britain "has an empire of her own which she seized exactly as Germany seized Poland and she sees the rise of a German empire threatening the safety of her English empire." German hegemony would threaten British control of the Mediterranean, which she had to maintain "to hold India and millions of people in Asia and Africa in subjection." Britain wanted to save her empire at the expense of her democracy, while Americans were being asked to risk their democracy on behalf of Britain's empire.

The war was another "chapter in the long, age-old struggle of European empires about dividing up the world." Flynn was opposed to empires—Roman, German, French, British, or American. The peace would resemble that of Versailles; the imperialist powers would make new deals. "And it is out of this abominable world of imperialism, the scramble for dominion, the

45. Max Lerner, "The People's Century," *NR*, April 7, 1941, pp. 465–466.

fight for trade backed by armies and guns, that I want to keep this great peaceful democratic America of ours."[46]

It was a "small minority," a "rich group, chiefly on the Eastern seaboard," that stood behind the interventionist drive. They agreed with Britain's desire to conquer the world. Although some were motivated by a humanitarian impulse to destroy Hitler, they all had been misled into working toward the destruction of the very institutions they had sought to defend within America. Those who sought to drive Hitler out of Europe did nothing to destroy the conditions that had created his original victory. The proof was their inability to do anything about preventing the collapse of the economy, which was kept alive only by "the immense war industries which the government is paying for with more borrowed billions." War, even victorious war, Flynn argued, "will destroy us."

The President had promised in October 1940 that no United States boys would be sent off to war. Yet administration spokesmen were saying that they opposed a law that would limit the service of American troops to the western hemisphere. Charging that the administration was part of a "gigantic conspiracy," Flynn argued that officials sworn to serve the nation were "busy fabricating new provocations, generating new and hotter hysteria," while leading internationalists threw off their disguises and demanded "war, open, undisguised war."[47]

Flynn's speeches, given under the aegis of the America First Committee, infuriated his opponents. It could not be denied, philosopher and educator John Dewey wrote Flynn, that the committee was a Nazi transmission belt. This charge, Flynn retorted, came from "the immature minds that make up the Park Avenue contingent of the war group in this country." As for Dewey's logic, it meant that "we must quit trying to keep this country out of war in order to displease Hitler." Like many

46. Talk by Flynn at an America First Committee meeting, Kansas City, Mo., Jan. 16, 1941.
47. Talk by Flynn at America First Committee meeting, National Theater, Wash., D.C., Feb. 2, 1941. Flynn, *War, What Is It?* (New York, privately published, 1941).

Socialists, Flynn argued that it was "under the influence of crumbling imperialism and of the enervated and dying capitalist regimes of Europe I see fascism spreading." Predicting that entrance into the war would end with domestic fascism, Flynn told Dewey that "because we want to save America from fascism" we are foolishly accused of being part of a Nazi front.

Flynn pointed out to Dewey the militaristic attitudes, and the praise of war itself, that had started to appear in the columns of liberal writers, as well as an increasing advocacy of an American corporate state and dictatorial powers for the executive branch of government. "Then ask yourself," he suggested to Dewey, "how far do we have to travel to find ourself in a nice, smiling, happy brand of American fascism all decked out in the terminology of democracy." Dewey had joined "up with the witch-hunt on Americans who are struggling to keep this country out of war." But when and if war came, the values Dewey cherished would be destroyed. Flynn would save Dewey's letter as "one of my melancholy souvenirs of this wretched era."[48]

The charge that America First was a Nazi transmission belt had first been voiced by an interventionist group, the Reverend Leon M. Birkhead's Friends of Democracy. They had accused the committee of serving to spread the antidemocratic ideas of Nazism into millions of American homes. The charge was a smear. But Flynn and the committee were not helped by the fact that Nazi and anti-Semitic elements were offering America First their support.

The Christian Front, the German-American Bund, and Joseph McWilliams' anti-Semitic American Destiny Party all moved to

48. Dewey to Flynn, March 17, 1941; Flynn to Dewey, March 19, 1941; Dewey to Flynn, March 21, 1941. Dewey's answer revealed that Flynn had partially reached him. It was others, he answered, who used the America First Committee as a Nazi transmission belt. He too opposed getting into the war, but was confused "when I find it said that we must keep out of war but arm to the teeth." If the U.S. must arm, Dewey argued, why not arm those nations defending themselves against the Nazis? Dewey also pointed to the differences between the two sides. He did not doubt that "Germany is the greatest menace to civilization and humanity that has occurred since Genghis Khan." He also did not like the name "America First Committee" because "it's too much like the nationalism that is a great cause of war."

endorse Flynn's New York chapter of the America First Committee. Flynn always did his best to keep these elements out. He was not always successful. On February 20, 1941, Flynn's chapter sponsored a rally with Socialist leader Norman Thomas and Senators Nye and Wheeler, who were to urge the defeat of Lend-Lease. Much to Flynn's chagrin, most of the 3,500 people in the audience were profascist and anti-Semitic. Most prominent was Joseph McWilliams, the self-styled American Nazi. Cries of "the Jews, the Jews" came from the audience. Although Flynn told the crowd that America First did not "approve doctrines which stimulate racial hatreds or religious hatred," it had little effect. America First's opponents were pleased. Flynn's group was castigated by his own former publishing outlet, the *New Republic*. "Willingly or not," their editorial proclaimed, "our most respectable appeasers are being drawn into a closely united front with the most vicious elements of American fascism."[49]

When 22,000 people packed Madison Square Garden for a major America First rally in mid-May, Flynn learned that McWilliams was in the audience. He immediately informed the crowd that America First was in no way responsible for McWilliams' presence. "What he is doing here, how he got in, or whose stooge he is I do not know . . . but I do know that the photographers for the war-making newspapers always know where to find him."[50]

The problem of America First's effectiveness being diminished because of the unsolicited support given the committee by anti-Semitic elements was most serious. Flynn wrote General Robert Wood that he felt the committee was composed of too diverse a group of people. He feared that some of the reactionary elements that had latched onto the committee would try to control it in order to advance their own objectives.

He was concerned, he told Wood, about the "powerful anti-Semitic under-current moving around the country." He had

49. "Fascist Pattern," *NR*, March 3, 1941, p. 293; see also Frey, "John T. Flynn," pp. 207–208.
50. *New York Times*, May 24, 1941, p. 6; Wayne S. Cole, *America First: The Battle Against Intervention, 1940–1941* (Madison, Wis.: Univ. of Wisconsin Press, 1953), pp. 125–126; Frey, "John T. Flynn," pp. 212–213.

observed it himself in New York "among some men who are both wealthy and powerful." Flynn believed that the Jews had "given plenty of people good cause to be indignant at them," and he often found it hard to hold his tongue when he heard prominent Jews demand intervention. But it was urgent that America First not be allowed to degenerate "into a piece of equipment in the hands of intolerance."

Flynn admitted that the charges made against the committee by interventionist groups had some substance. There were anti-Semitic and fascist elements giving it their support. Flynn himself saw signs of intolerant persons "snooping about and perhaps intruding themselves into positions where they may be able to grab this movement, at least its machinery, when its war job is done." Flynn was most concerned with the possible "rise of some kind of fascist movement in America when this damnable war hysteria runs out." Such a movement would be a "nice, respectable movement dominated by fascist ideas but never calling itself fascist." Since many of these elements had endorsed the America First Committee, it was conceivable that a new fascist group "would be a kind of America First movement," but in a "different sense" from their own noninterventionist group.

America First had to be kept from falling into fascist hands. If war was declared, America First should be dissolved. But if the war ended without U.S. involvement, some of the reactionaries in their group might try to organize themselves under the name "America First," in order to use "the prestige of this organization." Flynn thought the diverse coalition against intervention that was his America First would splinter and collapse. It would end up split "into three or four or more widely divergent political philosophies."[51]

Flynn was wrong. The war in Europe continued, and Hitler was evidently planning to move against England. But the attacks on the committee increased after Colonel Charles A. Lindbergh delivered his famous Des Moines, Iowa, speech on September 11, 1941. While identifying elements "responsible for changing our national policy from one of neutrality and independence to one of entanglement in European affairs," Lindbergh stressed that "the

51. Flynn to General Robert E. Wood, June 5, 1941.

three most important groups who have been pressing this country toward war are the British, the Jewish and the Roosevelt administration." Interventionist Jews were shortsighted, he asserted, and were "a danger to this country" because of their "large ownership and influence in our motion pictures, our press, our radio, and our government." Rather than agitate for war, Lindbergh continued, "the Jewish groups in this country should be opposing it in every possible way, for they will be among the first to feel its consequences. Tolerance is a virtue that depends upon peace and strength. History shows that it cannot survive war and devastation." As many Jews interpreted his statements, Lindbergh advocated a pogrom for their fellow Jews should war arrive.[52]

The America First Committee refused to reprimand Lindbergh publicly and deplored what it termed "racist smears" against him. Flynn, however, was enraged. Instead of receiving Lindbergh's speech in advance—the usual procedure—Flynn and the New York chapter of America First saw it for the first time in the papers. Lindbergh, Flynn wrote, had "never submitted a copy of this speech to anybody at all," and gave out copies to the press only when he had finished delivering it. "Not a soul in the organization knew what he was going to say and of course no one, so far as I can learn, dreamed of the blast he was about to deliver against the Jews." Flynn vowed to urge Lindbergh to explain publicly that the speech was his own, "that he did not consult anybody on the America First Committee and that the last thing he had in mind was to make an attack on Jews as such."[53]

His private reaction, Flynn revealed to Lindbergh, was "one of utter distress." The speech had alienated key supporters of the America First Committee, and within the group those who were "in daily eruption against the Jews were uproariously delighted." Those afraid of the issue "were equally depressed. Both groups were completely intolerant of each other." The danger was that many individuals would resign. Flynn was sure that Lindbergh was "as completely without anti-Semitism as I am." But he warned that the public did not take account of "shadings of

52. *New York Times,* Sept. 12, 1941, p. 1.
53. Flynn to Dr. Henry Noble MacCracken, Sept. 15, 1941.

meaning" and that his modifying statements would be ignored. Lindbergh had allowed the organization to be "tagged with the anti-Jewish label," and Flynn had been "struggling against great odds to keep [the committee] free of that label."

Flynn acknowledged that the Jewish population in New York almost unanimously backed entering the war. He also agreed that war mania did not serve their interest, since America could become quite intolerant "when its passions are aroused and when it is in search of a scapegoat for its misfortunes." Flynn further remarked that some Jewish leaders had sought to brand all those opposed to war as anti-Semitic. "It has seemed," he wrote, "that their responsibility for this should be brought home to them. But this is a far different matter from going out upon the public platform and denouncing 'the Jews' as the war-makers. No man can do that without incurring the guilt of religious and racial intolerance and that character is poison in a community like ours." Finally, Flynn chastised Lindbergh for delivering a speech "of such tremendous repercussive force without taking into your confidence the leaders of the movement who must share with you the responsibility for the consequences."[54]

Flynn's dissatisfaction with Lindbergh did not stop him from continuing his own activities with America First. He still saw World War II as a repetition of World War I—a perversion of humanity's quest for peace and justice. Moreover, he thought that the Western powers sought more than defeat of the Axis. Flynn presumed that the old capitalist nations were seeking new forms to structure their collapsing empires. To liberals who asked what was wrong with trying to save Britain, Flynn answered in June 1941 that this meant saving her "many colonies including India, Malay and countless other subject peoples."[55]

Another turn in world affairs affected the fortunes of the noninterventionists. On June 25, 1941, Hitler's troops invaded Soviet Russia, breaking the Nazi-Soviet Nonaggression Pact. The Soviets, who had attacked war talk as imperialist maneuvering, now advocated Allied intervention. Since they favored joint action with the West, what they had branded as an "imperialist"

54. Flynn to Lindbergh, Sept. 15, 1941.
55. Talk by Flynn on radio station WMCA, New York, June 18, 1941.

war became a "people's antifascist struggle." Flynn was not surprised. Hitler wanted the Ukraine and Russia's grainlands and the Baku and Rumanian oil fields. The irony of Western action was that the "free democratic states" were near collapse, while "the dark and bloody dictatorship of Stalin" had been saved. Flynn was furious that men such as Lindbergh, who had wanted Britain to build a powerful air force, had been condemned, while Western leaders kept on "driving one nation after another to fight without weapons . . . in the wrong places and against the wrong aims and getting whipped all the way, yet cursing and damning and vilifying those who tell the truth to save them."

Stalin had signed a pact with Hitler only to "postpone the evil day of war" against Russia; Hitler had only wanted to avoid conflict with Stalin while dealing with the West. Now that he had made his moves in Europe, he was free to turn against Russia. Now the interventionists were calling for aid to the Soviet Union, but both Hitler and Stalin, Flynn wrote, were "enemies of our form of society." The United States government had put Communist leader Earl Browder in jail and was purging Communists from jobs and from schools, while they urged us to "send millions of young men to Europe to fight the battles of Russian communism." Flynn did not want "to spill the blood of one American boy to make the world safe for either" Hitler or Stalin. Stalin's Russia was invaded and needed aid. Now Americans were being asked by Communists to bleed themselves "white with taxation, to disrupt our whole economic system, to plunge ourselves into bankruptcy" and to send millions to fight for a war "whose peace terms will have to satisfy Communist Russia."[56]

The Communist reversal had a lot to do with turning Flynn into an anti-Communist. Before the United States was even formally at war he was arguing that fighting on Russia's side would mean that the peace would cater to Stalin's demands. After the Yalta Conference this argument would become the staple of a new postwar right wing.

On September 11 FDR informed the nation that he had ordered naval and air patrols to clear all German and Italian

56. Talk by Flynn on radio station WJZ, New York, and the NBC Blue Network, June 26, 1941.

warships from waters considered vital to America's defense, and had in effect ordered American armed forces to "shoot on sight." The America First Committee believed that Roosevelt was looking for an incident on the high seas as an excuse for a declaration of war.

Although the nation was *not* at war, Flynn charged that the President was, that he had "committed acts of war against" Italy and Germany. American ships were convoying British war cargoes for the purpose of "pursuing a course designed to force the Axis powers into a corner where they will be compelled to attack us." Roosevelt had promised the American people he would not take them into war, but he meant to provoke an attack, after which he would "invoke all the gods of self-defense to take us full blast into the war which he has been clandestinely waging for many months." Roosevelt was "attempting to sneak into the war through the back door." Flynn promised to "denounce and resist" the President's "conspiracy until Congress, under the Constitution, declares that we are at war." The America First Committee, he believed, stood alone "as a bulwark between this country and war up to the present moment."[57]

One more fight engaged Flynn's attention—the effort to prevent further revision, repeal, or modification of the Neutrality Act. FDR had proposed on October 9 that Congress allow armed merchant ships to enter combat zones. After the German attack on the *Kearny* the House acted to repeal the prohibition. Flynn moved immediately to appear in opposition before the Senate Committee on Foreign Relations. He appeared on October 23, preceded by Oswald Garrison Villard and other noninterventionists. To allow merchants ships to be armed would only heighten the danger. Next they would be allowed to carry goods to British ports, inviting attack and causing the American people to ask for a declaration of war. Flynn's campaign was not successful. The House voted 212–194 to allow merchant ships to be armed.[58]

57. Flynn, statement, n.d. (1941).
58. U.S. Senate, Committee on Foreign Relations, *Hearings, Modification of Neutrality Act of 1939—H.J. Res. 237,* 77th Congress, 1st sess., 1941, pp. 201–216; see also Frey, "John T. Flynn," pp. 229–232.

Time was short. Minority leader Joseph Martin was under immense pressure to come out against the war and make the Republican party an out-and-out antiwar party. Flynn believed that the Republicans had to look to the future and "take a definitive position to protect this nation from the overthrow of constitutional government and the destruction of its economic system" by helping to keep America out of war. If the Republican party opposed war, but then advocated its successful prosecution once the nation was enveloped, its position would be "impregnable" at the war's end, and it could "come into power almost without effort."[59]

This was another shift. A lifelong, if lukewarm Democrat, Flynn was now engaging in a dialogue with Republicans. Flynn stated to Alfred Landon that the Republican party had to break with Wendell Willkie and the me-tooers who aped the Democrats. He urged Landon to purge the party of prowar Republicans such as Henry L. Stimson, since he saw in the Republican party "the only force now in existence which can mobilize the strength of the nation not only against this war but against the follies and madness of the New Deal when the war is over." Flynn was trying to get a statement by leading Republicans opposing FDR's war policies; at this late date he still believed America could keep out of the war.[60]

Flynn continued, therefore, to debate with liberal interventionists, arguing that Hitler's system was economically unstable and that after peace it would begin to disintegrate. The new order meant pouring "endless streams of government money into the economic bloodstream, subjecting the whole business world to the most bureaucratic regulation, spending vast sums on military establishments," and spending little on anything of substance. It was war, not victory of one or another side, that would destroy Europe. As far as Flynn was concerned, the "chief threat to our way of life" was not from Hitler but "from right inside our own

59. Flynn to Martin, Oct. 2, 1941.
60. Flynn to Landon, Oct. 8, 1941. See Robert A. Taft to Flynn, Oct. 21, 1941. Taft hoped to meet with Flynn, but he wrote that "it is quite difficult to read somebody out of the Party, no matter how much he differs with the Party's principles."

shores." It was the threat of depression and the failure of the capitalist system to create prosperity.[61]

Privately he was less optimistic. But a last chance for peace had to be grasped. Congress was considering total repeal of the Neutrality Act. If it were repealed, war was imminent. Flynn argued that "every dictate of strategy calls upon us to assert that the nation is not at war with Germany, that while the repeal of the neutrality act puts into the hands of the President the power to put us into war, nevertheless we will not be at war until he actually uses that power, that Congress has abdicated completely to the dictator, but that there are still the American people to reckon with and that the America First Committee will resist any involvement to the end." Flynn pleaded with Robert E. Wood to remain as chairman of the America First Committee and to think of the "hundreds of these plain, simple people who look to us to save them."[62]

Although they lost the fight, Flynn looked at the positive side. It was probably clear to Roosevelt, he thought, that he had "got his grant of power under circumstances which will make use of it extremely dangerous." The President would have to come to Congress for a declaration of war. Flynn suggested that America First remain quiet and that others who did not belong to their committee be encouraged to continue the resistance. Those in Congress who favored higher taxes and price controls but who opposed intervention should remain quiet "and let the war-makers take the blame."

They had 200 congressmen and 42 senators on their side. With work, Flynn hoped they could get 7 more senators and 10 more congressmen to support nonintervention. But rather than work through the controversial and discredited America First Committee, a "peace offensive" should be sponsored under the leadership of liberal clergymen such as Harry Emerson Fosdick. They should also work in local political primaries. Flynn thought that FDR was in a terrible spot and that "war-minded madmen around him grow more and more angry with him." Flynn hoped they could keep what he termed "the accident factor" out of the

61. Debate with Frank Kingdon, Bernardsville, N.J., Nov. 11, 1941.
62. Flynn to Wood, Nov. 11, 1941.

picture, because he knew that an accident might result in war, and thereby "make the President's war policy."[63]

The Japanese raid on Pearl Harbor—the kind of accident Flynn feared—occurred but a few weeks later. Hopes for a final peace offensive were shattered. Revisionists such as Charles A. Beard, and Flynn himself, would later argue that Pearl Harbor was anything but an accident. But, then, the war had plunged Flynn and his associates into despair. "The warlords wanted war, and they won," Burton Wheeler proclaimed. "You and I used what little intelligence we have in every honorable way to keep this country out of war, and we lost." Like Flynn, Wheeler had "no apologies to make for the part I played."[64]

As for Flynn, he thought in retrospect that "so many people were against the war for so many different reasons that the problems of amalgamating that sentiment into an effective driving force against war was a difficult one." Many were never concerned with what Flynn saw as the "broader aspects" of opposition. Given the task of "trying to keep them all together," Flynn explained, "I, for one, found myself confronted much of the time with an impossible task."[65]

But the war had taught Flynn new lessons, given him new allies, and shown him the need to work to create consciousness of the "broader" issues that moved a nation like the United States to war.

63. Flynn to Robert E. Wood, Nov. 16, 1941.
64. Wheeler to Flynn, Dec. 22, 1941.
65. Flynn to John Haynes Holmes, Jan. 6, 1942.

Among speakers at the Anti-War Congress in Washington on May 31, 1941, were, left to right: John T. Flynn, Chairman of the Keep America Out of War Congress; Mrs. Robert A. Taft; and Norman Thomas, Socialist leader. (ACME)

John T. Flynn, at Decoration Day, 1941, gathering in Washington, D.C., accuses the administration of "leading us down the road to war" which "only one out of five is ready to march down." (ACME)

John T. Flynn and the Cold War

JOHN T. FLYNN emerged embittered and distraught from his struggle against American intervention in World War II. He had been a classic *New Republic* liberal—antiwar, sympathetic to the Left, critical of capitalism and any drift toward fascism, dedicated to a nonimperial America, persuaded that we could have prosperity without recourse to war.

Nothing in his early career prepares us for the course he would follow in the 1950s, when he became known to a wider circle of Americans as a major supporter of Senator Joseph McCarthy's crusade against communism. Before the senator's name became a household word Flynn published a slim volume, *The Road Ahead: America's Creeping Revolution* (New York: Devin-Adair, 1949), which, according to liberal journalist Fred J. Cook, gained him a new reputation, that of a man who was "cultivating the radical right front." Flynn attacked Truman's efforts to prove he was tough on Communists "as a phony ploy designed to blind Americans to the real menace—which was not communism [but] the 'American edition of the British Fabian Socialist, who is engaged in a sneak attack here . . . who denies that he is a Socialist and who operates behind a mask which he calls National Planning.'" Fabian socialism was a step toward fascism. In America, "Fabians," CIO leaders such as Sidney Hillman and Walter Reuther, as well as economists such as Alvin Hansen, had moved into the Democratic party, where they would further advocate unsound economic policies that would lead to fascism. Socialist trends, deficit spending, a war economy, and centralized economic planning had to end. Republican government would be preserved only through the power of new American conservatives.[1]

1. Fred J. Cook, *The Nightmare Decade: The Life and Times of Senator Joe McCarthy* (New York: Random House, 1971), pp. 70–71; cf. Richard C. Frey, Jr., "John T. Flynn and the United States in Crisis, 1928–1950" (unpub. diss., Univ. of Oregon, 1969), pp. 310–312.

The Road Ahead became a best seller. A new edition was distributed by the Committee for Constitutional Government, accompanied by a blurb describing it as "the most important book of this decade [which exposed how] in secret, planners at top level in Washington have been working for a stealthy revolution in collaboration with labor monopolists . . . It shows that, in reality, the mislabeled 'Welfare State' is a handout, pickpocket state, by which bureaucrats buy, with other people's money, control of the entire nation and subject citizens to the serfdom of the state."[2] It was condensed in the February 1950 *Reader's Digest* and sold almost 4.1 million copies. In one chapter Flynn argued that a group of Protestant ministers and laymen were deliberately deceiving Christians by handing out socialist propaganda disguised as Christian literature. The charges received widespread attention. They were the most serious to be leveled against the Protestant Church prior to attacks made during the McCarthy period.[3]

Flynn wrote more McCarthyite volumes—*While You Slept: Our Tragedy in Asia and Who Made It* (New York: Devin-Adair, 1951); *The Lattimore Story* (New York: Devin-Adair, 1953), and *McCarthy: His War on American Reds, and the Story of Those Who Oppose Him* (New York: America's Future, Inc., 1954). He became a favorite of the right wing and the darling of the McCarthyites. What led Flynn to such a pass? Was there a link between his early libertarianism and his later support of a demagogue? These are tough questions, and the answers to them are not clear.

To begin an exploration, one must go back to the aftermath of Pearl Harbor. The sentiment that occurs time and again among the noninterventionists was a feeling that they had been misunderstood. "It seems to me," Charles Lindbergh had written Flynn, "that we must expect unjust accusations and mis-quotations for some time to come." Believing the record would be set straight some time in the distant future, Lindbergh said this time

2. Quoted in Cook, *The Nightmare Decade,* pp. 71–72.
3. Ralph Lord Roy, *Communism and the Churches* (New York: Harcourt, Brace, 1960), pp. 230–231: see also Frey, "John T. Flynn," pp. 322–333. The entire controversy is described thoroughly in the Frey dissertation.

was an "intolerant and immoderate period." He believed that America's fundamental danger was in Russia and Japan, not in Germany, and this was a view that moved many of the isolationists toward militant anticommunism.[4]

As the war went on, Flynn was concerned with the preservation of popular government. In 1943 he argued that the U.S. was "little by little adopting first one and then another policy that is beginning to make us look more like a National Socialist government than a democracy." Blaming German fascism on the old social democratic and republican governments that preceded Hitler, Flynn argued that their regimes had developed and cultivated the essential elements of fascism, including corporatism: "the organization of the economic society as a planned economy under the supervision of the State"; a "planned consumption economy"; "militarism as an economic weapon"; "imperialism"; and finally "dictatorship."

All these characteristics had been developed in Italy and Germany by civilian leaders. The Weimar Republic had engaged in planned consumption and had plunged Germany into debt on top of debt, causing a ruinous inflation. It had developed cartelization of industry and government partnership in industry. Under Article 31 of its constitution, the government had ruled by emergency decree. When Hitler took power, all he had to do was to add on the older militarism and imperialism of the empire and consolidate it by a strong dictatorship.

The essence of fascism, Flynn stated, was not in the ugliness of Storm Troopers and book burnings; it was in more commonplace elements, which also existed in the United States. In particular, he saw the threat of strong central government and "a plan for blank-check" government in the efforts of the National Resources Planning Board under Alvin Hansen, which sought to initiate similar planning. With FDR's third term, the New Deal was "forging the last link in the chain of American national socialism."[5]

4. Charles A. Lindbergh to Flynn, Jan. 6, 1942, Flynn MSS., Univ. of Oregon Library, Eugene, Ore. Unless otherwise indicated, citations of all correspondence, speeches, and radio scripts are from this collection.
5. "Are We Drifting Away from Popular Government?" address by John T. Flynn, Springfield, Mass., Adult Education Council, April 6, 1943.

U.S. soldiers were fighting Hitler's armies in Europe, and an attack on the President for harboring fascist tendencies was unwelcome. But the Socialist party chief, Norman Thomas, was impressed. "In the most effective possible fashion," he wrote Flynn, "you have made a very strong case," though Flynn had "dismissed some of the side-show features of fascism a little more summarily than I would." And he disagreed with Flynn's negative view that "the world drifts to fascism anyhow through processes which private capitalism has accepted to its own hurt." Thomas, of course, saw "an alternative to fascism," but he believed it could not "be a return to private capitalism that has steadily evolved toward the present situation." Still, Thomas informed Flynn that he had "quoted [his] definition of fascism in a footnote in my own book."[6]

Fascist trends were clear, in Flynn's analysis, in postwar international agreements that were effected by majority action of both houses of Congress rather than by a two-thirds vote of the Senate, which constitutionally must ratify peace treaties. "In the presence of a concerted drive by this administration to nullify the Constitution wherever it becomes onerous, by ignoring it outright or by various devices circumventing it, it seems to me Congress must now become more implacable than ever in resistance to any devices designed to break down the power of the Congress to resist the invasions of the President."

Flynn wrote Senator Arthur Vandenberg that avoiding a two-thirds Senate vote was a "complete surrender" to State Department New Dealers, who argued that any agreement made by treaty could also be made "by the President in the presidential agreements, provided Congress will cooperate." He demanded a "very high degree of certainty" requiring a two-thirds Senate vote before the nation put any international agreements into effect. These new methods were "the final success of the New Deal's ten-year drive to rid itself of the restraint of the Senate in its international relationships."[7]

Cordell Hull had met with Soviet leaders in Moscow. The United States had won an agreement with Stalin that he would

6. Thomas to Flynn, Aug. 31, 1943.
7. Flynn to Vandenberg, Aug. 18, 1943.

not make a separate peace with Germany. In the process it had created a military alliance with Stalin. But because Russia had "suffered vast and terrifying losses," Flynn was persuaded that Stalin was "firm that Russia will get something out of the war besides the defeat of Hitler." Having the enormous prestige of victory, and with a large and powerful army, Russia, Flynn predicted, would be regarded as "the great master state of Europe."

First Stalin would try to gain the land on Russia's western boundaries, annexing areas Germany had conquered after it had broken the Nazi-Soviet Pact. Since such actions would be "in complete defiance of the declaration of the Atlantic Charter," Stalin was aware that if his actions were discussed at the peace table an "effort would be made to deprive him of what he regards as his legitimate prey."

Stalin's goals were understandable. Flynn acknowledged that the Soviet leader had "been very uneasy at the delay of the Allies to open a second front," and thought there was reason for Stalin's suspicion "that Britain and America have been delaying it for political reasons." Churchill, he explained, had opposed a front until 1944 "in order to permit Hitler and Stalin to fight it out and exhaust themselves so that when the Allies do invade with their fresh armies and abundant supplies, an exhausted Russia and Germany would be ready to accept their terms." But Stalin, a realist, had had to make it clear that Russia would not fight "beyond the point where Russian armies were driven from Russian soil," and that he would not oppose the recreation of a strong Germany at the war's end. He could, in other words, threaten a separate peace and blackmail the Western powers to open a second front, or permit him to annex the desired territories. The West would either acquiesce or submit to a separate peace. Thus at the Moscow Conference Cordell Hull and Anthony Eden had made it clear that they would "yield to Stalin's demands" and open a second front. Like the postwar revisionist historians, Flynn was arguing that the West had implicitly supported Russian hegemony in Eastern Europe.

The absence of formal discussion about territorial demands meant that "these territories would be treated as Italy was being treated"; and Italy was under Western control after Mussolini's defeat. The Soviet ambassador, Flynn noted, had made it clear that Russia had no intention of yielding her claim to these territories. Flynn wanted Americans to comprehend the ramifications of the Moscow Conference. It occurred to ensure that Russia would not go its own way. Nevertheless "it was a victory for Stalin and not for Hull and Eden." In addition, the military alliance of the big powers meant that Russia and Britain would divide up Europe as they chose, and proceed to arrange "matters to suit themselves."[8]

Flynn's analysis of these wartime dealings reveals an emerging overpowering anticommunism. Like Charles Beard, Flynn judged Stalin's Russia to be no better or worse than Hitler's Germany. The belief that the war would produce worldwide democracy was myth. The grand alliance permitted one totalitarian power to triumph in place of another. Like other old isolationists, Flynn regarded the war's end from the perspective of Versailles. Because FDR wanted a new league of nations, he was willing to yield to Stalin's territorial demands. Winston Churchill was seeking a Big Three understanding in order to maintain British hegemony in Western Europe, the Mediterranean, and North Africa. This meant a new triple alliance, "in which Britain, Russia and the United States will manage the affairs of the world." The United States had repudiated the conditions it had laid down as indispensable for a successful new league. Military power was lodged in new great powers, "two of them imperial . . . [and its] council is equipped with . . . vast authority to make decisions, to dominate the world." It could hardly be described, Flynn wrote, "as according sovereign equality to all peoples."

The proposed new United Nations Organization might well create new spheres of influence. Disarmament would be forced upon the weak nations, but there would obviously be no disarmament of the all-powerful victors. The force to preserve peace would be that of the huge military establishments of a few imperialist nations that would enforce their own peace terms, and these would include "the subjugation of many peoples."

8. Flynn, "Moscow Pact," radio script, Dec. 1, 1943.

A new military alliance meant arms and territorial aggrandizement, as well as new worldwide tensions. True, Roosevelt sought
to confer with the Senate, which Wilson had not done. But the
League of Nations had floundered because of "mistakes in the
very structure of the vessel itself." As the Allies had handed over
Shantung Peninsula to the Japanese rather than to the Chinese at
Versailles, the Allies were now handing over conquered territory
to Russia. Again one would have "the cynical distribution of land
and peoples and resources among the victors without regard to
the rights of millions of people, most of them our allies."

Flynn remarked that the old distinction "between isolationist
and internationalist [was] no longer valid." All agreed on the
merits of international cooperation; they divided on the objectives and forms of cooperation. He favored a truly independent
league of nations that renounced claims against sovereign nations
and peoples and that favored disarmament. But the UNO that
Roosevelt was proposing meant to serve a quite different function: "But there is a difference between cooperation for peace
and justice and a combination of imperialist powers . . . to
perpetuate the injustices of allied imperialists. That is not cooperation for peace and justice. It is cooperation for peace and
imperialism. What we will get out of that is a league, not of
nations, but of imperialism, and such a league cannot ensure
peace. It can only ensure war and make it certain that we shall be
in it."

The seeds of war lay, Flynn thought, in the perpetuation of
imperial politics, and the Allies had betrayed the aspirations for
independence of the peoples of Poland, Rumania, and the Baltic
lands. On this point Flynn was at home with the right wing,
which had always regarded Russia as the real enemy.

But after making this point Flynn turned sharply from the Red-
baiters. The seeds of war lay as well, he stated, in the Orient, in
the "irrepressible aspiration of a billion people for freedom from
the indignity of white domination." And it was the United States
and the Western powers who proposed, "in the name of democracy, to deliver the seventy million people of the Indies back into
the hands of the Dutch, the millions of Burma and Malay into the
hands of the British, the millions of Indo-China into the hands of

the French and the great cities of China back into the hands of the British."

Western colonialism, which the Allied powers continued to support, stood in the way of peace. Along with the struggle to control Mideastern oil, the conflict between Russia and Britain would end in world conflict inevitably. There must be a league that would renounce aggression, demand disarmament, and grant all nations equality. Force would be used only by such a league, not by a small combination of aggressive powers. But those who fought for such things were now being "smeared with the title of isolationists." Whatever the smear, they would remain opposed to "that thing Mr. Roosevelt is preparing—which is the very antithesis of the dream of world peace and justice."[9]

The great war against fascism had not changed the characteristics of the world's powers. Flynn was trying to warn Americans of what he conceived to be basic—the starting point for a realistic assessment of the possibilities of achieving peace. He wrote what would be the most representative book of his career—which until recently lay neglected and relatively unknown—*As We Go Marching*. Its purpose was to define the meaning of fascism and "then to search for its elements in America."[10]

Given the response, his intention had an element of irony. Because he had opposed entrance into World War II, he was tainted with the label of "appeaser." When he came to speak at the University of Illinois in May 1944 thirty members of the faculty and student body protested against his appearance "on the ground that he was anti-Semitic, that he had trafficked with seditionists, was pro-fascist and that it was not good for the war effort to have him there."[11]

Despite the opposition he faced from those apparently on the political Left, Flynn's arguments bore some close resemblance to

9. Flynn, "What Is the President's Foreign Policy and What Is Wrong with It?" and "Memo for Mr. [Paul] Palmer from John T. Flynn," June 12, 1944.

10. Flynn, *As We Go Marching* (New York: Doubleday, 1944), p. vi. A new paperback edition of this work was issued by Free Life Editions of New York in 1973, and is readily available.

11. Memo of Flynn's remarks to questions at the University of Illinois, Urbana, Ill., May 18, 1944.

Marxist arguments about the nature of fascism. His book would give little comfort to the Right—which was itself so blinded by anticommunism that it often submitted to fascist efforts at repression.

It was statist institutions as solidified by the New Deal, Flynn argued, that had produced an American version of fascism—a "good" rather than the "bad" fascism that Americans detested in Nazi Germany. Its elements were planted in such corporatist institutions as the NRA. People responded to the word "planning," but New Deal planners conceived of it as "a change in our form of society in which the government would insert itself into the structure of business, not merely as a policeman, but as partner, collaborator and banker." The economy could be planned and coerced rather than free, one in which "business would be brought together into great guilds of an immense corporative structure, combining the elements of self-rule and government supervision with a national economic policing system to enforce these decrees."[12]

World War II had consolidated a business collectivism based upon "an economy supported by great streams of debt and an economy under complete control, with nearly all the planning agencies functioning with almost totalitarian power under a vast bureaucracy." The New Deal had tried to extend this system into foreign affairs in prolific government spending for military systems. There was no objection from Congress, business, or labor to expenditures for national defense. "Thus militarism is the one great glamour public-works project upon which a variety of elements in the community can be brought into agreement."[13]

Militarism and acceptance of war, both components of fascism and imperialism, were evident in the United States. Unlike many prowar liberals, Flynn had few illusions about the unique characteristics of the American democracy. He was especially concerned about the administration's efforts to impose conscription under the guise of "civilian training." There were arguments on behalf of a big army, he wrote Senator Vandenberg, but nations had tried militarism, "supposing it would advance some special

12. Flynn, *As We Go Marching,* p. 193.
13. Ibid., p. 207.

objective not necessarily connected with war, only to find that militarism in the end rides the countries. It sets in motion forces and pressures too powerful ever to be controlled."

Flynn presented Vandenberg with a copy of his book, telling him that he had "tried to depict the current of pressures and forces that slowly drew Italy and Germany along the road to Fascism." America, he said, had a unique position. It was not only the one remaining nonimperialist nation but it was "the only great power which did not use its strength for aggression." But he was "apprehensive that we may be lured along the road to imperialism—under the pious pretensions and false declarations as to our purposes."[14]

Like any other empire, America was not exempted from the rules of imperial decline. The large nations wanted to preserve the *status quo.* They appealed for support to well-meaning idealists who hoped for a peaceful world, but their own purposes were to build an order "in which they, all leagued together, will preserve a world which they have divided among themselves and in which the combined forces and might of the allied aggressors will hold for each what they have"; it was imperialism, disguised under "phrases of benevolence and as a dream of world peace." Americans "will do what other countries have done: we will keep alive the fears of our people of the aggressive ambitions of other countries and we will ourselves embark upon imperialistic enterprises of our own." There was no doubt that the "germs of a vigorous imperialist are here among us . . . the moral germs. And if the economic problems of the nation should seem . . . to lead us off into some imperialist adventures, the moral support of such ventures will not be lacking."[15]

14. Flynn to Senator Vandenberg, Oct. 30, 1945. Vandenberg answered (Oct. 31, 1945) that he thought anything Flynn wrote was important, and that he shared Flynn's "suspicions of this sugar-coated 'peacetime conscription.'" And he noted that he would endorse it if it was the *"only* recourse available to our national defense." At that date, however, Vandenberg did question "precisely what masses of foot soldiers are going to do in an atomic war." Vandenberg shortly became an archinterventionist, the major Republican exponent of bipartisanship in waging the cold war.

15. Flynn, *As We Go Marching,* pp. 213, 214, 224.

America had bases all over the world. There was "no part of the world where trouble can break out where we do not have bases of some sort in which . . . we cannot claim our interests are menaced. Thus menaced, there must remain when the war is over a continuing argument in the hands of the imperialists for a vast naval establishment and a huge army to attack anywhere or to resist an attack from all the enemies we shall be obliged to have. . . . We must have enemies," Flynn added sarcastically. "They will become an economic necessity for us."[16]

A public-debt-supported state would collapse unless it was run in a centralized, totalitarian fashion. America was moving in that direction. Centralized power was growing stronger as more power was concentrated in the hands of the executive branch. "Despite many differences in the character, customs, laws, traditions, resources of the people of Italy, Germany and America," Flynn wrote, "we have been drifting along identical courses and under the influence of the same essential forces." Free enterprise and constitutional government had been eroded. A new statist capitalism had replaced it. "The test of fascism is not one's rage against the Italian and German war lords."

> The test is—how many of the essential principles of fascism do you accept and to what extent are you prepared to apply those fascist ideas to American social and economic life? When you can put your finger on the men or the groups that urge for America the debt-supported state, the autarchical corporative state, the state bent on the socialization of investment and the bureaucratic government of industry and society, the establishment of the institution of militarism . . . and the institution of imperialism; under which it proposes to regulate and rule the world . . . and proposes to alter the form of government to approach . . . absolute government—then you will know you have located the authentic fascist.[17]

An American fascism would believe in "marshalling great armies and navies at crushing costs to support the industry of war and preparation for war which will become our greatest indus-

16. Ibid., pp. 225–226.
17. Ibid., pp. 251–252.

try," all conducted under "a powerfully centralized government in which the executive will hold in effect all the powers, with Congress reduced to the role of a debating society."[18]

Flynn's prototypical American fascist was not a thug in brown-shirt or SS uniform; he was an American politician who would erode the people's power in their Congress in order to concentrate undue authority in the hands of the President. In 1944 this analysis seemed to advocate reaction at home and isolation abroad. Few paid attention to Flynn's critique of militarism and imperialism. The principle of constitutional government was shortly to become a right-wing rallying cry. The hatred of many on the Right for Russia and communism—a sentiment Flynn shared—would obscure the substance of his argument.

Like other libertarian individualists, Flynn admired the staunchness of Taft's courage. He alone had defended a concept of law in his challenge to the legitimacy of the Nuremberg trials, which violated *ex post facto* laws of justice. Flynn was disgusted with New York Republican leader Thomas E. Dewey, who stooped to any "demagogic trick" to get votes. Flynn hoped that Taft would try for national office, and he advised him: "Keep your powder dry, stick to your high principles, talk up and out when the occasion arises." The people would reward him and turn to him in time of need.[19]

Socialist Norman Thomas was another leader with whom Flynn, like Lawrence Dennis, felt kinship. Indeed Flynn's positions on some issues were to the left of Thomas' stand. In a recent book of Thomas', Flynn wrote, the Socialist leader had "left out a discussion . . . of the one and really only great impediment to disarmament":

> If the U.S. agreed to disarm we would have to dismiss a couple of million men out of the forces, demobilize a whole legion of generals and admirals and other officers and the federal government would have to withdraw from the economic system some seven or eight billion dollars' worth of contracts for arms, clothing, food, ships, planes, oil, and all sorts of things, the production of

18. Ibid., p. 253.
19. Flynn to Taft, Oct. 9, 1946.

which account for another two or three million persons in employment. Every state that has an army camp would march to Washington to protest the removal, which would of course be a blow to all the patriotic merchants and producers in the community. I imagine even the steel, coal, automobile and maritime and shipyard unions would protest.[20]

The problem was to find a way to overcome the consensus in favor of an arms production on which the capitalist system seemed to thrive. To ask America to disarm was similar to asking a large business to liquidate itself. America had no economic equivalent to the arms industry. For Thomas to urge disarmament "without finding some means to fill up the gap in employment which politicians and business men believe would be created by disarmament [was] . . . to be fighting a hopeless battle." The issue was "economic resistance" to disarmament.[21]

Flynn's critique was radical, yet concerning an analysis of American foreign policy and United States-Soviet relations, he accepted the interpretations that would become the focus of right-wing and McCarthyite attacks on the Truman administration. The issue was the Yalta agreements and the idea that a conspiracy had taken place to sell out American interests to the Russians. In his 1948 study of FDR's Presidency Flynn had called Yalta the "final betrayal." The Polish question was settled with a formal proposal to hand over eastern Poland. Elections had been promised but never held. Poland was given a part of eastern Prussia, territory with a completely German population. FDR had ignored the terrible lessons of World War I and its aftermath, when French land had been awarded to Germany and German land had been given to the Czechs.[22]

At Yalta a tripartite occupation of Germany had been agreed on, with Russia allowed to take German labor as a source of reparations; this was a "diplomatic way of authorizing the seizure of human beings to work as slaves after the war ended." Stalin would enter the war against Japan three months after Germany's

20. Flynn to Thomas, April 2, 1947.
21. Ibid.
22. Flynn, *The Roosevelt Myth* (New York: Devin-Adair, 1948), pp. 388–389.

defeat, providing *"the political aspects of Russia's participation had been clarified"* (Flynn's italics). Stalin wished to "turn Manchuria into a Russian puppet state, which was precisely what Chiang Kai-shek so bitterly and properly opposed." But in return for Russia's participation in the war against Japan, "Roosevelt [had] agreed that the Kurile Islands would be handed to Russia, who would also get Sakhalin Island, internationalization of the Port of Darien, the lease of Port Arthur as a naval base and joint operation with China of the Eastern and Southern Manchurian railroads." Flynn called attention to a point that would prove difficult for the Truman administration to explain: the "secret agreement . . . was not made public and was concealed even from Byrnes who was Roosevelt's adviser at Yalta. He did not hear of it until after Mr. Roosevelt's death . . . by that time he was Secretary of State."[23]

Flynn did not push the blame for this treachery onto the new President, Harry S. Truman. Unlike Oswald Garrison Villard, who considered the Potsdam agreements to be the major postwar crime against humanity, Flynn sympathized with Truman's dilemma. "All the major decisions which make up the incredible record of surrender, blunder and savagery," he explained, "had already been made long before President Truman and Secretary Byrnes went to Potsdam. What Truman and Byrnes could have done at Potsdam rather than what they did is difficult to discover. The war was over. Europe lay in ruins. Roosevelt had conceded everything to Stalin." FDR had given away "the existence of little nations and the rights of little peoples he had sworn to defend." Truman knew little about what Roosevelt had done in private. He had made agreements which he had kept secret even from Churchill, and had made arrangements with Chiang Kai-shek which were secret from both Churchill and Stalin. Later, Roosevelt had made agreements contrary to Chiang's interests without the Chinese leader's knowledge. In fact, Roosevelt had "made many secret agreements which no one in our State Department knew about until his death and then [had] learned about . . .

23. Ibid., pp. 389–390.

the hard way, by having them flung in their faces at embarrassing moments by Molotov."[24]

At Yalta, and later at Potsdam, the United States had put into Stalin's hands the means of conquering a good part of Europe. It stood aside as Stalin accepted what had been offered. The U.S. gave Stalin the arms and support he needed, and withheld its attack on Europe until Stalin had what he wanted. "Then in a series of conferences with him we yielded it all in return for his promise to come into the United Nations on terms which enabled him to wreck that as an instrument of settling any serious international dispute." The upshot was that "Russia held in her hands a vast belt of land running from the Baltic Sea in the north to the Black Sea in the south."[25]

What are the realities in Flynn's analysis of Yalta? Which strategies of the Roosevelt administration encouraged the conservative's case of appeasement? How does a conservative analysis match the long-standing anti-imperialist and libertarian concerns that liberals such as Flynn had long stressed?

Flynn's arguments were not singular. Historian Athan Theoharis has pointed out that during the late 1940s and early 1950s congressional conservatives pointed to the secrecy surrounding Yalta provisions concerning Eastern Europe and the Far East to prove that the Roosevelt policy at Yalta contributed to the Soviet threat to America's national security. Conservatives addressed themselves to Yalta decisions that established new Polish boundaries, German agreements on occupation zones and reparation payments, and agreements in the Far East that gave to the Soviet Union preeminent rights to Port Arthur and Darien, joint ownership of the Manchurian railroad, and control of South Sakhalin and the Kurile Islands.[26]

There was also severe disapproval of the manner in which Roosevelt had conducted his diplomacy: the very fact of negotiating with the Russians in good faith, the secrecy as well as the

24. Ibid., pp. 393–394.
25. Ibid., p. 395.
26. Athan Theoharis, *Seeds of Repression: Harry S. Truman and the Origins of McCarthyism* (Chicago: Quadrangle Books, 1971), pp. 68–69.

agreements themselves, and the President's failure to consult or inform Congress. When Truman assumed the Presidency, the rationale of supporting further negotiations with the Soviets was rejected in favor of a doctrine of containment and the achievement of superior military strength. Truman's policy, Theoharis wrote, "the continual recitation of American omnipotence, and the regular rejection of summit diplomacy all served to discredit the diplomacy of Yalta. In the context of the administration's representation of the Cold War as a confrontation between good and evil, Yalta emerged as an immoral compromise and a distinct betrayal of American ideals . . . By augmenting Soviet power, the Yalta Conference had made a third world war possible."[27]

The conservative analysis gained a following after the Truman administration made it seem credible. Moreover, it gave conservatives ammunition for their own interpretation. The United States had kept secret its Far Eastern concessions at Yalta in order to delay negotiations on a treaty with Russia. This was to gain time to avert an extension of Soviet influence, because of successful U.S. military operations, without having to repudiate any terms laid down at Yalta. By June of 1945 the Far Eastern theater had picked up, and the administration acted in the belief that Soviet military action against Japan was no longer imperative.

The U.S. strategy had failed and then backfired. The Soviet Union honored its commitment and went to war against Japan. Without conclusion of a Sino-Soviet treaty, and without formal United States request, the Russians declared war on Japan on August 8, and quickly moved troops into North China and Manchuria. On August 14, under pressure, Chiang Kai-shek acceded to Soviet demands and signed a treaty with the Russians. It was the Roosevelt administration's "dual strategy of postponement and inflexibility," Theoharis wrote, which "had left the Nationalists in the lurch, completely vulnerable to Soviet intervention. . . . It was indeed the Truman administration's shortsightedness that had in essence 'betrayed' the Nationalists."[28]

Flynn, and others in the conservative camp, attacked the secret cession of territory to the Russians. The U.S. sought to have

27. Ibid., pp. 70–71.
28. Ibid., pp. 88–89.

Japanese troops surrender to the Nationalists south of Manchuria and to the Russians in Manchuria. This was supposed to prevent surrender by Japanese to Chinese Communist troops and to limit the Soviet's occupation role.

Publication of the agreements made at Yalta, Theoharis pointed out, "would have bound the administration to fulfilling them, and this it was not prepared to do." Flynn's error, one now can see, was to have assumed that the administration had always sought to implement them. But if the agreements had been made public at the time of Yalta, Theoharis argues, they would have been "generally accepted by the American public in September. Trust of the Soviet Union was still in force; the Sino-Soviet treaty was being praised, and . . . Soviet occupation of the Kuriles was by and large considered a necessary check upon Japan." But James Byrnes was duplicitous when he publicly denied that the status of the Kuriles had been defined at Yalta, and when he failed "to report the existence of other Far Eastern agreements." He did so in order to avert a Soviet occupation role. But it was his duplicity, nevertheless, "and the attendant necessity not to publish the Far Eastern agreements or even, for that matter, admit their existence," which "seriously compromised the administration's position."[29]

When Byrnes faced a Senate probe, especially under questioning by Senator Styles Bridges of New Hampshire, he neither affirmed nor denied that any agreements had been made concerning the Far East. But he did make an innocuous statement implying personal ignorance of any China agreements. In February 1946, when the United States announced it had turned over to international trusteeship certain Pacific islands captured from Japan during the war, Dean Acheson was asked whether the Soviet Union would be required to turn the Kuriles over to a similar trusteeship. Acheson replied that the Yalta agreements provided only for Soviet occupation of the Kuriles, not permanent acquisition, and that final disposition awaited determination by a peace conference. These remarks were immediately challenged by the Soviet Union, and Molotov announced that both the Kuriles and

29. Ibid., pp. 90–92.

South Sakhalin had been formally ceded to the Soviet Union at Yalta.

At a January 29 press conference Byrnes admitted that the Russian allegations were correct. What was dramatic was not the disclosure but the attempt to explain the administration's earlier evasions. Although Byrnes had been present at Yalta and had stated in September that he was aware of all the discussions that took place there, in December he had denied that any Far Eastern concessions had even been made. In his explanation to the press Byrnes tried to shift responsibility for the secrecy from the Truman administration to Franklin D. Roosevelt.

The failure to publish the Yalta agreements meant that Truman could not admit that his administration sought to repudiate them by not publishing them. His public position since 1945 had been that of promising to honor the agreements made at Yalta by FDR. Now the Truman administration argued that it was the Soviet Union that had begun to violate the agreements signed at Yalta.[30]

The domestic implications of this had an equally important effect, Theoharis explains:

> Domestically, the administration's secrecy and duplicity furthered popular doubts and suspicions about everything and everyone connected with the Yalta Conference. Moreover, they legitimated the McCarthyites' contention that, since Roosevelt's "secret" diplomacy at Yalta—a brand of diplomacy continued by Truman—had contributed to the "loss" of China, Congress must reassert its authority and restrain the executive branch. Administration secrecy in the instance of initially withholding publication of the Wedemyer Report and the secret conduct of the Marshall Mission only increased the effect of the McCarthyites' charges.
>
> There had to be, conservative Congressmen now claimed, an extensive congressional review of past policy decisions to uncover the "full" secrets of Yalta and to expose and dismiss those who had acted disloyally. Only Congress could do this.[31]

The Roosevelt and Truman administrations had lied about the nature of wartime agreements. The Truman administration, in-

30. Ibid., pp. 93–96.
31. Ibid., p. 97.

tent upon backtracking on the agreements, lied to save face, and got caught in the web of its own tissue of fabrications. Had the administration officials published the secret agreements, they would have had to repudiate what Roosevelt had signed. When conservatives discovered their secrets, they assumed the facts had been kept secret for different reasons—a desire by the administration to implement the agreements without having to admit to the public that it was a sellout.

By the time Joseph McCarthy took up these charges the Korean war was raging and the anti-Communist hunt was on full blast. To older conservatives McCarthy seemed to be an agent through whom to fight against centralized executive power. The executive had usurped the power of Congress, had lied about its foreign dealings, and was refusing to supply Congress with documents on the grounds of national security.

Joining McCarthy's crusade, conservatives such as Flynn were somehow continuing their long battle with the power grab of the executive. Flynn had turned in that direction back in 1945 when he sought out Congressman Martin Dies, chairman of the House Committee on Un-American Activities. HUAC, he thought, had important information about Communist-infiltrated groups. They had to expose the activities of those parlor pinks who hid behind patriotic rhetoric, and who were paving the way for national planners who would destroy the free-enterprise system. Dies and HUAC would continue the work carried out by Ferdinand Pecora and Gerald Nye, congressional investigators of an earlier time. They would be the nation's new saviors.

Facing great difficulties in finding publishing outlets after Pearl Harbor, and finding that pro-administration journalists were calling for censorship of his writing, Flynn naturally turned to those anti-Roosevelt publications that welcomed his articles—the *Reader's Digest,* the Chicago *Tribune,* and the Hearst papers. Flynn saw Republicans as the group best suited to carry on the old liberal fight against expansion of the powers of the executive branch. After 1945 Flynn began to work with conservative lawyer Merwin K. Hart and the National Economic Council, and Edward A. Rumely and the Committee for Constitutional Government. Fascism, Flynn now argued, would destroy the economy, and the Communists would move in to pick up the pieces.[32]

China's impending fall indicated to the conservatives how serious the world crisis was. China had begun to collapse, Flynn would argue, when FDR met with Chiang Kai-shek and told him to form a united government with the Communists, thus "opening the way for Stalin to take Manchuria by compelling China to give him a half interest in the Chinese and Manchurian railroads." At Yalta the United States had made the mistake of bribing Stalin to enter the war against Japan, even though Stalin wanted only to enter at the war's end, when he could take what he wanted as a partner in victory. Stalin then asked for all of Asia. The fault was not Chiang's, as Dean Acheson had claimed. It was Franklin Roosevelt who had put China into Stalin's arms back in 1941. Flynn also had praise for domestic anti-Communists. It was HUAC that had the foresight to "put the finger on . . . traitorous elements inside our own government." At Yalta, under the influence of Communists, the United States had "betrayed our Chinese allies and handed over to Stalin Manchuria and the means of destroying China."[33]

The only way Flynn could explain such appeasement was by attributing the motivation to a domestic Communist conspiracy. Once he had said that American policy had caused the loss of China, however, Flynn denied the other major premise of the cold war—that the Soviet Union was "going to send any armies against us or our possessions." Russia had already been given East Germany, and would not go to war for more territory. To those who claimed she would attack West Germany, Flynn noted that there was "an awful lot of war talk to keep the people frightened and excited." His warning was sharp: "We must not picture Russia as itching for war, because that just is not so." Flynn thought Russia would act in a reasonable way to get what she wanted.

Stalin was a cold, sober, and calculating leader who accomplished his purposes with Western acquiescence, and Western

32. Frey, "John T. Flynn," pp. 276–277, 284–286.
33. Flynn, "Why China Is Lost," script No. 16, "Behind the Headlines," Aug. 21, 1949. Flynn had both weekly and daily radio programs, sold on a syndicated basis. The scripts are to be found in the Flynn MSS.

policy was so shortsighted that it might actually be contributing to the coming of world communism. If there was "to be a war with Russia we will have to start it," he stated, "because Russia banks on attaining her ends without a war." An American-inspired war was a possibility. War would give Americans "a chance to hate something with a grand fury and it seems virtuous instead of anti-Christian and barbarous." Flynn had one answer: stop "spending so much time talking about war with Russia and . . . begin thinking about peace in America."[34]

Russia's goals, he stated, were traditional Russian aims. Stalin had but "the same objectives as the Russia of the Czars . . . to dominate the affairs of Eastern Europe—the Balkans, the Baltic. Second, to make her way down to the Mediterranean, and third to dominate China."[35] She had won these without force. America had to completely revise her foreign policy. World War I had destroyed the economic life of Europe; World War II had changed the economic system and altered the nature of government; World War III would make the "Constitution and our traditional free life" a thing of the past. The United States had to abandon the theory "that we must make ourselves responsible for the well-being of the world." Like Robert A. Taft, Flynn favored a strong defense by stocking H-bombs and using air power. But he also advocated a realistic policy based on acceptance of the fact that "China is gone" and that the battle to win her back was "lost."[36]

The contest with Bolshevism was a contest between social systems, and time was on the side of the proponents of democracy. To end the cold war would be to loosen Stalin's grasp on Russia's internal society. Rather than move to fight Soviet Russia, Flynn suggested that "the course of wisdom for the American people would be to sit tight and put their faith in the immutable laws of human nature," which would work to weaken Stalin's reign. To do this, he argued, Americans would have to "make an end of the cold war."[37]

34. Flynn, "Is War Inevitable?" script No. 27, Nov. 6, 1949.
35. Flynn, "War and Taxes," script No. 39, Jan. 29, 1950.
36. Flynn, "A Foreign Policy for America," script No. 43, Feb. 26, 1950.
37. Flynn, "A Plan on Our Russian Front," script No. 44, March 5, 1950.

The cold war was soon to grow much hotter. For Korea the Truman administration gained a new, enormous defense budget, which had been called for in the secret National Security Council Resolution 68. Drafters of NSC 68 requested a $35 billion budget. Truman considered it hopeless to obtain this amount, since a reluctant Congress would grant at the most $17 billion. But the Korean crisis allowed him to recommend the higher amount. The Korean war was a boon—politically, economically, and socially—to American imperialism.

Flynn was aware of the economics involved. Tremendous spending for war was "going into the hands of factories, farmers, working men and is producing what the President calls great prosperity." But it was not a natural prosperity. Given a choice between risking war or facing "the danger of a frightful economic collapse in this country," Flynn thought American political leaders would choose war, which was politically safe. Economic collapse would ruin those responsible; war would not. On the contrary, war would cause the people to rally around those who caused it.[38]

As to Truman's assertion that the war was a "police action," Flynn replied that the first casualty of war is truth, and the obvious truth was that the war was not a police operation but a war. The administration's myth was a legal excuse to justify Truman's refusal to go before Congress for a declaration of war.

At the end of World War II the United States had allowed Russia to occupy North Korea, and was a party to partitioning. Eventually the North was governed by local Korean Communists and the South established a Western-style republic. The Koreans "didn't approve of this partition," and Flynn thought it inevitable that either North or South Koreans would try to reunite their country by a "civil war." If it were civil, the conflict could not be a case of North Korean or Russian aggression, even though Russia supported the North.

Flynn was alarmed that American leaders would use the war as preparation for a third world war. He warned Americans against

38. Flynn, "Stalin and the Cold War," script No. 59, June 18, 1950.

being influenced by "warriors infatuated with war," and he asked, at a time when most Americans were hearing about the need to defeat communism by military victory, "What can possibly be gained from victory?" While he stopped short at condemning Truman, Flynn attacked events that had "got us into the position which forced the President's action." Americans had to find a way to "disentangle [themselves] from these grim and tragic necessities." Unlike liberals who supported the Truman intervention, Flynn called depiction of the war as a UN action a "pathetic comic opera."[39]

One should pause at Flynn's analysis of Korea. At a time of almost total consensus he showed political courage and independent judgment. Most ironic is that Flynn's criticisms were voiced in spite of his belief in the Yalta myths—or maybe because he thought that the time when communism might have been stopped had passed. Now he asked Americans to "get tough" with themselves and find a way out.

Flynn may have been the first American to take public notice of the Truman administration's seemingly innocuous increase of American aid to the French military effort to pacify Indochina. There were, Flynn informed his weekly radio audience, other potential war areas in the cold war. One of these was Vietnam, which "was and is a French dependency." Explaining that "a rebellion has been in progress there for some time led by . . . Ho Chi Minh," Flynn reported that the "guerrilla war" had enabled the revolutionaries to gain "possession of a large part of the countryside." Truman, he reported, "has promised to send military equipment" to the French, and "an American military mission is . . . on its way to that country."

Either Indochina or Malay, he predicted, could replace Korea as a new area of military conflict. The question was how much the effort would cost the American taxpayer and how many soldiers would be required. Americans had to think of what lay beyond, and stop to ask where it would lead.[40]

It was an error to believe that Americans could bring freedom

39. Flynn, "After Korea—What?" script No. 63, July 16, 1950.
40. Flynn, "Who Is Next on Stalin's List?" script No. 65, July 30, 1950.

to Asia by fighting. "If we are preparing to make war to save Asia from dictatorships we will waste every dollar, every pound of steel and every precious life that is snuffed out in that foolish adventure." The end of such a great effort could not be to keep Asia from going Communist. China had done so, with U.S. approval. Without big-power interference, he thought, "almost all of Asia would go socialist." Because U.S. policy makers put the blame for Communist strength on Russia, the danger of American intervention existed anywhere that Russian-inspired revolutions broke out. Flynn rejected that course, as well as an attempt to fight Russia in Europe. Intervention would only produce a statist and totalitarian domestic government. America itself would become socialist, and would be destroyed.[41]

Flynn's worst fears began to materialize. A few months after he had warned his audience about Vietnam, Flynn reported that the "Communist army in Indo-China has trapped and captured 5,000 French soldiers." Vietnam was a "colonial dependency of the French empire," and the army protecting it was mainly composed of Frenchmen. Now they were being beaten "by the Indo-Chinese Communists instructed and armed by Russia." But the French were failing and needed arms. "So now," he noted, "we are going to send $2,450,000,000 to France, a large part apparently to be used to help the French whip the Indo-Chinese Communists." This was a clear case of U.S. "aggression," even though the "President says we are prepared to resist aggression anywhere in the world." How many billions the Indochinese war would cost America was anybody's guess. The only thing sure was "they will be our billions."[42]

The Korean war, Flynn thought, had been a defeat for genuine American needs. Even if the U.S. had won militarily, for American society Korea meant "the shifting of our activities to war measures . . . the piling on of the taxes, the prices and the prospect of a further and enormous increase in our debt." This all fitted in with Russia's plan to bankrupt American capitalism by dragging it into little wars. But during 1950 Flynn believed that

41. Flynn, "America's War Policy," script No. 69, Aug. 27, 1950.
42. Flynn, "Revolution Here and Abroad," script No. 78, Oct. 29, 1950.

the United States "dare not send soldiers" to Indochina. If it did, it would "only be proving the case of the Communists against America that we are defending French imperialism in Indo-China."[43]

John T. Flynn's criticism differed from that of both the Left and the Right. He rejected equally the view that victory in Korea could bring democracy to Asia and the plea for an all-out atomic war with Russia. He saw Korea as a "terrible disaster" in which at least 12,000 young American men had been killed and another 20,000 wounded. And what was worse was that "ahead of us lie more Koreas." We "could be at war in Indo-China," he said, and if the United States won or lost, "the price would be appalling." If war came, it would be due to American intervention in Asia, not to the presence of Russian armies in the United States.[44]

Flynn's analysis closely resembled the traditional socialist argument that the American economy depended on war produc-tion for prosperity. "The biggest industry in the United States," he wrote, "is the military industry." Americans had to ask themselves whether it was a "good thing . . . to get our whole economic life built on a huge industry like war." Getting out of war production would be six times worse than if the automobile business folded. It would be the equivalent economically of closing all car factories, all the oil companies, and the entire food and clothing industries. But now, Flynn gloomily wrote, America was "coming to resemble more and more the Europe from which men fled to America for safety and freedom." It was on the brink of a new major war. The President's budget for 1951–52 called for $58 billion, most of which went for defense. America was at the "edge of the precipice," he warned, and the next step would take it "over the brink and our destiny for a generation will be fixed in the dark and savage culture of war and a war-supported world."[45]

At a time when liberals as well as many conservatives united

43. Flynn, "What Is Stalin Driving At?" script No. 82, Nov. 26, 1950.

44. Flynn, "Fighting for Survival—of What?" script No. 88, Jan. 7, 1951.

45. Flynn, "War—America's Biggest Business," script No. 91, Jan. 28, 1951.

behind the presidential war in Korea, Flynn's attention was riveted on Vietnam. Prophetically, he perceived the direction in which the nation was moving. As the presidential primaries loomed in 1952, Flynn reflected that "it is entirely possible we may be getting casualty lists out of Indo-China before long." Giving his audience a brief history of that region's political development, he informed them that when the Japanese left, "a nationalist movement known as Viet-Minh took control of a large part of the country and in 1945 proclaimed the Republic of Viet-nam with Dr. Ho Chi Minh as its President." He was a Communist, Flynn acknowledged, "but he is an Indo-Chinese Communist."

Under Ho's leadership the "revolutionary movement had forced France to recognize Viet-Nam as a free state within a future Indo-Chinese federation." But when the French reneged on their agreement a war took place, which was "sapping the strength of France." The French now faced 400,000 armed Vietnamese. Quoting *The New York Times,* Flynn reminded his audience that the U.S. government was giving "hundreds of millions of dollars in materials and arms" to the French. The equipment included planes, tanks, and trucks. It was only a matter of time, he thought, when "the United States may have to make a decision as to whether or not it will get into another Asiatic war." Vietnam was rich in rubber, tin, rice, and other materials. Native governments were fighting nations they viewed as imperialist aggressors. Now, it grieved Flynn to note, the United States would be "put in the position of aiding the aggressors against the people, while Russia will pose as the defender of the natives against the European aggressors."[46]

Flynn objected to the cold-war rhetoric of press reports stating "that the free world faces a set-back in Indo-China." Asking Americans to keep their sights straight, he declared that "Indo-China is [not] part of the free world. It is a captive country. The captors are the French." To take the side of France meant that "we are put in the position of being not the free world but the

46. Flynn, "LBS No. 96," Jan. 15, 1952. The radio scripts are catalogued at this point in the Flynn MSS. as LBS.

imperialist world that has seized and exploited and dominated an Asiatic country." France *was* "the imperialist exploiter." The United States had become its ally.[47]

Flynn had a warped view of what he considered to be the conspiratorial origins of American-Soviet tensions. His opinion of Franklin D. Roosevelt prevented him from standing aside and looking objectively at the process that had led to the cold war. Yet despite the Yalta myths and his own McCarthyism, Flynn was waging a fundamental assault on the premises of the cold war.

The United States had not as yet created the Southeast Asia Treaty Organization, but Dean Acheson was beginning to talk about the need for such an organization. Flynn opposed such a pact, which, he argued, had failed in Europe and which ignored the basic *ideological* challenge of Soviet communism. It was insane to spend billions to arm Western Europe to defend itself against a Russian invasion when Russia had no intention of launching a military crusade.

Flynn thought a major issue in the 1952 presidential campaign might be Indochina. The U.S. had been spending great sums of money to rearm France, and now the French were demanding more funds or threatening withdrawal. They were asking for another $700 million in U.S. dollars, "to be spent in France to put workers to work in the arms factories." There would be no "limit to this drain on our resources," especially when the money went for fighting a French war that did not help America. Most surprising was Flynn's description of the Indochinese war: "The revolution in Indo-China was begun by Indo-Chinese against the French imperialist master in Indo-China. The truth about the matter is that France, Britain and Holland are all hated in Asia because these three countries have carried on their imperialistic aggressions in Asia for over a century. Now the United States is put in the position of being the partner and financial backer of the European powers most hated in Asia."

Despite this, Dean Acheson wanted to involve the United States "in a pact to defend the possessions of these European

47. Flynn, "LBS No. 126," Feb. 26, 1952.

imperialist countries." Flynn favored instead the alternative of arming Japan to defend herself and the Philippines. But the problem was that the State Department was dominated by its attachment to Britain in the Pacific, which meant an attachment to imperialist interests. The people of Asia, he wrote, were "aroused against those European nations which exploited them," and he called it "sheer madness for us to be identifying ourselves with this dying era." If France could not "defend her conquest of Indo-China certainly we have no business stepping in to take her place in the hatreds of the Asiatic peoples."[48]

America's evolving intervention in Indochina was not an aberration: the huge defense budget, growing debts, and autarchy were manifestations of consensus behind a globalist ideology. Both Democrats such as Dean Acheson and Republicans such as John Foster Dulles made "decisions about our foreign policy on the basis of the security of Britain or some other country." They thought that "for the United States to live in security" it must "police the whole world, fight the battles of the whole world, make every country in the world like the United States." Globalists tried to "frighten us by telling us Stalin will come over to eat us up, just as they told us Hitler would come over here." He rejected one popular view of Soviet Russia as a parallel to Nazi Germany. And he noted that the globalists backed Eisenhower in 1952 because "they believe he has taken his stand with Truman and Acheson and Dulles for the mad program of scattering our wealth and our income all over the world."[49]

Flynn rejected the bipartisan consensus that was at the heart of the cold-war strategy. Describing the forces behind globalism, Flynn predicted the New Left's emphasis on the role of corporate liberal policy-making bodies. A particular target was the Rockefeller-dominated Council on Foreign Relations, out of which policy makers Acheson and Dulles had both emerged. It had as its purpose "to take this great big globe on its lap and coddle it and exploit it." Sixty-four percent of its membership, Flynn noted, favored a *modus vivendi* with Communist China two short

48. Flynn, script No. 58, Aug. 13, 1952.
49. Flynn, "LBS No. 179," May 9, 1952.

months before the Korean war broke out. The globalist ideology was "supported by a strange partnership of leftists, politicians and certain business groups interested in trade."[50]

Like other prewar isolationists, Flynn attacked various schemes of the globalists, including universal military training, which they backed because it would provide jobs, even though it would glorify militarism as a way of life. The most powerful reason for attempts to save the world, Flynn reasoned, is that it keeps the factories working. This meant a commitment to put the country on a permanent militaristic basis. Of course, he commented sarcastically, it would all be done "under the banner of progress."[51]

Flynn was moved once again to state that America's leaders were "borrowing from Fascism." The popularity of fascism among liberal intellectuals was not unique. Flynn listed the many notables who had been admirers of Mussolini. Included were Columbia University President Nicholas Murray Butler, Congressman Sol Bloom of New York, diplomat Richard Washburn Child, and financier Thomas W. Lamont. Fascism promised jobs and security by large spending of money raised through taxes and government borrowing; the money was spent on arms production.

Mussolini had initiated "a kind of statism in which the govern-

50. Flynn radio speech, July 31, 1952; cf. G. William Domhoff, "Who Made American Foreign Policy: 1954–1963?" in David Horowitz, ed. *Corporations and the Cold War* (New York: MR Press, 1969), pp. 25–69.

Domhoff attempts to show how the power elite controls the making of U.S. foreign policy: "The most important institutions in foreign policy decision making are large corporations, closely related charitable foundations, two or three discussion and research associations financed by these corporations . . . the National Security Council . . . and specific committees appointed by the President." There is "no better starting point than the Council on Foreign Relations."

Domhoff treats the council as a middle ground "between the large corporations on the one hand and the federal government on the other." It is the link in the mechanism "by which the corporate rich formulate and transfer their wishes into government policy." It is, he concludes after lengthy discussion, "a key connection between the federal government and the owners and managers of the country's largest corporations." Its policy is one "of international involvement, as opposed to isolationism, for which it is called 'communist' and 'un-American' by older fashioned, nationalist critics" (pp. 27–28, 35–36).

51. Flynn, radio script No. 1, May 26, 1952.

ment should be responsible for the material welfare of the
people." Flynn would have called it socialism, but he noted that
Mussolini had called it fascism because that "didn't have a bad
name." But the only new industry to keep Italy prosperous was
"militarism and war." By 1937 Mussolini was spending 37
billion lire on the armed forces; now Americans were emulating
him. Since 1939 America had been floating on government
military spending. In Italy such a path had led only to war.[52]

With the presidential election nearing, Flynn adopted a partisan note: the responsibility for the Korean war lay with the
Democratic party. "The decisions which have involved us in this
frightful disaster . . . were made not by the military but by the
State Department." Military decisions had been made "under the
influence of Acheson and his Communist-ridden State Department." Like Taft, Flynn was alluding to Acheson's portrayal of
Korea as outside the U.S. defense perimeter.

Flynn's election-time analysis was close to the McCarthyite
position. The critical decision regarding Korea had been made at
Yalta. There FDR had "agreed to allow Russia to enter the war
in Asia and . . . to arm with American arms and munitions an
army of over a million Russians to invade Manchuria and
Korea." Communists in the State Department had wanted Russia
in the war so it could "get a foothold in China." United States
troops withdrew from South Korea in 1948 when Russia agreed
to withdraw simultaneously from the North. But by that time
North Korea had built up a Communist army of 150,000 trained
soldiers, while the South had only a token police force of 15,000
men. Dean Acheson had stated publicly in January 1950 that
Korea lay outside the defense perimeter of the United States.
"With that assurance," he concluded, "the Reds struck in
Korea."[53]

52. Flynn, "Borrowing from Fascism," script No. 227, K 263, Sept. 15,
1953.
53. Flynn, script No. 101, Oct. 13, 1952; see also Flynn to Demaree
Bess, Dec. 7, 1953. The State Department, he wrote Bess, had given out a
statement at the time of troop withdrawals that the entry of the Russian
Army into Korea was the result of an agreement between military com-
manders, who held to an arrangement to keep their respective armies at
different sides of the 38th parallel. "This statement I have known to be un-

The victory of the Eisenhower administration, as it turned out, gave Flynn little cause to rejoice. Events in Indochina continued to propel the new administration along the interventionist course Flynn had feared. He turned his attention to Vietnam, where, by early 1954, the Vietminh controlled over half the countryside. The French had put their finest troops into an isolated garrison north of Hanoi—Dien Bien Phu—and had invited the Vietnamese revolutionary army to come after them.

As the desperate situation at Dien Bien Phu became known, Flynn expressed relief that Eisenhower had "barred the sending of any American troops to Indo-China." The President had stated that the United States would not "get involved in an all-out war in any of those regions, particularly with large units." But Flynn worried still that Eisenhower contemplated a halfway war. He would have preferred that Eisenhower state "that we're not going to get involved in any kind of war in Indo-China, hot or lukewarm, all out or part-way."

Unlike Korea, in which the United States had become involved because of FDR's perfidy, any war in Vietnam would be inexcusable. Forty thousand Frenchmen were ruling 25 million Indochinese. "That's not," Flynn proclaimed, "the kind of thing we're supposed to be fighting for."[54] Events at the end of March 1954 indicated that the administration was edging toward military involvement. Behind the moves was Secretary of State John Foster Dulles, who, Flynn reported, had "told the American people that the Communists in Indo-China must be defeated" even if the U.S. had to go to war, and who "declared that if necessary the President of the United States can take this country into war in Indo-China without asking Congress." In the light of such statements Flynn concluded that "the greatest danger to the peace of this country is John Foster Dulles."

Flynn was suspicious of Dulles because he had been bred in Roosevelt's State Department and had had as protégé Alger Hiss,

---

true," Flynn wrote. "There existed a document signed by Stalin and F.D.R. at Yalta which allowed Russian armies to move North, but never to this day made public."

54. Flynn, script No. M-3, Feb. 14, 1954.

the very symbol of appeasement. The same globalists who had appeased communism at a time when Russian advances in Asia might have been stopped were now ready to risk war for a small strip at the bottom of Asia—a clear violation of constitutional government. Dulles was arguing on behalf of "instant massive retaliation," and he wanted the President to have power to declare war "and carry on war anywhere" if retaliation was deemed necessary.

There was hope, Flynn thought, only if Congress asserted itself. To those who asked what the consequences would be if the Communists conquered Indochina Flynn answered that the French had conquered it years before and that his own sympathies were with the Indochinese. He would prefer that the Indochinese "expel both the Chinese Reds and the French imperialists," but he did not favor sacrificing "the life of one American boy for this purpose."[55]

The hawks in Washington were not listening to Flynn, and neither was John Foster Dulles. Flynn accused the Secretary of State of personally declaring war on Indochina and of trying "to drag the United States in with him." He suggested "giving him a gun and sending him over there." The United States was already paying 56 percent of the cost of the French war—one billion, one hundred million dollars. That money was producing jobs in America. Conscripted Frenchmen were not sent to fight there, but if the U.S. entered, "we will draft American boys to save Indo-China for France whose government will not draft Frenchmen to fight for their imperial possession."

A few days earlier President Eisenhower had invoked the now famous domino theory: Southeast Asia was like a row of dominoes; if you knocked over the first, it was certain that the last would go over very quickly. "How silly can politicians get?" Flynn challenged. The time to weep over the loss of Asia had passed. "The Reds," he noted bluntly, "already have Asia." If the United States sent in troops, China would be likely to send in

55. Flynn, script No. M-10, April 4, 1954. Flynn ended with a cryptic aside on Dulles, who was "very keen about driving the Communists out of Indo-China, but [who] seems to be outraged at Senator Joe McCarthy, who wants to drive them out of the United States Government."

hers. Moreover, America's "noble allies" wanted "no part of this war." Britain, and even France, wanted to trade with Communist China. Flynn's advice was that Dulles "stop fighting Communism in Europe and Asia"—a bit of advice that would have meant ending the cold war.[56]

Flynn was not only an opponent of the cold-war consensus but of the new aggressive right wing in American politics. Vice-President Richard M. Nixon had suggested on April 16 that, "if to avoid further Communist expansion in Asia and Indo-China, we must take the risk now by putting our boys in, I think the Executive has to take the politically unpopular decision and do it." The Geneva Conference was due to convene on April 26, and Flynn regarded Nixon's trial balloon as monstrous. It indicated that the administration was opposed to abandoning Vietnam and to allowing Ho Chi Minh to make gains by a negotiated settlement. General Nathan Twining suggested dropping three small atomic bombs on the Vietminh troops. Winston Churchill gagged at this plan, which had been endorsed by Nixon and the Joint Chiefs of Staff, and eventually Eisenhower vetoed it. On May 7, 1954, Dien Bien Phu fell to the Vietminh.

The Eisenhower administration, Flynn concluded, had "been flirting with another war in Asia—ten thousand miles away," which the French were losing and had no stomach for fighting without aid from the United States. "These last few weeks Mr. Dulles has been making desperate efforts to keep the French fighting and to induce the British to join us in action." Flynn found it frightening that while President Eisenhower maintained "that he would engage in no war without a declaration of war by Congress," he continued to state that "he had the right to send troops anywhere in the world where he thought they might be needed, and without the consent of Congress." If he did send troops, Flynn assumed the "next step must be a declaration of war."[57]

Flynn was furious that Dulles was planning to "sprinkle [Asia] with American boys." To prevent an executive war in Indo-

56. Flynn, script No. M-11, April 11, 1954.
57. Flynn, script No. M-15, May 9, 1954.

china, Flynn supported a resolution introduced in the House by Congressman Frederic Coudert of New York, who "recently proposed an amendment to the defense budget to prohibit the sending of troops to Indo-China without the authority of Congress." But Eisenhower opposed and defeated it. Flynn feared the President was getting ready for some kind of action, maybe military, in Asia. And Dulles was openly seeking to get the United States into an alliance in Southeast Asia.[58]

Commenting on the Geneva Conference, Flynn stated that Eisenhower and his administration were "trying to decide whether they are going to spend their summer in Indo-China fighting another war." They had not as yet reached a decision to ask Congress for authority to enter such a war, and Flynn found it disconcerting that military staff talks had been held with officials of Britain, France, Australia, New Zealand, and the United States. Eisenhower was facing "the same trap that President Roosevelt" had faced in 1939. In Depression years only war had saved the country from continuing unemployment. Since 1941, Flynn reported sadly, America had "been living on the big business of war."

Without a new war to keep prosperity intact the 1950s' business boom would collapse and no means would exist to finance American capitalism. Eisenhower had been unable to find any substitute for war to keep fifteen or sixteen millions employed. The national debt was $274 billion, and the government was spending $2 billion per month on munitions production. But without a new war that business would drop. War spending could not be stepped up without a war. If war was the basis of the prosperity, the domestic cost was the "slavery of militarism for millions of young men," increased debts piled upon debts, high wages and prices, and continuing inflation.[59]

Flynn was relieved when the United States did not then send troops to Indochina. But the increased financial commitment of the Eisenhower administration led the United States into the circumstances that resulted in the subsequent military interven-

58. Flynn, script No. M-16, May 16, 1954.
59. Flynn, script No. M-19, June 6, 1954.

tions of the John F. Kennedy and Lyndon B. Johnson administrations. Flynn, who opposed the bipartisan cold-war consensus, would not have been surprised at the turn of events. One can wonder what the future would have been like had support emerged for the resolution introduced by Coudert, the conservative congressman from New York. It was only the conservatives who introduced and supported a resolution to limit the executive power, which they feared might be used to lead America into an Indochinese war.

How did Flynn, who saw America depending on war for prosperity, who courageously condemned the interventionist policies of both Democratic and Republican administrations, come to support and sponsor the anti-Communist crusade of Joe McCarthy? How did Flynn, who had attacked the FBI as an agency that harassed political dissidents, support McCarthy's smear campaign against Owen Lattimore?

Flynn had first turned against the Communists when they became militant advocates of collective security, before U.S. entrance into World War II. During the war the American Communists backed the Roosevelt administration, which they saw pursuing an antifascist united-front policy. Flynn believed that the Communists approved FDR's plan to have the big powers divide up the world with the Russians. That was the only time Communist advance could have been stopped. While Flynn had opposed the cold-war program of the Truman and Eisenhower administrations, he had always argued that the time to have prevented Communist triumphs was in 1945, when Roosevelt presided over the selling out of Eastern Europe to the Russians and China to Mao Tse-tung's troops.

Flynn first became acquainted with McCarthy in 1949, when the then unknown senator was carrying out an investigation into alleged mistreatment of accused Nazi war criminals by American troops in France. Flynn attempted to get McCarthy's charges published in the *Reader's Digest*. The magazine refused to go along with his request. McCarthy, however, thanked Flynn for trying. A year later, when McCarthy began his hunt for Communists in government, Flynn rushed to his defense. He solicited money for McCarthy's re-election campaign in 1952, generally praised the senator's efforts on radio, and accepted a medal on McCarthy's behalf from a right-wing women's group.[60]

McCarthy rode to power at the start of the Korean war, by repeating and popularizing the Yalta conspiracy theory as well as by impugning the patriotism of General George Marshall and the entire State Department. Flynn shared the analysis that Mc-Carthy evidently learned from the pen of World War II revisionist scholars Charles C. Tansill and Stefan Possony of Georgetown University. Scholars such as Owen Lattimore, who had been affiliated with the Institute of Pacific Relations (IPR), had served as researchers and China experts for Roosevelt's State Department. These individuals, Flynn argued, were either "members of the Communist Party" or had "promoted the Communist line . . . the Soviet line in Asia." It was their work that induced the State Department to sell out China to the Reds. The IPR, and Lattimore in particular, had "introduced its members into the most important sections of the State Department dealing with Asia and which, at an official conference of the State Department, formulated the final decisions to abandon Korea and China and even Formosa to the Communists."[61]

When the Senate initiated an investigation of McCarthy, Flynn argued that "the only crime he [has] committed has been to investigate communism in government." Flynn denied that Mc-Carthy had invaded the rights of freedom of speech and thought. He was not "investigating any man's right to be a Communist"; he was only investigating "whether Communists ought to be employed in the American army, the American State Department, the radar installations, the atomic energy laboratories and other government departments."[62]

Flynn did not pause to examine the logic of his own rationale for McCarthyism. His argument implied that belief in com-

60. McCarthy to Flynn, Aug. 1, 1949, and Nov. 28, 1952; Flynn to McCarthy, June 18, 1951; Flynn, address to the National Society of New England Women, May 6, 1954—all cited in Frey, "John T. Flynn," p. 335.

61. Flynn, "America's Unknown War: The War We Have Not Yet Begun to Fight," address before the Pennsylvania Manufacturers' Association, Feb. 24, 1953 (America's Future Publishers, Inc.).

62. Flynn, script No. M-16, May 16, 1954.

munism was automatically equatable with commitment to acts of treason, and that therefore an individual could be deprived of employment in government jobs because of his beliefs. McCarthyism, of course, affected many more individuals, depriving them of employment in private areas and occupations. Flynn had nothing to say about their plight. He did not ask whether it was valuable to have the right to be a Communist if it meant losing one's job. Flynn produced a strange justification, given the circumstances of his dismissal from the *New Republic* because of his antiwar beliefs. It was that episode that probably made Flynn personally vulnerable. As Murray Rothbard writes:

> Driven out of the media and journals of opinion by their erstwhile allies, condemned as reactionaries and neanderthals, the left and liberal opponents of war found themselves forced into a new alliance with individualists and with *laissez-faire* Republicans from the middle west. Damned everywhere as "ultra-rightists," many of the old liberals and leftists found themselves moving "rightward" ideologically as well; in many ways this move "rightward" was a self-fulfilling prophecy to the pro-war left. It was under this pressure that the final forging of the "Old Right" was completed. And the vanguard role of the Communist Party in vilifying these anti-war progressives understandably turned many of them not only into classical liberals but into almost fanatical anti-Communists as well.[63]

And FDR's tactics at Yalta, hidden from the public by the Truman administration, provided Flynn with further evidence that postwar administrations were carrying on with pre-Pearl Harbor diplomacy. But in this case the new administration was appeasing the Communists. Anticommunism strengthened Flynn's concern that Truman, like FDR, was attempting to divide the world with other big powers, behind the backs of Congress and the people.

In this context Flynn's emphasis on conspiracy at Yalta added up. Administration treachery had led to the communization of Asia, the tragedy in Korea. When Senator Joe McCarthy stepped into the breach opened by the void of bankrupt liberalism, Flynn

63. Murray N. Rothbard, "The Foreign Policy of the Old Right," unpubl. MS., p. 11.

considered him capable of forcing a change in the policies pursued by the statist postwar governments. McCarthy would be the vehicle for a new campaign to reassert congressional power against the pervasive power of the executive.

In addition, McCarthy was opposed by the very practitioners of the bipartisan cold war. One of their favorite arguments was that McCarthy was serving the interests of Russia and communism, since his spurious charges were weakening the world's confidence in America's stability and sense of justice. The liberals' charge only revealed that they also accepted the context in which McCarthy operated. If McCarthy called many liberals Communists, they responded by countering that his charges were aiding the Communists. Flynn saw the senator as an individual who also challenged the very political system favored by those liberals.

Both political parties, Flynn argued, no longer accepted the liberal political formula of "private enterprise functioning in a free society managed politically by a highly limited form of government." Many had come to favor the fascist form of rule he had tried to warn Americans about. Now the job was "to get all of the enemies of the welfare collectivist state into one camp and all of the proponents and beneficiaries of the welfare state in a different political camp." This meant that "one of our parties would have to go out of business." The first job was to "purge the Pinkoes out of the Republican Party." Flynn favored formation of a conservative group that would have the same role Americans for Democratic Action played vis-à-vis the Democrats—a caucus that could threaten to withdraw its support from the Republicans and work for their defeat at the polls.[64]

Flynn saw McCarthy as the man for that job. Eisenhower was untrustworthy. Before he was President, Flynn wrote, "Eisenhower was up in Columbia [University] literally surrounded by Communists." In that "heavily poisoned atmosphere" he never moved his finger against the Reds. Most important, Flynn argued that Eisenhower was definitely a "collectivist." Even if his life were at stake he would prove unable to state "the limits to his collectivism."

64. Flynn to Senator Karl E. Mundt, May 21, 1951.

Flynn admitted that McCarthy's "forthright stand" often made it difficult to accept him, and he too read McCarthy's charges "with some misgivings." But he thought Eisenhower was preparing to make a "deal of some kind with Russia," which would prove that the President was continuing the policy initiated by Roosevelt.[65] So he persisted in coming to McCarthy's support just at the time the senator was finally challenged by the Senate. He told Senator Karl E. Mundt that Americans were all living in "this miserable world built by Messrs. Roosevelt, Truman, et al." McCarthy was an antidote to this world, a "brave man" who stood up against "the calumny, the abuse and the talent for persecution which these revolutionary scoundrels have." Flynn found it understandable that Eisenhower had capitulated to the anti-McCarthy forces, since he "owes practically everything he has to the gang now under attack." But Flynn was not going their route. It was "no time for weakness," he wrote Mundt, "on the part of those who should stand with McCarthy holding up his hands."

Flynn was sickened that "those who should stand behind him at a difficult moment" were "running to cover." For Flynn, defense of McCarthy was a matter of principle. His hatred of the cold-war liberals had blinded him to McCarthy's demagoguery. He swallowed and propagated McCarthy's most questionable attacks. Although Flynn offered no evidence that McCarthy was developing an alternative foreign policy, he evidently thought his simple disdain of Communists guaranteed a fresh start. At this point Flynn's own critical judgment deserted him. It was enough that McCarthy was leading the fight against the architects of the new statist order.

Thinking perhaps of his own career and the agony he had suffered at the hands of liberals, Flynn saw triumph for McCarthy as validating his own lifelong fight. He himself, Flynn told Mundt, had had his "share on a scale equal to almost anyone's"; it had been easier to "liquidate writers than politicians."[66] Flynn embraced McCarthy as the liberals' major foe, and in so doing, he turned against his libertarian beliefs.

That Flynn's support of McCarthy was based on his view of

65. Flynn to Mundt, Dec. 9, 1954.
66. Flynn to Mundt, March 15, 1954.

him as an opponent of corporatism is indicated in his unusual account of what lay behind the Senate resolution of censure, which was spearheaded by the attack on McCarthy made by Senator Ralph Flanders. Flynn describes the "conspiracy" to destroy McCarthy as coming from his attack on the U.S. Army. Secretary of the Army Robert Stevens is described as former "head of a large textile business which he inherited from his father. He is a man of large wealth and apparently, left to himself, is a fairly decent person." John G. Adams, legal counsel to Stevens, was appointed to his position in October 1953. Flynn continues: "On January 21st, a group met in the office of the Attorney-General. Present were Attorney-General Herbert Brownell, Jr., Deputy Attorney-General William P. Rogers, hatchet-man John G. Adams . . . Sherman Adams, the top Presidential advisor from the White House, Gerald Morgan, another White House assistant, and Henry Cabot Lodge, United States representative to the United Nations."

These conspirators, Flynn argues, agreed to contact Senators Mundt, Everett Dirksen, Potter, and McClellan and enlist them in a plan to "file a series of charges against McCarthy and his aides Roy Cohn, Frank Carr, and G. David Schine." The "war on McCarthy," Flynn concludes, "got nowhere until the White House took a hand."[67]

According to Flynn, the White House moved only after McCarthy had attacked the scions of big wealth. Implicit in Flynn's analysis is that McCarthy was cut down because he opposed the interests of the governing powers and their corporate allies. In one sense Flynn was correct. McCarthy was stopped because eastern business interests began to feel that he was a threat to their legitimacy and their position. It was one thing to attack Communists, quite another to attack Robert Stevens. As one eastern businessman, president of a large manufacturing corporation put it: "When McCarthy starts doing that to one of us, it puts a whole new complexion on affairs."[68]

67. Flynn, *McCarthy, His War on American Reds and the Story of Those Who Oppose Him* (New York: America's Future Publishers, 1954), pp. 13–14.
68. Charles J. V. Murphy, "McCarthy and the Businessman," *Fortune* (April 1954), p. 190.

McCarthy *was* indeed a reactionary—but the large and stable corporate interests were not behind his fight. And it was hardly surprising that Flynn's support of McCarthy continued his isolation. Flynn broke with McCarthy only in 1956, when he was disillusioned to find that the senator advocated intervention in the Suez crisis by the "international marauders" Britain and France.[69] When McCarthy backed policies also favored by the liberal empire builders, Flynn could no longer go along with his fight.

Now Flynn was to be separated as well from his new conservative allies. Once McCarthy was cut down, conservatism began to move in new directions, to function as a right wing of the liberal establishment. "A new breed," Murray Rothbard has pointed out, "was marching on the scene to take over and transform the American Right wing." This group was led by another McCarthy backer, William F. Buckley, Jr. When he created the *National Review* in 1955, it soon became the undisputed leader of a scattered and fragmented right wing:

> Moreover, the Buckley forces brought to the fore of right-wing leadership in the Republican Party two internationalists; Senators Barry Goldwater, who had been an Eisenhower delegate at the 1952 convention, and William F. Knowland, who had been a follower of Earl Warren in California and who had voted against the Bricker amendment. *National Review* also brought to the intellectual leadership of the right-wing a new coalition of traditionalist Catholics and ex-Communists and ex-radicals whose major concern was the destruction of the god that failed them, the Soviet Union and world Communism. This change of focus from isolationism to global anti-Communism had been aided, in its early years, by the advent of Senator Joseph McCarthy, with whom Buckley had been allied. Before he launched his crusade, incidentally, McCarthy had not been considered a right-winger, but rather a middle-of-the-roader on domestic questions and an internationalist in foreign affairs.[70]

The new right wing discarded the anti-interventionism of a John T. Flynn and Oswald Garrison Villard with a ferocious

---

69. Flynn to McCarthy, Nov. 2, 1956, cited in Frey, "John T. Flynn," p. 336.
70. Rothbard, "The Foreign Policy of the Old Right," pp. 28–29.

commitment to a globalist struggle against world communism. It shared the fundamental assumption of the cold-warriors. Once the New Right had become an extreme wing in the cold-war consensus, Flynn would find that he was not a welcome member of the club. Flynn's sharp criticism of U.S. foreign policy and the cold war had been contemporaneous with support of McCarthy's domestic fight against the Communists.

Flynn had found in the late 1940s that his work was no longer welcome in the *New Republic*. Now he was to be rejected in the 1950s by Buckley's *National Review*. In the piece he sent the magazine Flynn had repeated his fondest arguments: militarism was a "job-making boondoggle"; its purpose was not defense but a means of bolstering "the economic system with jobs for soldiers and jobs and profits in the munitions plants." The Eisenhower administration was no better than its predecessors. Most of the national budget went for "so-called 'national security.' "[71]

Buckley, trying to humor Flynn, sent him $100 with his rejection of the article. His reasons for turning it down were instructive. It was difficult to defend Flynn's thesis, he wrote, "in the absence of any discussion whatever of the objective threat of the Soviet Union." His own opinion and that of the "other anti-Socialists on *National Review* is that the Communists pose an immediate threat to the freedom of each and every one of us." Buckley suggested that Flynn read William Henry Chamberlain's piece in *National Review* describing "the difference in the nature of the threat posed by the Commies and the Nazis."[72]

Flynn was rejected as not understanding the nature of the Soviet military threat, just as Bruce Bliven and the war liberals had attacked him for underestimating the Nazi threat in the 1930s. His argument was the same. The threat was not abroad—either in 1940 or in 1950. William Buckley's New Right ideology, which lay within the context of the cold-war consensus, did not countenance John T. Flynn's antiwar heresy, his persistent argument that the Soviet threat was not military.

Flynn returned the money, adding that he was "greatly obli-

71. Flynn article, n.d. (1956) enclosed in William F. Buckley, Jr., to Flynn, Oct. 22, 1956.
72. Ibid.

gated" to Buckley for "the little lecture."[73] Although Buckley apologized to Flynn the next day and attributed his arrogance "to gaucheness or inexperience for a clumsy effort at elucidating a profoundly felt conviction," and although he referred to Flynn as a "mentor in whose writings I never cease to delight and from whose courage I draw strength," Flynn's piece was not published.[74]

Flynn ended his public career in 1960, isolated from the radicals of the Left and from those who, in the name of conservatism, were propagating globalism and perpetual intervention abroad. The old globalist alliance had captured one more component for the consensus. Against all odds, Flynn insisted that the only threat was domestic militarism and fascism.

He devoted his efforts to pointing out that no Soviet threat existed, and to trying to get Americans to look at themselves rather than devoting their energies to shadowboxing a nonexistent menace. He fought the executive branch, which he feared would draw America into another Asian war in Indochina. Few heeded his warnings; he was just a fanatic of the Right. It was the greatest of ironies that Flynn's McCarthyism served, not to interfere with the efforts of the cold-warriors but rather, to permit liberals to ignore his warnings and to comfort themselves with the thought that their military actions in Asia were bringing democracy to a totalitarian world.

Flynn's fight was lonely and his efforts warped by his naïve adoption of McCarthyism—a wrongheadedness partly growing out of personal reasons. His prophecies came to be realized. American participation in an Indochinese war was a few years away. Once again the United States would be drawn into a quagmire without any awareness by the people or resolve by the Congress. The executive would act in secret and on its own initiative. Flynn's fight was marred by poor tactics and by his perverse support of Joe McCarthy, but it does not take away from the magnitude of his courage and the accuracy of his effort.

73. Flynn to Buckley, Oct. 23, 1956.
74. Buckley to Flynn, Oct. 24, 1956.

Lawrence Dennis (UNITED PRESS INTERNATIONAL PHOTO)

America's Dissident "Fascist": Lawrence Dennis

THE NAME Lawrence Dennis is more likely now to bring back vague memories only in an older generation of Americans of a time when Franklin D. Roosevelt's New Deal was thought by its defenders to be menaced by powerful and shrewd enemies of the far Right. Dennis was considered to be a major figure among the New Deal's opponents. As a supposed speech writer for Charles A. Lindbergh—advocate of a corporatist collectivist state—and as a member of a group of war opponents indicted for sedition in 1944, Dennis takes a front seat in the pantheon of conservative critics of the New Deal. A best-selling text in American history calls him "the intellectual leader and principal adviser of the Fascist groups." Along with William Dudley Pelley, Fritz J. Kuhn, and Gerald L. K. Smith, Dennis is accused of flooding "America with Nazi propaganda, [nurturing] anti-Semitic passions, and [being part of] an important component of the large isolationist faction after 1939."[1]

Dennis differs from the other subjects of this book in a major regard: he was self-defined as a fascist. Still, even liberal intellectuals show him a certain regard. Unlike the others, Arthur M. Schlesinger, Jr., writes, Dennis "brought to the advocacy of fascism powers of intelligence and style which always threatened to bring him . . . into the main tent." He "had Goebbels-like qualities," was "clever, glib and trenchant," and his "analysis cut

1. Arthur S. Link and William B. Catton, *American Epoch: A History of the United States, 1921–1945,* 4th ed. (New York: Knopf, 1973), II, 18.

Pelley, Kuhn, and Smith were overt anti-Semites and leaders in American-style pro-Nazi groups. Pelley lead a group called the Silver Shirts, modeled after Mussolini's Blackshirts. They were activists and pro-Nazi. The contents of their organizations and ideology were different from the fascism espoused by Dennis. Kuhn led the German-American Bund, and Smith was a supporter of Father Charles E. Coughlin.

through sentimental idealism with healthy effect"; his writing "had an analytic sharpness which made it more arresting than any of the conservative and most of the liberal political thought of the day."[2]

At first glimpse Dennis appears an unlikely candidate for America's leading fascist. Charles A. Lindbergh described Dennis as a man with a rugged look and dark complexion, who would seem more in place at a frontier trading post than in Washington.[3] Educated at Phillips Exeter and Harvard, he served briefly with the armed services, and was chargé d'affaires in Nicaragua during the revolution of 1926. From 1927 to 1930 he represented the banking house of J. W. Seligman in Peru.

After he left Seligman in 1930 Dennis became a critic of U.S. loans abroad and of investment banking practices. In the liberal *New Republic* Dennis revealed how American investors were defrauded by being coaxed into purchasing large amounts of foreign bonds on which the issuing governments had defaulted.[4] His experiences in Latin America had turned him into a confirmed noninterventionist. He had concluded that those peoples did not wish American intervention.[5]

In Nicaragua he had witnessed "continuous occupations under the hollow pretexts of protecting American lives and property and assisting the Nicaraguan Government with the supervision of elections, the maintenance of order and economic rehabilitation." Calling this just one of "many bloody phases of . . . prolonged adventures in dollar diplomacy," Dennis noted that 135 of our marines had been killed and 66 wounded, while the "Nicaraguan patriots who opposed our intervention, lost over 3000." Dennis could write "advisedly as well as feelingly" of these minor episodes of American imperialism because, as a member of the

2. Arthur M. Schlesinger, Jr., *The Politics of Upheaval: 1935–1936* (Boston: Houghton Mifflin, 1960), pp. 74–78.

3. Charles A. Lindbergh, *The Wartime Diaries of Charles A. Lindbergh* (New York: Harcourt Brace Jovanovich, 1970), p. 391 (entry of Sept. 17, 1940).

4. Lawrence Dennis, "What Overthrew Leguia?" *New Republic,* Sept. 17, 1930, pp. 117–120; and " 'Sold' on Foreign Bonds," *New Republic,* Dec. 17, 1930, pp. 131–134.

5. Dennis, "Reminiscences," p. 31, in Columbia University, Oral History Collection. Hereafter this source will be referred to as COHC.

Foreign Service in Nicaragua and Haiti, he had actually sent the telegram requesting the presence of marines.[6]

Dennis came to public attention with his first book, *Is Capitalism Doomed?*, which argued that the business community in the United States had destroyed the balance and stability of the old American capitalism. With a nostalgia for the age of small-scale production for a limited market, Dennis proposed measures prohibiting farmers from borrowing funds to expand and mechanize, suggested taxing large fortunes to prevent monopoly, and favored protection to exclude mass-produced foreign goods and the exit of U.S. capital.

"Our frontier days are over. . . . Capitalism has run down for want of new worlds to conquer." The internationalist bankers were leading America toward communism, and only new leadership could save the nation. The state must act decisively, planning consumption patterns, maintaining spending to keep up employment, and instituting protective tariffs. In lieu of that, war would become the only solution for unemployment. "Keeping six to eight million men unemployed," Dennis wrote, ". . . is the best known way to prepare for war. The day a war starts somewhere in the world, millions of unemployed . . . will heave a grateful sigh of relief. As American business picks up, American idealism will get acquainted with the moral issue of the New Armageddon, and history will repeat itself."[7]

Dennis' argument was welcomed by some radicals. The British intellectual and then Marxist John Strachey called him admirably realistic when "showing the fatal contradictions inherent in large-scale capitalism. He is especially powerful in his exposure of the rapidity of the present drive towards war." Strachey disagreed with the alternative of a return to modest, small-scale early

6. Dennis, *The Dynamics of War and Revolution* (New York: Weekly Foreign Letter, 1940), p. 108; see also Dennis, "Revolution, Recognition and Intervention," *Foreign Affairs* (Jan. 1931), "Nicaragua: In Again, Out Again," *Foreign Affairs* (April 1931), and "Columbia and the State Department," *New Republic,* March 2, 1932. After Dennis' book was turned down by a commercial publisher, he published it himself under the imprint of his own weekly newsletter, *The Weekly Foreign Letter.*

7. Dennis, *Is Capitalism Doomed?* (New York: Harper, 1932), pp. 91–93, 316.

capitalist methods, but concluded that Dennis had offered a more penetrating analysis than any professional capitalist economist.[8]

Dennis' advocacy of a return to laissez-faire was to be short-lived. Within a few years he had turned to formal advocacy of and identification with the doctrine of fascism. To Dennis, fascism was a system that provided the stability missing from either unrestricted competitive capitalism or from communism. A new managerial class pledged to centralized control and national unity was the only sound answer to America's developing crisis. Dennis did not advocate Nazism and Hitler's brutality as features of his own fascist system. But the very use of the term forced him into intellectual isolation. He was charged with favoring a Nazi victory and wishing for an American Hitler who would save the people from the Communistic New Deal.

Publication in 1936 of *The Coming American Fascism,* he later thought, got him labeled as a fascist, more because of the book's title than its contents, which few people read. Its thesis was that the world was faced with a choice between communism and fascism, both variants of socialism, "or a more or less equalitarian type of collectivism." Fascism was preferable to communism, because while the Communists would liquidate 40 percent of the labor force, a fascist regime would use and value the talents of businessmen. It was less evil, and more likely to succeed in America, because it would be easier on existing capitalists. Dennis denied that he was a member or a promoter of any party or "ism." He saw himself as an "objective student, observer and interpreter of current trends."[9]

Whether or not Dennis was simply an objective social analyst, he was arguing definitely that liberal capitalism had failed, that war would force the United States to move toward fascism, though it would remain disguised as democracy. Dennis was for a "desirable fascism," that would be instituted before it would become "an accomplished fact in the United States" by vile means. Fascism would preserve private property and the market

8. John Strachey, *The Coming Struggle for Power* (New York: Covici Friede, 1933), pp. 149–150.

9. Maximilian St. George and Lawrence Dennis, *A Trial on Trial: The Great Sedition Trial of 1944* (New York: National Civil Rights Committee, 1946), pp. 398–399.

system; efficiency could be maintained with a minimum of government regulation and control. "The ultimate objective," Dennis wrote, "is welfare through a strong national State, and neither the dictatorship of the proletarian nor the supremacy of private rights under any given set of rules." Unlike communism, which would end in a blood bath, a fascist regime could be organized by a managerial class around centralized control and national unity. A disciplined state, run by an elite devoted to the national interest, alone could avoid war.[10]

Dennis later argued that he had not called for fascism as much as for an American response to Hitler's and Mussolini's dependency on the power of the state. Rather than seeking an American Hitler or Mussolini, Dennis was pointing to the reality that the United States would have to go fascist in the same way that Germany and Italy had gone in order to respond to the Depression.[11]

The question is what exactly Dennis meant by fascism. Certainly not a totalitarian system based on the repressive mechanism of Hitler's and Mussolini's regimes. Dennis was firmly opposed to the probings of Congressman Martin Dies and the House Committee on Un-American Activities, which he thought was being used by the Roosevelt administration "for warmongering purposes," developing war hysteria and smearing isolationists. Rather than break diplomatic relations with Nazi Germany, which would eliminate Nazi agents in the U.S. overnight, Dennis noted that "the technique of the Dies smear is to identify opposition to American entry into war with activities of German agents too terrible to particularize." As a sequitur, any American who opposed "America's entry into war is a fellow conspirator and a criminal . . . The big idea is to damn, persecute or punish people for offenses which are not punishable under statutory laws." This "legalized smearing where legal indictment would be impossible," Dennis charged, "is a part of the American drift to Fascism and War."[12] Here Dennis was seeking to

10. Dennis, *The Coming American Fascism* (New York and London, Harper, 1936), pp. xi, 170–172, 190.

11. Dennis, COHC, pp. 11–12.

12. Dennis, "The Story Behind the Dies Committee," *Weekly Foreign Letter,* Nov. 28, 1940.

show that the regular policies of the Roosevelt administration were leading America unconsciously toward the "bad" fascism typical of the European regimes.

Dennis could be accused of moral neutrality. Nazi aggression, he argued, was hardly unique: "Germany, Italy and Japan are only doing what Britain, France and we ourselves have done repeatedly in the past."

> Have we forgotten our conquest of Mexico or our conquest of the entire continent from the Indians? What of England's countless conquests of the past three hundred years? Even today England is bombing defenseless Indian and Arab villages in wars of pacification. France has had on her hands a war of subjugation in Africa almost continuously since the end of the World War. In March Hitler united Germany and Austria virtually without bloodshed and our press raved over the "brutal rape of poor Austria." Between 1927 and 1932 the United States Marines in Nicaragua, a country of 600,000 inhabitants, killed some 3,000 natives. Did the European press rave over the wilful slaughter in a futile, undeclared war of American intervention?[13]

It did not seem to occur to Dennis that British, French, and American imperial brutality and oppression were neither sufficient nor logical justifications for Nazi expansion. Dennis was uncritically admiring of Hitler, whom he saw as a rational and practical politician who had transformed Germany from vanquished nation to Europe's master. Hitler knew how to lead the masses by means of emotion. He would not be stopped by a hysterical Western response.

Only appeasement, accommodation, and sharing with the "have not" powers, of which Germany was one, would avert a new war. Force, Dennis believed, had always ruled the world. When the democracies and the "have" powers held the upper hand, their rule of force was the rule of law. The logic of the West meant that "the rule of my force is the rule of law; the rule of your force, if it is against me, is the rule of lawlessness and violence." Instead of universally condemning reliance on the use

13. Dennis, "Propaganda for War: Model 1938," *American Mercury*, XLIV, No. 173 (May 1938), p. 7.

of force, Dennis recommended moral and political neutrality.[14]

Dennis became a serious contender for intellectual respectability with publication in 1940 of *The Dynamics of War and Revolution*. Here he treated nineteenth-century capitalism as triumphant because of abundant land, cheap labor, expanding markets, huge populations, and easy wars. These sources of success were about to dry up. Capitalism would become increasingly vulnerable to overproduction and depression, which meant the inevitable triumph of collectively directed societies.[15]

Capitalist rivalry would lead to war, and in such a contest only the "have not" nations had the necessary order and discipline to succeed. Unlike Marxist revolutionaries, Dennis did not call for the abolition of the existing social order. He believed an evolving corporatism would replace the existing chaos and guarantee national welfare by leveling income and increasing public ownership. A new socialism would center around the nation-state and lead to a genuine folk unity. The state would build public housing, institute socialized medicine, subsidize fuel and transportation, and supply free milk and food. A powerful elite would develop economic controls that would support full employment. The groundwork was being laid in the New Deal's corporate collectivism. It would be easier to maintain full employment through public works and fascist methods of control than through useless foreign conflict. Dennis despaired that such a course would be followed, however; he suspected that only an "anti-axis crusade for righteousness" would have the appeal necessary to mobilize the people and ease their suffering.[16]

War might be inevitable, but the Allied cause was "counterrevolution"; it upheld "the status quo and oppose[d] redistri-

14. Dennis, "After the Peace of Munich: Is Hitler a Madman?" *American Mercury*, XLVI, No. 181 (Jan. 1939), p. 15.

15. See the discussion in Justus D. Doenecke, "Lawrence Dennis: Revisionist of the Cold War," *Wisconsin Magazine of History*, LV, No. 4 (Summer 1972), 275–286, and Doenecke, "Lawrence Dennis: The Continuity of Isolationism," *Libertarian Analysis*, I, No. 1 (Winter 1970), 38–65. It is appropriate here to note my indebtedness to Professor Doenecke, whose two articles have led the way in the re-evaluation of Lawrence Dennis.

16. Doenecke, "Lawrence Dennis: Revisionist of the Cold War," p. 277.

bution [of wealth] according to the indications of need." The Allies proposed "a crusade in the name of moral absolutes to prevent world-wide redistributon of raw materials and economic opportunities." Either redistribution would be achieved at home or it would be fought abroad:

> The plutocracy that opposes redistribution at home is all for fighting it abroad. And the underprivileged masses who need redistribution in America are dumb enough to die fighting to prevent it abroad. The probabilities are that we shall have to come to the solution of the domestic problem of distribution through a futile crusade to prevent redistribution abroad. If it so happens, it will prove the final nail in the coffin of democracy in this country.[17]

Dennis was not advocating such a forbidding future, he hastened to explain, but only explaining the irreversibility of the new world revolution. America, as he later put it, would "go Fascist fighting Fascism," and he could not see "the sense of America fighting a war to stamp out Fascism to make communism master of Europe . . . and to establish Fascism in America."[18]

Dennis was not a simple Nazi. He believed fascism was rising in America because of the way he analyzed what was being accomplished by the Roosevelt administration under the guise of New Deal statism. "Capitalism is doomed and socialism will triumph."[19] Many of his readers were irritated or confused with Dennis' argument that fascism was just another word for a special kind of socialism; that the people who were called fascists were socialists, and that he looked up to Norman Thomas with admiration.[20]

Taking socialism as "broad and elastic in meaning," Dennis was arguing that it could be thought of as an operational concept. "I grant Norman Thomas's right to call himself a socialist but not to deny to Hitler or Stalin the right to call themselves socialists." Russian communism, Nazism, and Italian fascism were variants

17. Dennis, *Dynamics of War and Revolution,* p. 216.
18. St. George and Dennis, *A Trial on Trial,* p. 399.
19. Dennis, *Dynamics of War and Revolution,* p. xvi.
20. Dennis, COHC, p. 15.

of socialism, and the United States would develop "an American brand of national socialism."[21]

"The frontier was to Americans," Dennis wrote, "what the empire was to the British. . . . Getting rid of the American frontier amounted to getting the American empire." The American empire was informal. "Being Republican and Puritans we could not well call ours an Empire. We had no emperor. Besides, our governing . . . imperialists, the Eastern plutocracy, felt that the less said about their ownership and power, the better. They were interested in the take, not the glory. They wanted to rule indirectly and anonymously. Their principal device for ruling eventually . . . came to the modern corporation."[22]

Decades before historian William Appleman Williams' revisionist discussion about the connections between frontier ideology and foreign commercial expansion Dennis had argued that "what we now call capitalism, democracy and Americanism was simply the nineteenth-century formula of empire building as it worked in this country." The process of American expansion was the growth of the frontier, and now "the empire building along the lines of the nineteenth-century formula is over."[23]

The frontier, the classic gate of escape, had gone. America was necessarily moving toward national socialism—a path toward the "escape from escape." The contradictions of American capitalism had fully matured:

> Capitalism faces a dilemma it never faced before: it cannot raise living standards without reducing profits and the incentives to new investment and enterprise; at the same time it cannot maintain the necessary market for full production and employment without raising living standards of real wages at the expense of profits. This dilemma never existed for capitalism as long as it had a frontier, rapid growth, migration and a flourishing industrial revolution in progress.[24]

21. Dennis, *Dynamics of War and Revolution,* p. xxvi.
22. Ibid., pp. 67–68.
23. Ibid., pp. 68–70; cf. William Appleman Williams, "The Frontier Thesis and American Foreign Policy," in *History as a Way of Learning* (New York: New Viewpoints, 1974), pp. 137–157.
24. Dennis, *Dynamics of War and Revolution,* p. 81.

The corporate state, Dennis believed, would not be realized by development of domestic plans that would guarantee full employment. Rather, it would occur as a result of war with Germany and Japan. War "could be sold to the American people"; full employment would be a by-product. War collectivization would "replace the traditional American system with a totalitarian dictatorship by the Chief Executive in the exercise of his war powers." These measures, Dennis noted sarcastically, would be patriotic and applauded by men of goodwill. He should not "be prosecuted, investigated or even criticized for applauding it with all the enthusiasm of one who sincerely hopes for the revolutionary achievement of the new order which this plan and its governmental agents are eminently well suited to initiate under the smoke-screen of a war to preserve the American system and check the march of dictatorship abroad."[25]

Just as the Civil War had led to liquidation of slavery as a result of military and economic necessities, Presidential war powers exercised during World War II would lead to a complete socialization of American industry.

From the present perspective, Dennis' ideas were only some among many critiques of the collapse of the old capitalism, his solutions among many offered by dissident groups during the late 1930s. The conviction that Roosevelt and the New Deal were moving America toward fascism was not unique.[26] Still, Dennis' consistent advocacy and use of the term "fascism" guaranteed that he would not invite dispassionate response. Others could ignore his criticism easily and use Dennis as a scapegoat. Such was the case with the American Communist party. Dennis had confused them early in the game when he gave a favorable review to John Strachey's *The Coming Struggle for Power*. Strachey, an

25. Ibid., pp. 242–243.
26. See, e.g., John Haynes Holmes to Amos Pinchot, April 13, 1935, Amos Pinchot MSS., Box 56, Library of Congress, Wash., D.C. Holmes, the noted liberal minister, wrote that "the whole drift of governmental power into the hands of the Executive, during the last two years, represents a danger of formidable proportions. Taken together with certain other facts . . . it indicates a movement toward Fascism which may well alarm us all. I think that Fascism is definitely on the way, and may possibly be with us before we know it."

upper-class Englishman who was the major voice of the British Left, was helping to make Russian communism palatable to many Western liberals, and Dennis judged his arguments about the collapse of capitalism to be "impressive," although he disagreed that communism would replace it. Strachey had not proved that "in the classless society of the Communist millennium, after the dictatorship of the proletariat is no longer necessary for the liquidation of the bourgeoisie, there will not remain the classes of the governing and the governed."[27]

Recognizing Dennis as an opponent the Communists found it convenient to depict him as an American Adolf Hitler. Billing Dennis as the "Leader of Fascism in America," the CP sponsored a debate between him and one of their leaders, Clarence Hathaway. Hathaway said that a true debate was impossible: "Between a Fascist and a Communist nothing can be settled by debate. This issue will be decided on the barricades."[28]

Yet they did hold the debate. And top Communist leader William Z. Foster reviewed *The Dynamics of War and Revolution* in a 16-page essay in the *Communist,* proclaiming it "the most comprehensive statement . . . that has yet been made of the sprouting fascist movement in this country." Although Foster acknowledged that Dennis had no "organized movement" behind him, he called attention to Dennis' "wide contacts among big business and reactionary circles and [that] he is obviously seeking to become the intellectual head of the many spontaneous and confused fascist and semi-fascist tendencies, groups and organizations in the United States."[29]

27. Dennis, "A Communist Strachey," *Nation,* March 8, 1933, pp. 264–265. Strachey had an equally high regard for Dennis; see also St. George and Dennis, *A Trial on Trial,* p. 280. When Strachey "came to this country back in 1938 and was for a time detained at Ellis Island as a communist . . . he dropped Dennis a line with a copy of his newest book . . . Dennis had him out to his home for dinner and they sat up into the wee small hours talking politics and discussing the state of the world, about which they had as many disagreements as agreements."

28. Clarence Hathaway, "Fascist on Parade," *New Masses,* March 13, 1934, pp. 9–10.

29. William Z. Foster, "American Fascist Speaks Out," *Communist* (April 1941), pp. 333–349, quote on p. 333. Page nos. in the following text refer to this article.

What had infuriated Foster was Dennis' insistence on calling fascism a form of socialism. At that time the Nazi-Soviet Pact was in force and Russia had not yet been invaded. This posed a problem. Dennis also wanted to keep the United States out of war. But, Foster argued, Dennis opposed a belligerent role because he preferred "to let Hitler himself dispose of the British Empire, while the United States picks up the pieces and establishes fascism here in doing so" (p. 337).

The Communists could not ignore Dennis, because, as Foster explained, his "central fascist ideas represent the basic trend of finance capital and similarly of the policies of the Roosevelt Government." Dennis had argued that fascism would be brought in by FDR, a point that Foster interpreted quite differently from Dennis. The grouping of Russia, Germany, Italy, and Japan as socialist or national socialist countries was without foundation. The "socialism of the U.S.S.R. and the national 'socialism' of the fascist lands," Foster stated, "are opposite poles of modern social organization" (pp. 338–339).

To use government control of industry as a criterion of socialism was ridiculous, for it could point only to state capitalism, which had reached its highest point under fascism. It was, Foster retorted, a "crystallization of the capitalist counter-revolution" (pp. 338–339). "Socialist countries will not make war against each other," Foster predicted confidently, "but will live together harmoniously." Only a fascist world would be one beset with imperial war; "a socialist world will be a world permanently at peace" (p. 343).

If Dennis was a Nazi, why did his works reveal no anti-Semitism or racism? The answer was clear: Dennis [deemed] "it advisable not to arouse the antagonism of the workers by talking plainly on this matter." It was simple trickery that made Dennis "soft pedal anti-Semitism and anti-Negroism, which are organic to his fascist thesis." Dennis was one demagogue who did not "care to buck the widespread mass disapproval of such reactionary propaganda" (p. 343).

In contrast to Dennis' prescription for a new "folk unity," Foster held out "Soviet socialism" as the only basis for creating a "real national unity." Instead of "the false 'folk unity' of Hitler and Dennis with its terrorism, demagogy, cultivated ignorance, anti-Semitism and division of the people . . . the Soviet Union . . . has abolished classes and class hatreds." It was along the path they were treading that the world's peoples would find "unity, freedom, prosperity and maximum cultural development" (pp. 348–349).

Dennis received attention from more than the Communists. When other isolationists were discovering the liberal press closed to them, *Nation* readers shared a full-fledged debate between Dennis, pro-Soviet political scientist Frederick L. Schuman, and the Left-liberal columnist and political theorist Max Lerner.[30] The text reveals that American intellectuals took Dennis seriously, even though they disagreed with him fundamentally.

Schuman praised Dennis for having the courage to analyze the world in revolution. But as a Left nationalist he could not support Dennis' position of neutrality. Instead, Schuman favored a new dynamic America acting in concert with Britain and France, to impose "its will on the world by force." The Russians would respect such a show of strength, and the big powers could then remake the world in a fashion favorable to Americans.[31]

Dennis was pleased that Schuman took him seriously. But he attributed America's backwardness to capitalism in collapse, and pointed again to the need for a new dynamic system. War with capitalism's challengers could only be averted by creating an "expansive totalitarian collectivism directed by a non-hereditary functional elite." If such was developed, America would have no need to combine with other nations to restrain opponents of the *status quo*. He agreed with Schuman that Soviet Russia was acting rationally, because her system was in tune with the direction in which the world was moving. "The totalitarians are the rationalists," he argued, "the democracies the irrationalists." Instead of building its own vital system, Americans were likely to raise taxes, lower living standards, increase the class struggle,

30. "Who Owns the Future?" *Nation,* Jan. 11, 1941, pp. 36–44.
31. Frederick L. Schuman, "The Will to Survive," ibid., pp. 36–39.

and embark upon military adventures. Meanwhile a victorious Nazi Germany would undertake cooperative relations with dynamic totalitarian nation states.[32]

Dennis' analysis enraged liberal theorist Max Lerner. Lerner argued that American democracy was in reality "substance as well as dream." It was capable of controlling capitalism to serve the people's needs, and was worth fighting for. The culture was strong, not dying. American democracy would restore order in the world and defeat the fascist gangsters who fought for power and booty. Like the Communists, Lerner charged Dennis with seeking to develop an ideology for an American Nazism. Appealing for an end to friendly dialogue with Dennis, Lerner accused Dennis and his associates of being "political forerunners of the barbarians."[33]

Lerner's argument failed to sway Dennis. Those Lerner termed the barbarians would win, because they were leaders of all those nations engaged in creative social forms and expansionist systems. Dennis explained that he had no sympathy for Germany's and Japan's effort to create vast empires. But totalitarianism was inevitable; America itself was moving that way in the guise of fighting it abroad. Ironically, Dennis claimed to be working to oppose such totalitarianism by keeping America out of war. It was Lerner and the liberals who denounced totalitarianism, but who were actually "hastening it by crusading for American intervention in the war."[34]

Dennis' message may have been misunderstood by the Communists and the liberals, both of whom sought to depict him as an American proponent of Nazism. But Dennis received a different reception from a small group of Left Socialists and Communists. Left Socialist Freda Utley dissented from Dennis' conclusions but found much to agree with in his analysis of capitalism. His point, she noted, was that "the Haves want peace to enjoy the plenty won by past wars but the Have Nots refuse to accept peace with poverty." Utley saw Dennis as a courageous thinker in a world

32. Dennis, "The Party-State and the Elite," ibid., pp. 39–41.
33. Max Lerner, "The Dynamics of Democracy," ibid., pp. 41–44.
34. Dennis, Letters to the Editor, *Nation,* Jan. 25, 1941, pp. 111–112.

given to illusion, and she hoped that his views would be assessed dispassionately.[35]

Dennis' work was given its most subtle and penetrating evaluation by the small group of council Communists—individuals whom the Bolshevik leader Lenin had condemned as "infantile Leftists" and as "ultra-Left" sectarians. Karl Korsch, a German emigré and former Communist deputy in the Weimar Reichstag, understood that Dennis' writing did "not constitute a handbook and pocket guide for the American Hitler to come." Korsch saw his work as rational and consistent, and he argued that liberal intellectuals simply had no answer to Dennis' case for fascism. Korsch also accepted Dennis' treatment of Germany, Russia, and the United States as similar nation-states. He differed in the assessment of these nations only as revolutionary, viewing them instead as equally reactionary powers.[36]

Korsch and fellow emigré Paul Mattick viewed Dennis as a supporter of the new rationalized capitalism. In his journal, *Living Marxism,* Mattick treated Dennis as part of "a group of reactionary writers" who had begun to attack the old capitalism and its social organizations more vehemently than had exponents of the radical labor movement. Their prognosis of the growth of state capitalism had nothing in common with the fascist political movement, and Mattick argued that Dennis' book would find little appreciation among fascists or their opponents.

Mattick praised Dennis for understanding that capitalism's days were numbered, although he argued that any form of fascist system could not solve the problems inherited from old-style capitalism. Dennis was merely an advocate of state capitalism, fighting a family feud with the men of old wealth. Yet Dennis had insights into contemporary brutality. In the battle with the old capitalists, Mattick contended, Dennis would emerge the winner: "In this feud all the advantages are on the side of Dennis. . . . A liberal democrat could not possibly oppose his arguments with

35. Freda Utley, "Mr. Dennis' Dangerous Thoughts," *Common Sense* (Sept. 1940), pp. 23–24.
36. Karl Korsch, "Lawrence Dennis's Theory of 'Revolution,' " *Partisan Review,* VIII, No. 3 (May–June 1941), 244–247.

any measure of success. And in fighting Dennis' 'socialism' the laugh will be on Dennis' side, because his enemies will certainly in the process of fighting fascism have turned themselves into fascists."[37]

Mattick may not have realized exactly how, in the process of fighting Dennis, his enemies would "turn themselves into fascists." Dennis' opposition to the war and his talk about fascism would eventually make him a prime target. In 1944 Dennis and twenty-nine other right-wing opponents of Roosevelt whom the President believed guilty of "seditious" conduct were indicted and charged with conspiracy. FDR had prodded Attorney General Francis Biddle for months, asking him when he would indict the seditionists. Biddle finally acted, and they were brought to trial in Federal District Court in Washington, D.C.

"A grand rally of all the fanatic Roosevelt haters," James MacGregor Burns commented. It included Joseph E. McWilliams, chief of the Christian Mobilizers, who had called Roosevelt the "Jew King"; Elizabeth Dilling, anti-Communist author of *The Red Network;* admitted German agent George Sylvester Viereck; and William Dudley Pelley, leader of the Mussolini-like Silver Shirts.

The defendants, Burns wrote, "were charged with conspiring to overthrow the government in favor of a Nazi dictatorship and stating that the Japanese attack on Pearl Harbor was deliberately incited by Roosevelt and his gang; that the American government was controlled by Communists, international Jews, and plutocrats; that the Axis cause was the cause of morality and justice. The trial got under way amid histrionics but dwindled into endless legalism and obstructions; it lasted over seven months; the judge died before the conclusion; no retrial was held, and in the end the indictment was ingloriously dismissed. The trial did serve to muzzle 'seditious' propaganda, but it also revealed

37. Paul Mattick, "Fascism Made in U.S.A.," *Living Marxism,* V, No. 3 (Winter 1941), 1–30. Dennis was taken so seriously by the editors that they invited him to reply to Mattick's critique. His reply, "The Dynamics of War and Revolution," appeared immediately following the Mattick article, pp. 30–33. Dennis, however, only reiterated the theme of his book, arguing that the masses were "growing dissatisfied not with capitalism, but with the way it is working."

Roosevelt as a better Jeffersonian in principle than in practice."[38]

Dennis had been indicted under the Smith Act on the charge of conspiring with others to cause insubordination in the armed forces. The prosecution had attempted to prove its case exclusively by placing in evidence seven excerpts from his public writings, reprinted in the publication of the German-American Bund rather than as originally published.

Dennis and his lawyer, Maximilian St. George, defended on civil-libertarian grounds, accusing the government of using the methods of fascism against Dennis and invoking a vague use of conspiracy law. The trial, in fact, can be seen as similar to the great Communist trials of the 1950s, the Chicago Conspiracy Trial of 1969, and the Berrigan Harrisburg trial. The defendants, pulled together because of their views, were accused of conspiring because of their supposed common goals. "We see no sense of fairness in the use of the term Fascist or Nazi in connection with a trial for conspiracy to cause insubordination in the armed forces," Dennis wrote, "unless the defendants are all members of a party knowing all its criminal purposes, that calls itself Fascist or Nazi and that aims to cause insubordination in the armed forces."[39]

The question was whether his views made him a fascist and whether his publicly stated views proved he had conspired to bring about insubordination in the armed services "as a means to Nazifying the world." Fascist-baiting was "identical with red-baiting . . . the methods by which certain defendants were made to appear Fascists or Nazis were identically the . . . methods the people behind the Trial had complained of as having been used to make them out to be communists" (pp. 399, 402).

Like many on the postwar Left, Dennis charged the FBI and the Justice Department with having shown little respect for free speech during the war. The FBI, Dennis asserted in 1945, was an instrument of crime detection and prevention, but had not demonstrated a scrupulous regard for civil liberties. He called it a

38. James MacGregor Burns, *Roosevelt: The Soldier of Freedom: 1940–1945* (New York: Harcourt Brace Jovanovich, 1970), pp. 453–454.

39. St. George and Dennis, *A Trial on Trial,* p. 397. Page nos. in the following text refer to this work.

tool of partisan politics, whose actions added to "war hysteria against certain minorities" (pp. 409–411).

All conspiracy prosecutions had to cease, and Dennis tried to call attention to the dangers of abuse of conspiracy law and practice in politically motivated criminal indictments. Public interest, he argued, "does not require the mixing of non-criminal political utterances, writings, activities or doctrines in a charge of criminal conspiracy . . . There was no more reason to bring out, in a charge of conspiracy, the facts that most of the defendants were anti-semites, isolationists or anti-communists than there would have been in a trial of a group of New York City contractors on a charge of conspiring to defraud the city to bring out the facts that the defendents were all Irish or Jews and had always voted the Democratic ticket" (pp. 409–411).

> In the Sedition trial, the people with the bad intent were the Nazis who were not put on trial but were named as co-conspirators by [O. John] Rogge in the indictment and bill of particulars and throughout his opening statement. The Nazis were supposed to have had the evil intent of wanting to cause insubordination among the armed forces, while the defendants were supposed to be linked with the Nazis by reason of the fact that both Nazis and the defendants favored an isolationist policy for America, were against the communists and said uncomplimentary things about the Jews. (p. 419)

They had been indicted under the Smith Act, passed to prosecute Communists, because it did not, as in the espionage law, which was entirely court made, require proving an overt act by the alleged conspirators. Rather, the government could seek to gain indictment for insubordination by alleging a conspiracy as part of a worldwide movement (p. 91).

The defendants, in Dennis' view, were scapegoats, chosen because they had opposed administration policy. Still, American law did not allow for ideological prosecution. The trial took place because of pressure from many groups that wanted to quiet right-wing opponents. But thought and ideology, Dennis asserted, should be debated freely, not suppressed with the "soldier's rifle nor the policeman's club." Those who supported the trial supported the methods of Moscow, Nazi Germany, and Fascist Italy (p. 52).

Aside from the issue of law, Dennis' inclusion with the defendants was another matter. He was of a different caliber from that of the Bundists and anti-Semites indicted with him. Yet the prosecutor called him "the Alfred Rosenberg of the movement in this country," making an analogy between Dennis and the chief intellectual and cultural adviser to Hitler's Nazi movement in Germany. Dennis supplied ideas to the other defendants, was the "mentor and advisor" of American Nazi organizers, and was regarded by them as "the No. 1 American Nazi" and was himself "proud of the label" (p. 136).

Dennis retorted that the evidence introduced hardly proved that charge. He had also been in close contact with many Communists, leftists, and liberals. "The idea that a man is to be judged by the company he keeps," Dennis answered, "is not a safe rule to apply to writers who have to make a business of familiarizing themselves with all . . . points of view and causes" (pp. 279–280). As for the charge of being pro-Nazi, no evidence had been introduced to show him as head of "any organization or group or that he was a mere member of one in which he was recognized as a Nazi." Nor had he ever stated that he was for any form of Nazism in America. As for being an American equivalent of Nazi intellectual Alfred Rosenberg, Dennis noted that he was virtually unknown to members of the German-American Bund and that not one witness linked him with "any member or official of the Nazi party." He had been simply singled out by the prosecution as the best available man for the role of *eminence grise* to Nazi groups. "Proving that he fitted the role was simply a matter of defining the movement so as to include Dennis, and showing that Dennis had been quoted seven times by the Bund newspaper" (p. 282).

The tactic, in spite of the indictment's eventual dismissal, worked. Dennis' name indeed conjures up the image of Nazism. Some of Dennis' friends, however, disagreed. A totalitarian development in America was inevitable, revisionist historian Harry Elmer Barnes wrote, because of the refusal of capitalist democrats "to make reasonable reforms while reform is still possible."

But in the United States social crisis would produce a move to the Right, "because of the absence of a strong radical *bloc*." Referring to the "reality of American imperialism," Barnes argued that it produced a "proto-fascism" revealed in the "power of the FBI and intimidation of opponents." The trial's purpose, he suggested, was to make "the FDR Administration *seem* opposed to Fascism" and at the same time smear those who sought to "expose the Fascist trends" actually emerging through the "State Syndicalism or Capitalistic Syndicalism" initiated by the Roosevelt administration itself.[40]

The truth was, a friend wrote to Oswald Garrison Villard, that despite his reputation, Dennis was a socialist. He had shown exemplary conduct by refusing "to bow to the war crowd, coupled with his costly and courageous Sedition Trial fight," as well as by his "protest of policy back in Nicaragua." Taking into account the charge of fascist, Richard Koch wrote that Dennis differed "from other 'socialists' not in heart, but in practical realism." Liberal circles, "like the obtuse Tories, will some day regret their disregard of Dennis."[41]

Villard, who admitted that there was "a certain basic kinship" between his own "liberal ideas and those upheld by certain honest and fearless conservatives," perhaps because they had also been willing to criticize "Roosevelt and the war policies," admired "greatly [Dennis'] fight in the sedition case and much that he writes seems to me to be sound and entirely defensible." Dennis' ability was beyond question, but Villard wondered aloud whether his "leaning philosophically toward the fascist idea" could classify Dennis "as a liberal socialist."[42]

It would be stretching matters to judge Lawrence Dennis a liberal socialist—or a socialist libertarian. By his own words he favored an organic community—a collectivist society run by a small elite. But unlike those he was persuaded were introducing such a state—one that would develop without an overt revo-

40. Harry Elmer Barnes to John T. Flynn, Sept. 15, 1943, John T. Flynn MSS., Univ. of Oregon Library, Eugene, Ore.
41. Richard Koch to Oswald Garrison Villard, Sept. 8, 1946, Oswald Garrison Villard MSS., Houghton Library, Harvard Univ., Cambridge, Mass.
42. Ibid., Villard to Richard Koch, Sept. 12, 1946.

lution—Dennis insisted on announcing such goals and describing them as fascist. That error of judgment, more than any other, invited detractors and misapprehension of his analyses of the crisis of capitalism and his critique of the old order. Liberal circles never got around to regretting the disregard of Dennis, because they were not tempted to look back and find out what he had argued. Instead, they joined in celebrating firm action taken to prosecute the native fascists, and like Max Lerner, thought of Dennis as an apologist for barbarism.

Among the speakers at a political forum held February 5, 1935, under the auspices of the Beekman Hill Neighbors at the Beekman Tower in New York, were, left to right: James S. Sullivan, Socialist representative; Chase Mellen, Jr., for the Republicans; Lawrence Dennis, for the Fascists; James Roosevelt, eldest son of the President; and Henri Hart, for the Communists. (ACME)

Laissez-Faire Critic of the Cold War: Lawrence Dennis

LAWRENCE DENNIS was concerned with how mass attitudes and public opinion were formed. The answer to him was clear. Concepts advanced by journalists such as Walter Lippmann were passed on to teachers, professors, and writers, and were eventually heard on the radio and in the slant of the news as it appeared in evening papers. Walter Lippmann's statements about the issues would become FDR's policies in the 1944 campaign. Republicans had no answer as yet. They could straddle the issues and come up with an evasive platform, nominate Wendell Willkie or another candidate who approved the President's postwar plans, or nominate someone such as Colonel Robert R. McCormick, who, as publisher of the Chicago *Tribune,* opposed the President's expansionist policies. The first or second response would ensure a Roosevelt sweep. Dennis predicted, however, that the Republicans would avoid the issue and nominate Thomas E. Dewey.

"Foreign policy is the irrepressible issue," he argued. Lippmann had made the Democrats' position clear, and Republicans would have to respond firmly. The masses of people did not need to read Lippmann. Schools such as Columbia University's Teacher's College held classes for teachers from "back in the sticks," in which they were indoctrinated with theories such as Lippmann's, which they in turn taught to the children of farmers and factory workers in Iowa and Mississippi. "To know what is going to happen in America," Dennis advised, "you must read the *Nation* and the *New Republic,* not the *Wall Street Journal.*" What the liberal and radical papers had plugged twenty years before was now being put over. The Republicans had to develop a different policy.[1]

1. Lawrence Dennis to Clarence B. Hewes, July 17, 1943, Robert A. Taft MSS., Box 552, Library of Congress, Wash., D.C.

Rather than consistently opposing the New Deal world of global internationalism, the Republicans were to choose to support the over-all dimensions of Roosevelt's administration. Dennis retired to his farm to write his bitter response to the liberal press. Back in the 1930s, and until he was indicted in 1943, he had published the *Weekly Foreign Letter*. Now he began a new "private weekly news letter," a five-page mimeographed sheet, with the name—probably coincidental—of an old Socialist party newspaper, the *Appeal to Reason*. At a subscription price of $24 per year, it had about 300–500 subscribers, people prominent among the conservative elite.[2]

The war is over, announced the first issue; "it was never a religious war for any one ideology or ism about which all good Americans must be agreed." In the postwar era a political-ideological world unity was "to be imposed by force rather than sought exclusively by means of peaceful persuasion." It was the "world menace of the hour." Many misguided internationalists who now shape U.S. policies "appear to cherish this dangerous ideal"—UN supporters, one-worlders, as well as the champions of an Anglo-American military alliance.

These internationalists were preparing Americans for a new world war. Dennis advocated a return to formal neutrality, a path we had abandoned in 1914, while "interventionism [had] been given . . . the fullest and most expensive trial conceivable only to prove completely unworkable." It had been claimed that Germany and Hitler had forced the United States into the world war, "just as they will say tomorrow that it is Stalin and not they who will be getting America into the Third World War. Everything said against Hitler can be repeated against Stalin and Russia."[3]

2. See Justus Doenecke, "Lawrence Dennis: Revisionist of the Cold War," *Wisconsin Magazine of History*, LV, No. 4 (Summer 1972), 277. Doenecke notes that subscribers included Herbert Hoover, Burton K. Wheeler, General Robert E. Wood, General Albert C. Wedemeyer, Amos Pinchot, Truman Smith, and Bruce Barton.

3. *Appeal to Reason*, No. 1, March 30, 1946, pp. 1–3; cf. Les K. Adler and Thomas G. Paterson, "Red Fascism: The Merger of Nazi Germany and Soviet Russia in the American Image of Totalitarianism, 1930s–1950s," *American Historical Review*, LXXV (April 1970), 1046–64. Adler and Paterson argue that the American public came to accept an oversimplified

Alluding to "the war and spy hysteria" and the "total militarization of America through peacetime conscription," Dennis attacked Winston Churchill's speech at Fulton, Missouri, as a call to a new cold war, a political "bid for a come-back in a new coalition government which a Russian war scare might bring about." What was to be done about it? On this point Dennis differed from some of his conservative friends. Although "isolationists at heart," he commented, and truly alarmed over the growth of leftism, statism, bureaucracy, and intensified domestic class warfare, they had endorsed internationalism only to denounce its consequences.

Such conservatives wanted an Anglo-American world domination. They wanted to "get tough with Russia." Yet such a policy would "create for the communists just the conditions their internationally minded counterparts in Czarist Russia" had created before the Bolshevik victory. There was a choice—Churchill's alliance for war against Russia or neutrality. Churchill's policy would mean preventive atomic war. Since that was unthinkable, even to the policy makers, there would be efforts to provoke Russia into a war by tough talk, a policy already adopted by Senator Arthur Vandenberg and Secretary of State James F. Byrnes. America's interventions abroad were making more enemies than friends. The only solution, Dennis concluded, was to return to the traditional American policy of neutrality, as well as to the Enlightenment and the principles developed by humanity from the seventeenth through the nineteenth centuries.[4]

Dennis no longer considered himself an exponent of fascism. He had returned to a classical laissez-faire economic theory of a premonopolistic age. He saw himself as an old-fashioned capitalist, a follower of the free market, an exponent of the capitalism of "the dissenters, the rebels and the nonconformists whose main

---

thesis that the Soviet Union after World War II would operate internationally in the same way Germany had during the 1930s. "Once Russia was designated the 'enemy' by American leaders," they write, "Americans transferred their hatred for Hitler's Germany to Stalin's Russia with considerable ease and persuasion."

4. *Appeal to Reason*, No. 1, March 30, 1946, pp. 3–5. Hereafter *Appeal to Reason* will be cited by number, date, and page numbers, without the title.

motivations were not profit or money-making but either religious or intellectual self-expression, freedom and independence." American big business, whose representatives ruled the state and directed foreign policy, were not capitalists but bureaucrats, "the entering wedge for the socialist or statist bureaucracy." They were yes-men and conformists, not managers of independent free enterprise.[5]

America had become a socialist nation. Government spending on war, the military, and defense revealed the true character of the American state. "The most socialist institution of the State in America today," Dennis wrote, "is that of the armed forces . . . the free market or freedom of contract is out. The members of the armed forces, their dependents and their widows and orphans must be virtual wards of a paternal state." Just as Hitler had built his war machine through a strong national socialism, the U.S. defense program was "the most obvious and practical way imaginable to convert America to a totalitarian socialist basis." The same liberal leaders now calling for war on Soviet Russia would transform the United States into a "socialist society by conscription, controls and rationing."[6]

Major governmental subsidies to develop foreign markets meant socialism at home and war abroad. "Most people still think that the essence of socialism is a shift from private to public ownership, greater equalization of wealth and income and certain so-called economic reforms." Dennis disagreed. "They are all wrong. State planning and control of the economy, with enough spending of government or bank-created money to maintain full employment—that is now the essence of socialism in action."[7]

Dennis applied himself carefully to the day-by-day events of the growing cold war. Like a future generation of revisionist historians, he judged the Soviet Union at the war's end as weak and unprepared for war, but quite ready to seize advantage of Western political weaknesses. The spy scare and domestic anti-Soviet policies encouraged the notion that Russia had to be

5. No. 210, April 1, 1950, p. 5.
6. No. 251, Jan. 13, 1951, p. 5.
7. No. 170, June 25, 1949, p. 5.

halted. The truth was that the Soviet Union was only "exploiting our own irrationalities." The time to have stopped Russia was in mid-1943, when Germany's armies were deep in Russian territory. Having neglected that opportunity, it was absurd to try in the aftermath.[8]

World communism might spread in influence, and Russian foreign policy might be successful. But the United States could not make its policy rely on the imposition of our way on any foreign people. If the Communist revolution should surge forward, "we have to ride it out."[9]

Dennis opposed a postwar economic loan to Great Britain—an attempt to subsidize that country so that it would stand with the United States against Russia. "The enterprise is anti-Russian," he noted, "and we are against the enterprise, not the loan."[10] The new tension with Russia was itself a smoke screen to disguise our inability to create a healthy domestic program. "War unity [was] against a foreign devil. Yesterday it was Hitler; soon it will be Stalin."[11]

Dennis cited articles in *Life* attacking Stalin written by "well informed former leftists and Soviet sympathizers," individuals who had previously advocated unity with Russia against Hitler, the world's only devil. The *Appeal* "agrees with nearly everything bad the Russian war-mongers have to say against the Soviet regime, except the statement that it has a monopoly of sin."[12] One had to see whether Russia's European neighbors wanted to stop Russia. And Charles de Gaulle had given Americans the answer. "Americans may think they can lead a world crusade against communism but Catholic de Gaulle makes it plain that they cannot count on his kind in France to furnish cannon fodder for such a crusade as did the western European fascists for Hitler."[13]

The first major cold-war crisis, over the Dardanelles, was a logical and old Russian objective, as "logical and inevitable for

8. No. 2, April 6, 1946, p. 3.
9. No. 3, April 13, 1946, p. 4.
10. No. 5, April 27, 1946, p. 5.
11. No. 14, June 29, 1946, p. 1.
12. No. 14, June 29, 1946, p. 4.
13. No. 19, Aug. 3, 1946, p. 3.

Russia as our military control of Panama or Britain's of Gibraltar and Suez." Do American national interests require millions to die over the Dardanelles, in a bid for world domination, as opposition to Russian expansion as well as a bolstering of the declining British Empire?[14]

Truman dismissed Wallace from his Cabinet for persisting publicly in calling for an accommodation with Russia, while Byrnes and Vandenberg were applying the "get tough" line in negotiations in Paris. Dennis was glad for the apparent rupture in the bipartisan cold-war consensus. "We are against national unity based on fraud and leading to war." Byrnes and Vandenberg "are doing an FDR-Willkie." Dennis disagreed with Wallace's endorsement of separate spheres to be under mutual Soviet and American control. "We believe . . . that America and democracy means local self-government, not attempts by one or two nations at world domination."[15]

The Republicans were not providing a viable alternative. They were still trying to "give the impression that if they got in, they would run the Byrnes-Vandenberg foreign policy better and get us into war with Russia sooner than Harry." Dennis favored letting Stalin work things out on his own, a process that would make his neighbors rebel. War would only lead Europeans to regard the United States as imperialist.[16] American policy *was* based upon "continuous American subsidy for the operating deficits of British, French and Dutch imperialisms," and war preparation was costing every American $100 per year. The Republican failure to talk about that reality would be a boon for the Wallace movement.[17]

Truman's stance was meant to rationalize the continuing totalitarian trend within America as political leaders denounced communism in order to confuse issues. Truman, described by Dennis as "that pathetic little man from Missouri," was accused of fostering totalitarianism through his plan for universal military training. "Nothing could be more in the totalitarian and less in

14. No. 22, Aug. 24, 1946, p. 1.
15. No. 26, Sept. 21, 1946; quoted in Justus Doenecke, "Lawrence Dennis: Revisionist of the Cold War," p. 282.
16. No. 27, Sept. 28, 1946, pp. 1–3.
17. No. 41, Jan. 4, 1947, p. 1.

the great Anglo-Saxon tradition of the past three hundred years," Dennis wrote, "than a state ordained and militarily administered course of political indoctrination of the youth of this country with a view to 'insuring the continuation of our form of government.' "[18]

More ominous was the appointment of General George C. Marshall as new Secretary of State. The result would be "to put our most important policy above debate." It meant, as Dennis headlined, "NO CRITICS, NO FOES, NO POLITICS. 'RALLY ROUND THE FLAG, BOYS.' " Truman would use Marshall "to make foreign policy do for him what the war [had done] for FDR." Foreign policy would be, as was the social system in Russia, beyond criticism. It would make "little difference whether a Truman or a Dewey carrie[d] out our present foreign policy."[19]

The only division worth recording was between those who wanted a policy that could lead to war with Russia and those for whom avoiding such a war was a major objective. Dennis acknowledged that the Wallace camp sought to excuse and defend Russia, and on that score the anti-Soviet group had the better argument. Nevertheless Dennis insisted upon "good, old fashioned American neutrality." Russia was indeed sinful, but Dennis complained about those who say that sin anywhere in the world is something that the United States must do something about. "We don't believe in wars to prevent sin." Only local forces "acting more or less spontaneously and autonomously" could check Russian communism. Like Oswald Garrison Villard, Dennis was skeptical of Henry Wallace because of his prewar interventionism. He acknowledged, however, that "the strength of his position is that war with Russia can be shown to be bad business and a real danger."[20]

The announcement of the Truman Doctrine confirmed Dennis' fears. Marshall, he wrote, "says we must take over Greece and the mid-east to stop Russia and red sin. Another rat hole down which to pour American millions."[21] The doctrine, the "opening

18. No. 42, Jan. 11, 1947, p. 3.
19. Ibid., pp. 4–5.
20. No. 44, Jan. 25, 1947, pp. 4–5.
21. No. 49, March 1, 1947, p. 2.

gun of World War III," meant a policy "to bribe the unwilling and subsidize the incapable to stop communism and Russia." Totalitarianism would conquer, he warned, "as we scuttle American tradition for a messianic crusade all over the planet." Accepting the "Truman doctrine for a holy war on communist sin" would commit America to a permanent war economy. It would guarantee Truman's presidential victory, because a war President never lost an election. The Republican opposition, once it accepted the need to crusade against foreign devils, would be incapable of preventing his victory.[22]

The internationalist doctrine meant that "the executive has unlimited discretion to wage undeclared war anywhere, any time he considers our national security requires a blow be struck for good against sin." The congressional right to declare war was abandoned. Congress had to vote the funds for permanent executive war. Why was the conflict going to take place in Greece and Turkey rather than in China? The answer was obvious—"the Standard Oil monopolies in mid-east oil."[23]

Economically, the Truman Doctrine was "a substitute for the unsound foreign loans of the twenties which financed a large exports surplus." American leaders thought that large exports were needed to maintain domestic prosperity. The Truman Doctrine laid the basis for an exports surplus of $8 billion per year, which produced inflation. The doctrine was a "super W.P.A. project based on war, which, unlike welfare projects, is acceptable to Republicans." It meant statism, compulsion, and declining freedom, a move "leftwards with Truman to war against the left."[24]

Dennis called attention to a little-noticed speech by Undersecretary of State Dean Acheson, given at Cleveland, Mississippi, on May 8, 1947. It would later receive a detailed examination by many revisionist historians. Walter LaFeber noted that the speech revealed the motives and substance of the Marshall Plan for Western Europe. Acheson's advisers had concluded that U.S. exports were approaching $16 billion annually, while European

22. No. 51, March 15, 1947, pp. 1–3.
23. Ibid., p. 3.
24. No. 57, April 26, 1947, pp. 4–5.

imports added up to only half that amount and Europe did not have the dollars to make up the difference. If the United States did not grant credits to European importers, they would be unable to purchase American products.[25]

Dennis had grasped the relationship between economics and foreign policy: the Marshall Plan was based on a $5 billion–$10 billion deficit-financed exports surplus, and the Acheson speech was "the tip-off for those who needed one." The $5 billion exports surplus was being financed by the United States for our own national security, but the real dynamic was the excess of exports over imports. The function of foreign trade since 1914, Dennis argued, "has been to provide a means of dumping American products or selling a surplus that could not be marketed at home." It was made possible by banks giving foreigners "purchasing power to buy our exports surplus."[26]

Marshall had outlined the principles of his plan for European reconstruction at the Harvard commencement on June 5. The question he did not pose, Dennis wrote, is whether "we should cut this exports surplus and with it present levels of employment, business activity and inflationary prices." It could be done by ceasing to give away money. United States funds were being given to foreigners "to keep up war inflation to prevent post-war deflation, depression and unemployment." These subsidies made no sense, because they were only "stop-gap pump priming until we get another world war," which could occur over a Russian refusal to cooperate with the Marshall Plan and what might be their general obstruction.[27]

In truth, Dennis concluded, one purpose of the plan was to "enable foreign imperialist governments like those of Britain, France and Holland to spend billions a year on foreign military commitments to hang on to empires and imperial rackets now everywhere being challenged by local revolt." Wall Street would be the major beneficiary, since the plan would account for $5

25. Walter LaFeber, *America, Russia and the Cold War: 1945–1971* (New York: Wiley, 1972), p. 49; see also Thomas G. Paterson, *Soviet-American Confrontation* (Baltimore and London: Johns Hopkins Univ. Press, 1973), pp. 209–210.
26. No. 60, May 17, 1947, pp. 3–4.
27. No. 65, June 21, 1947, pp. 2–3.

billion per year of American production. It was the old prosperity formula of the 1920s in a new form, except "instead of getting the added money supply by expanding bank credit for brokers loans for a speculative boom, the boys now get it shovelled out of the US Treasury as an outright gift." Eventually it will be "1929 all over again only worse."[28]

Dennis was emerging as the most vociferous conservative critic of the cold war, the regular Republicans, in his opinion, having capitulated to the consensus. Following Truman on foreign policy, they had failed to develop a strategy for political victory.[29] Only Walter Lippmann had "pointed out the absurdity and bluff nature of our foreign policy—containing Russia." Pointing to Lippmann's critique of George F. Kennan's famous containment statement, Dennis seconded the journalist's observation that the Western European nations were no longer to be counted upon as members of a coalition led by the United States against the Soviet Union. If the Republicans persisted in their metooism, they would continue to fail.[30]

Dennis pointed to the close connection between our foreign policy and the demands of business and government for an expanding foreign market. Although the U.S. had never been in a better economic condition, plans for a new world war were "providing a foreign market for an American exports surplus four times as big as anything ever achieved in the twenties." The new exports would be financed by domestic taxation.[31] The demand for such foreign markets was not new:

> The big argument of the internationalists for over fifty years, or since the early nineties, was that the U.S. had reached a point in industrial development beyond which it would have to seek foreign markets for its otherwise unmarketable surplus. Thus we could no longer be "isolationists" or observe neutrality towards foreign wars. Taking sides in a war provided a foreign market, as

28. No. 67, July 7, 1947, pp. 1–4.
29. Ibid.
30. No. 77, Sept. 13, 1947, p. 2. Kennan's article appeared as "The Sources of Soviet Conduct," *Foreign Affairs*, XXV (July 1947), 566–582. Lippmann's book was *The Cold War: A Study in U.S. Policy* (New York: Harper, 1947).
31. No. 74, Aug. 23, 1947, p. 1.

when the Morgans floated a half billion loan for the British in World War I. . . . And after the war America had to make large foreign investments every year to provide for the marketing of otherwise unmarketable surplus.[32]

Like Charles Beard, who called for an Open Door at home, Dennis did not believe that America's domestic prosperity depended on acquiring more and more foreign markets. The belief that Americans could not consume all they produced was "imbecilic and anti-social." In classical laissez-faire terms, Dennis argued, foreign trade was only a matter of "nations exchanging things which they can spare for things which they cannot advantageously produce in sufficient quantity to meet domestic needs." A surplus of cotton and wheat could be exchanged for imports of coffee. But to search for foreign markets to get rid of over-all surplus was "asinine and idiotic." It ended by domestic financing of the exports surplus by new investments abroad or by gifts in the form of aid. "A people should consume all it produces and it should never know underproduction or large scale lack of employment for want of effective demand for peak output."[33]

Dennis was suspicious of this new globalism, and he concluded that those who had fought to limit the powers of the state had lost their old battle. Conservatives were now divided between those who wanted to limit the cost of new policies and those who wanted no limitation as to ends *or* means. Most wanted only to "keep it cheap," not to reassess policy itself. "President Truman, the shapers of American policy and opinion, the bureaucrats, military and F.B.I.," Dennis wrote, "are trying to make our system conform to the requirements of the new interventionist crusade." He wanted to fight the growth of government's power and its interventions. But the battle could not be won, as Taft would have it, "by supporting unlimited intervention abroad." Waging cold war via the Marshall Plan was not a substitute for sound trade or a way to solve Europe's economic problems.[34]

32. No. 239, Oct. 21, 1950, p. 2.
33. Ibid., p. 3. Dennis' view of the importance attributed to foreign markets by U.S. leaders may be compared with that taken by William Appleman Williams, *The Tragedy of American Diplomacy,* 2d rev. ed. (New York: Delta, 1972), pp. 30–32.
34. No. 95, Jan. 17, 1948, pp. 1–4.

As the election drew near, Dennis continued to reprove the Republicans for not supplying a meaningful opposition. "The only real opposition Truman is getting comes from persons and publications not in the odor of sanctity: *The Chicago Tribune,* the communist *Daily Worker,* Vice President Wallace, Senator [Claude] Pepper."[35] Republicans had joined in the official crusade. Former presidential candidate Alfred Landon had told an audience that the United States was against imperialist expansion. "Apparently he never had any American history," Dennis commented, "or he would know that is exactly how we grew: the Indian wars, the Mexican War, etc."[36]

This imperial tradition, Dennis argued, came from "the great Republican elder statesmen of the preceding generation—T.R., Hay, Root, Wickersham, Knox, William Howard Taft, Stimson and Nicholas Murray Butler, inspired by the teachings of our Mahan and Britain's Matthew Arnold, Rudyard Kipling and Cecil Rhodes." Aided by Carnegie money, they had made Anglophile internationalism fashionable. It was the Democrats who had made it work. And again, in 1948, the people could not "vote for peace because there will be only internationalist candidates in the running." Both parties were asking Congress to vote billions for war preparations and peacetime conscription. The voter was left no choice: "The Republicans offer war prevention internationalism with tax reduction and without economic controls. The Democrats offer it with more austerity and less dishonesty as to the costs and police state implications. Taft offers it with penny-pinching economy. Stassen offers it with oomph. It's a case of whether you want your internationalism served up by a corporation lawyer or a crusader."[37]

American policy was moving rapidly toward confrontation with the Soviet Union. Policy makers were planning to prevent war, but were acting on the assumption that it was inevitable. To admit reality was bad for the war campaign waged by both political parties. For that reason Dennis hoped the Republicans

35. No. 52, March 22, 1947, p. 5.
36. No. 67, July 7, 1947, p. 5.
37. No. 107, April 10, 1948, pp. 1–2.

would win in 1948. They would have a slight chance of avoiding war, especially if Henry Wallace polled a large vote. Support to Republicans was similar to sultans "picking their grand viziers and palace personnel from among the eunuchs." It might lead to a dissolution of the cold-war consensus.[38]

The nomination of Thomas E. Dewey, however, dampened Dennis' hopes. At the convention the Republicans dodged the issues and smothered discussion. "The atmosphere was that of an Elks convention rather than of a meeting of a major party confronted by the gravest crisis in modern history." If Dewey became President, he would appoint John Foster Dulles as Secretary of State. "For getting America into war," Dennis believed, "nothing could be better than a Wall Street lawyer who can preach peace through power to the church folks." Dewey meant more "statism, totalitarianism and dictatorship." The Republicans had accepted the central fallacy of U.S. policy—that controlling the world is purely a matter of power. But the more power is used compulsively, Dennis charged, the more uncontrollable are the consequences.[39]

When Tito broke firmly with Moscow, Dennis noted that Yugoslav developments vindicated his analysis of Soviet bloc affairs. Nationalist communism meant that Moscow could not control its ideological compatriots, and a precedent for schism within the Communist world had been set. Although he did not believe that the Russians would communize Western Europe, he argued that nationalism would keep a Communist West Europe out of their hands.[40]

Though he recognized that he was part of a tiny minority, Dennis said he got tired of hearing that he was fighting for a lost cause. It was now practical politics, he wrote, "to whoop it up for the lost cause of one's countrymen and personally disastrous to advocate its abandonment." It proved that "when a people have been sold the idea of committing suicide, the only safe course to follow is to help them do it." This "is the defense being made by

38. No. 108, April 17, 1948, pp. 1, 4.
39. No. 118, June 26, 1948, pp. 1–4.
40. No. 119, July 3, 1948, p. 1.

thousands of Germans now accused of having aided Hitler when his policies and actions ran counter to their best judgment."[41]

Truman won in part, he argued, because the Republicans had failed to challenge the anti-Communist foreign policy. They objected to increased government spending, higher taxes, new controls, and the welfare state, "but they fall, like the suckers they are, for the war and anti-red-sin features." There is "nothing you can't put over on American conservatives," Dennis lamented, "if you spice it with war and anti-red" talk. The "dumb Republicans thought they would win on a pedulum swing to the right and as an anti-communist party. What saps!"[42]

Truman's victory increased the danger of a new world war. "The Marxist assumption that the American capitalist-dominated West needs war," Dennis remarked, "is correct enough." But the Marxists argued that the West needed war to maintain high profits, while in truth it risked war to keep consumption and production high enough to avert mass unemployment and to maintain subsidies for Western Europe in order "to pay for a necessary imports surplus while they go socialist."[43]

Like Taft and Villard, Dennis saw the North Atlantic Treaty Organization as a culmination of a bankrupt foreign policy. Its ratification by the Senate would mark the high point in a long trend toward internationalism, scrapping the constitutional provision giving Congress the exclusive power to declare war. And it would confirm this country and its European satellites in a permanent state of war with Russia. NATO marked "the official beginning of our transition to a totalitarian society."[44]

Dennis condemned NATO as an American version of the German-Japanese agreement of November 1936. America was trying to ape Hitler, Dennis wrote, and was now paying him the homage of imitation. Already, in Germany, "Nazism is rapidly reviving under our military government." In seeking to turn Germany against Russia, the U.S. was pursuing a policy similar to Hitler's.[45]

41. No. 136, Nov. 30, 1948, p. 4.
42. No. 148, Jan. 22, 1949, pp. 1–2, 4.
43. No. 154, March 5, 1949, p. 1.
44. No. 156, March 19, 1949, p. 1.
45. No. 159, April 8, 1949, pp. 1, 3.

In addition, Dennis argued, NATO would promote and finance a European arms race, "aggravating the results of having fought the last war and of now preparing for the next." The theory of the pact was based on the assumption that if the State Department let the Soviet Union know that any move against Western Europe would produce an American attack on Russia, the Soviet leaders would hold back. That was a false historical analogy. Russia would not act as Hitler's Germany had acted. NATO would only help the Russians, by putting the United States on the losing side in the contest between western imperialism and its opponents.[46]

Dennis thought it an illusion that the goals of colonial subjects and those of western imperialists could be brought together through gradual solutions such as local autonomy. NATO was a firm military commitment to fight on the side of discredited European imperialism. Could war with Russia, he wondered, be sold to Europeans when it would be fought over the defense of empire? Dennis thought not. "Why die for Hong Kong, Britain's Opium War loot?"[47]

When Truman accompanied NATO with a demand for a new Military Assistance Program (MAP), Dennis branded the call as tantamount to a demand for a declaration of war against Russia. Quoting Marshall's statement that the U.S. had "to get the respect of Russia for the combined strength of the Allies," Dennis responded that without an armed Germany, no European war machine could be effectively created. And if Germany were rearmed, he demanded to know why our policy makers thought Russia would "stand idle while we do it."[48]

Unlike some on the political Right, Dennis condemned the fruits of interventionism in Asia. General Marshall was "messing around in the Chinese civil war with $400 billion of our money" as a result of policy that was "anti-communist, anti-Russian and anti-Nationalist." Declaring that policy to be "negative, preventing and restrictive," Dennis attacked the illusion that the U.S. could get the Kuomintang and the Communists to stop fighting,

46. No. 174, July 23, 1949, p. 1.
47. Ibid., pp. 3–5.
48. No. 176, Aug. 13, 1949, pp. 1–3.

when one or the other must eventually dominate. Mao Tse-tung's Communist army were not agents of Russian expansion. "If the communist nationalists win out in China," Dennis predicted, "they are bound to be anti-Moscow," just as Chiang's side would be anti-American if they won.[49]

Dennis' position on Asia did not fit the supposed pattern of the political Right—a group of Asia-firsters who supported a hardline anti-Communist policy in China while ignoring events in Europe. Rather, he argued that the task of Asian intervention was too large to undertake. The victory of the Chinese Communists proved that the United States was unable to master Asia by dollars or military force.[50]

Dennis ridiculed those who urged nonrecognition of the new Chinese Communist government. If the U.S. aided Chiang's troops in blockading Chinese ports and bombing cities, it would only strengthen the Communists and harm western nations with stakes in Asia. The U.S. had intervened and lost. Dennis was one of the few who urged diplomatic recognition. "Extending recognition of a state of facts is not a duty but a practical necessity if a nation wants to be practical. America doesn't. So we eat crow."[51]

On that issue Dennis split with Taft and Herbert Hoover, who had suggested that the U.S. Navy interpose itself between Taiwan and the Chinese mainland to contain the further spread of communism. Dennis was heartened that both the left- and right-wing press came out against "the Hoover-Taft demand for further U.S. armed intervention in China on the side of Chiang."[52]

When the Korean war broke out, Dennis became one of its staunchest opponents. He saw the Rhee government as corrupt, incompetent, and unpopular, and talk of victory was meaningless to him. Intervention would take 100,000 men, $2 billion of equipment, and an annual mobilization cost of $500 million per year. It would be undertaken to back one faction in a civil war. Korea reminded him "of the Battle of Tippermuir in 1644, when

49. No. 8, May 18, 1946, pp. 4–5.
50. No. 136, Nov. 30, 1948, p. 5; No. 141, Dec. 4, 1948, pp. 1, 4–5.
51. No. 192, Nov. 26, 1949, p. 1.
52. No. 198, Jan. 7, 1950, pp. 1–3.

the Knoxite Presbyterians fought the Cromwell religious fanatics, the two gangs being as much alike as two peas, under the banner proclaiming 'Jesus and No Quarter.' "[53]

The reality, he argued, was that the United States would be unable to win. The will of 450,000,000 Chinese opposed to Western imperialism could not be broken so easily. Dennis rejected the callous calls of those who favored dropping the atomic bomb on China or North Korea. Almost alone, he offered one viable alternative—unilateral withdrawal. Realizing that it was unlikely, Dennis asked: "How many American graves in Asia and how much austerity . . . in America" would it take "to generate opinion and popular demand for calling off America's crusade?"[54]

But the crusade was not to be called off. America's intervention was causing the Chinese to enter, and Russia and China were acting as allies. Alluding to Truman's little noticed announcement of economic aid to the French forces in Vietnam, Dennis forecast a possible result of U.S. intervention: "Indo-China is now beckoning thousands of Americans to fresh dug graves."[55]

Unlike other conservatives, Dennis did not support the position taken by Douglas MacArthur. Favoring diplomacy over the use of force, Dennis feared that frustration would lead to American atomic bombing of Chinese cities. Such a course would be "mass murder by American bombers." Terming such actions crimes against humanity, Dennis believed that bombing might take place if the only options were withdrawal or an endless land war. At a moment when Republicans could offer real opposition, they were still trying to criticize the conduct of the war and refrain from opposition. Dennis called for a bold and radical opposition that would refute arguments treating Mao as Stalin's stooge and would truthfully point out that China's entrance into the war was logical. MacArthur had approached China's borders, and it was irrational to think she could stay out. "Would America

53. No. 223, July 1, 1950, pp. 1–2.
54. No. 227, July 29, 1950, pp. 2–4.
55. No. 235, Sept. 23, 1950, pp. 4–5; No. 239, Oct. 21, 1950, p. 5.

bow to the fiat of a European bloc . . . and stay out of Mexico while a European nation dominated Mexico and approached our border with a large armed force?"[56]

Dennis was most upset about the arrogance of those who wanted to use American air power to unleash mass destruction on the Chinese. Even without atomic warfare, the U.S. was turning large areas of Korea into scorched earth. Millions were being rendered homeless and left with no means of subsistence. America waged war of a new sort—"mass murder by American technology."[57]

His forthright opposition led Dennis to approve Truman's abrupt dismissal of MacArthur. Total victory desired by the General was an illusion. Given a choice between all-out global war and Truman's limited war, Dennis opted for the latter. It was better only because it was smaller. Taft and other conservatives who supported MacArthur simply did not understand his desires. Dennis caught those conservatives in an ironic contradiction. In June 1950 they failed to demand impeachment of President Truman for starting a war without a declaration of war by Congress. Yet in 1951 they were demanding impeachment of the President "for sacking a general in command who wanted to spread that war"—despite the fact that the MacArthur course could only mean more mass murder, huge expenses for the American population, and the use of U.S. troops to back up Chiang's beaten forces.[58]

Dennis persisted with his hard questions. "If the new military magic of strategic bombing can lick red China without the use of American combat troops in land action on the Chinese mainland, why couldn't . . . such magic make possible our speedy mopping up of the criminal aggressor in Korea?" How could Chiang's

56. No. 241, Nov. 4, 1950, pp. 1–4; No. 242, Nov. 11, 1950, pp. 2–5.

57. No. 251, Jan. 13, 1951, pp. 2–3; No. 253, Jan. 27, 1951, p. 5; see also Joyce and Gabriel Kolko, *The Limits of Power* (New York: Harper and Row, 1972), pp. 615–616. The Kolkos refer to the "process of utter destruction" engaged in by the U.S. bomber command during the Korean war. By the end of the first year of combat the U.S. had dropped 97,000 tons of bombs and 7.8 million gallons of napalm on Korea. Over one million South Koreans died as a result.

58. No. 264, April 14, 1951, pp. 1–4.

troops, licked in battle, be expected to do the job? "Mac thought and gambled that the Chinese would not fight after they had seen him in action. He now thinks the Russians won't fight after our forces give China the air works." Dennis was beginning to sound like some of the liberal critics who were condemning the support given MacArthur by Robert A. Taft. Like these liberals, Dennis failed to see how a bigger war could be won when the U.S. proved itself capable only of losing a smaller war.[59]

America had lacked an opposition for the past decade. Americans were propagandized consistently on the application of force. If MacArthur and his supporters united America around their program, it would be disastrous. Dennis hoped for enough disunity to check the impulse toward war. But he was fearful of Eisenhower's candidacy in 1952, believing him more dangerous than Truman, smarter and more popular. The General, he feared, might unify the American populace behind a new international global crusade.[60]

Dennis was also critical of Taft, who had supported MacArthur and who had not challenged the basic premises of U.S. foreign policy. Still, Dennis thought Taft the least likely candidate to engage in crusades or holy wars. Eisenhower's electoral victory and Dulles' appointment as Secretary of State were alarming. "Nothing short of total global victory over red sin," he wrote, "will satisfy Dulles." Dennis was also alarmed by the doctrine of "massive retaliation," and as other conservatives had done, he endorsed Senator John Bricker's proposed constitutional amendment restricting presidential power in treaty making. With Dulles' new doctrine of massive retaliation, Dennis thought the U.S. might retaliate "when and wherever sin starts popping."[61]

Dennis had begun to warn his readers about the possibility of a new war in Southeast Asia. When it appeared that full-scale intervention in Indochina might occur in 1954, Dennis was pointing out that the U.S. was still incapable of choosing a

59. No. 266, April 28, 1951, pp. 1–2.
60. Ibid., pp. 4–5.
61. No. 310, April 26, 1952; No. 336, Aug. 30, 1952; No. 348, Nov. 22, 1952; No. 408, Jan. 16, 1954; cited in Doenecke, "Lawrence Dennis: Revisionist of the Cold War," pp. 282–283.

winner. When the French forces collapsed at Dien Bien Phu, he remarked: "Don't forget. We told you so." As for SEATO, the Pacific equivalent of the North Atlantic Treaty Organization, Dennis opposed it as a contemporary manifestation of the Spanish Inquisition.[62]

Dennis' record of opposition to cold-war foreign policy makes clear that he was not the Asia-firster described by critics of "rightwing" isolationism. That mythical person is most often described also as a domestic McCarthyite. In John T. Flynn's case a critique of the cold war was accompanied by an uncritical commitment to the domestic crusade against communism. But Dennis fought domestic repression, placing the roots of what came to be known as McCarthyism in the anti-Communist policies of the Truman administration. "Accepting the Truman doctrine for a holy war on communist sin all over the world," he commented, "commits America to a permanent war emergency." Witch hunts and loyalty tests, "ostensibly aimed at the communists, are counted on to take care of any opposition."[63]

Talk of a world Communist menace distracted attention from

62. No. 421, April 17, 1954; No. 518, Feb. 25, 1956; cited in Justus Doenecke, "Lawrence Dennis: Revisionist of the Cold War," p. 283.

63. No. 51, March 15, 1947, pp. 2–3; No. 52, March 22, 1947, p. 5. Dennis' analysis bears striking similarity to the works of new revisionist historians. See Richard M. Freeland, *The Truman Doctrine and the Origins of McCarthyism* (New York: Knopf, 1972), p. 360. Freeland's thesis is that in "1947–8, in order to mobilize the country behind his foreign policies, Truman himself employed and permitted his subordinates to employ many of the same means of restricting democratic freedoms that he would later condemn. He legitimized or tried to legitimize for use in peacetime restrictions on traditional freedoms that had previously been limited in application to wartime emergencies. The practices of McCarthyism were Truman's practices in cruder hands, just as the language of McCarthyism was Truman's language, in less well-meaning voices."

Cf. Athan Theoharis, *Seeds of Repression: Harry S. Truman and the Origins of McCarthyism* (Chicago: Quadrangle Books, 1971), p. vii. Theoharis writes: "McCarthy's charges of communist influence in fact paralleled, in an exaggerated way, the popular obsession with national security that arose after World War II. The Truman administration committed itself to victory over communism and to safeguarding the nation from external and internal threats; the rhetoric of McCarthyism was in this sense well within the framework of Cold War politics. The Senator and the administration differed not so much over ends as over means and emphasis."

America's warped policies. "As the world conspiracy the Mundt-Nixon bill and the anti-communist crusaders depict," Dennis wrote, "communism is a joke and a nuisance to Russia. The communism we hear denounced these days is no menace to us . . . The communist atrocities which consist solely of actions and words exploiting our mistakes and weaknesses are the real communist menace, but they are almost never the subject of the diatribes of our anti-communist crusaders." Communists could gain power only when a total breakdown in society took place—as a result, perhaps, of a disastrous war. And in that condition, no laws could prevent their victory. The anti-Communist measures were therefore "silly and futile." Americans had to make an effort to prevent collapse of their economy, and that, Dennis argued, "can never be done by means of laws or police acts of the state."[64]

To sell its foreign policy to the American people, Dennis wrote, the administration had to keep the people fooled about its imperatives. Thus it prepared indictments under the Smith Act of the twelve top Communist party leaders. Dennis criticized those liberals who were arguing that one had to wait and see the government's evidence. They were ignoring the "peculiar nature of the indictment." Dennis pointed out how the government prosecuted such cases, as a result of his own indictment under the Smith Act in 1943. The evidence would be introduction of the "Communist classics, mostly antedating the Russian revolution and all antedating 1945." They would try to show that the Communist leaders followed "the line of the communist classics," which supposedly favored use of force and violence. Asserting that Communists had always taken power in a legal fashion, Dennis argued that even if their doctrines and classics advocated force, "the fact that any given person is a communist no more proves that the given person is now in a conspiracy to overthrow the government by violence than the fact that the golden rule is a Christian doctrine" meant that every Christian obeyed the golden rule. The truth was, he stated, that the Communists had adopted a new line in 1945, and the party

64. No. 119, July 3, 1948, pp. 2–3.

expressly forbade membership to anyone who favored overthrow of the government by force or violence.[65]

The Smith Act indictments were political trials, attempts to prove a political thesis that was inadmissible as a prosecution under Western law. Cases of espionage or sabotage were criminal charges that could be proved under legal rules. But whether the accused was a Communist would then be irrelevant, as it would be to a charge on a regular criminal case. "What is needed in a criminal case," he noted, "is facts showing criminal intent and the commission of a criminal act, not a lot of bilge about ideologies and the war of ideas which has absolutely no place in any decent, properly run Anglo-Saxon court of law."[66]

"Burning witches or lynching subversives," Dennis wrote, would not save America from the consequences of its policies. "Any Russian spy dumb enough to get caught by our FBI," he wrote, "is a good riddance for the reds." The Hiss case, which assumed major proportions in terms of the supposed evidence of Communist perfidy in the top levels of government, was not a serious matter. Agreeing with Truman that the Hiss case was a "red herring," Dennis argued that it was practically impossible to prove a charge of perjury. To jail Alger Hiss, "a Carnegie Foundation parlor pink for perjury," he wrote, "makes the same sort of sense that jailing Al Capone on an income tax evasion charge made." In Dennis' view, FDR and policy makers such as John Foster Dulles, who pursued international policies that strengthened communism, were those who should be standing trial. The guilty ones were the "eastern internationalists of great wealth and power," not men such as Hiss.[67]

While security would not hinder spies, the people's right to know would be taken away in the guise of protecting national security. The pumpkin papers Hiss was supposed to have passed on contained no secrets, Dennis wrote, only revelations about proposed negotiations between the U.S. and Nazi Germany, which Stalin knew about on his own. Whatever concessions Stalin won at Yalta, Dennis reasoned, did not come from "purloined

65. No. 123, July 31, 1948, pp. 3–4.
66. Ibid., p. 5.
67. No. 125, Aug. 14, 1948, pp. 1–2; No. 143, Dec. 18, 1948, pp. 1–2.

papers from the State Department." Ex-Communists such as Whittaker Chambers and Elizabeth Bentley, who were testifying against their former comrades, were "anti-red renegades and squealers . . . neurotic, nutty apostates" whom the Communists were fortunate to lose. It was absurd to jail anyone because of the testimony presented by this "on again, off again, rice-Christian variety."[68]

When Senator Joseph McCarthy first gained national attention, Dennis remarked sarcastically that he was doing a "grand job . . . giving the American people what they love, crime and mystery stories." Dennis feared that to prove himself sufficiently anti-Communist, Harry S. Truman would "have to start a foreign war to stop the domestic witch hunt."[69]

The Republican leaders seemed excited about McCarthy's spurious charges, hoping that the accusations would outweigh the denials in the public's mind. Dennis insisted that they were wrong to blame Russian strength on the "machinations and foul deeds of reds and pinks who infiltrated into our State Department and thus shaped policies . . . favorably to Russia and communism." The Republicans were trying to win elections by lies, rather than by attacks on the catastrophic globalist policies. Taft, Dennis charged, "thinks it is easier to sell the American people the idea that the reds and the pinks in the State Department are responsible for the present might and menace of Russia" than to engage in a meaningful critique of American foreign policy. Taft's problem, he suggested, was his admiration for "Republican internationalist elder statesmen" who had developed that policy. The Republican high command simply did not want "a real debate."[70]

Dennis could not see how a few individuals, such as Asia scholar Owen Lattimore, could be singled out and blamed for the success of communism abroad. Lattimore, who had been attacked by McCarthy as the "top Russian espionage agent" in the United States, may have been pro-Russian, but so was American foreign policy during the war. "To brand anyone as disloyal today because he was pro-Russian or pro-Communist during the

68. Ibid., pp. 3–4.
69. No. 209, March 25, 1950, p. 5.
70. No. 210, April 1, 1950, pp. 1–2.

late war" was simply an insult to one's intelligence. The government was once again using the techniques developed during the 1944 sedition trial to gain support for its policies.

> The reasoning is the same. . . . Hitler wanted to keep America out of the war and made communism his number one devil after July 1941. All Americans wanting to keep America out of the war . . . were, ipso facto, playing Hitler's game, pro-Nazi and in a world conspiracy with the Nazis. Now the corresponding theory is that any American who spoke well of Russia and communism, when they were our noble allies to save the world from Nazi devils, or who supported policies . . . helpful to Russia and communism was or is a pro-communist . . . If the U.S. Government, in wartime, with war hysteria to help it, could not put over this crazy prosecution theory and if the case had finally to be dismissed by the Court itself, just why do the Republicans and many anti-Reds now think they can win on an identically similar theory based on a similar historical lie?[71]

Law enforcement rested on the unity, consent, and consensus of a community. Legislation such as the McCarran Internal Security Act could not prevent advocacy of an alternative social system. The bill, which passed over Truman's veto, required that Communists and "Communist-front" organizations register with the government; that "detention" camps be established for internment of suspected "subversives" during a national emergency; and that Communists no longer be employed in defense plants.

That act was "a big step towards the worst features of communism in action . . . those of the police-garrison state." A law against "subversive activities" was irrational, since "Communist" was a term impossible of satisfactory legal definition. When Hitler favored keeping the U.S. out of war, those Americans favoring neutrality were branded as Nazis; in the postwar era "anybody fighting Truman is a co-conspirator of world communism." The McCarran Act proclaimed a holy war on "isms." Waging such a war revealed an inability to "tolerate opposition."[72]

71. Ibid., p. 3.
72. No. 220, Aug. 12, 1950, p. 4; No. 235, Sept. 23, 1950, pp. 1–2.

McCarthy's antics served an even more destructive purpose than imagined by many of the senator's critics. His charges kept the nation's attention away from the cold war that was being waged by the nation's liberal leaders. Dennis suggested that McCarthy would have to be cut down once he had undertaken a war against the army and its businessman secretary. The likes of Joe McCarthy, Dennis argued, would not be entrusted to wage the cold war. "For leading an Anglo-American world crusade to wage global religious war on red sin," he commented, "a Woodrow Wilson, a Churchill or a Franklin D. Roosevelt, not material for New York or Boston ward politics, is indicated." Flynn predicted that the forthcoming army-McCarthy hearings would cut McCarthy "down to size." When McCarthy died, Flynn summed him up as a "typical, sincere, roof-raising American—a most authentic type," who "never quite grasped that sin is here to stay and has to be lived with."[73]

Lawrence Dennis had moved a long way from being the unpopular exponent of fascism before the onset of World War II. Reverting to his earlier laissez-fairism, he had developed a consistent and firm opposition to the waging of cold war, whether carried on by liberal Democrats or conservative Republicans. Aware of the charge of appeasement leveled against critics, he argued that such a course might indeed be warranted. "The avoidance of war has often been in the past and will often be in the future," he wrote in 1969, "made possible by concessions which can only be called appeasement."[74]

A proper analogy with prewar behavior, he maintained, was the similarities that existed between Hitler's preparations for war and U.S. cold-war policy. The basic similarity was the "big, basic fact of a crusading anti-communism, the . . . rationalization—both of Hitler's preparations and of America's preparations for war in the nineteen sixties." The second was the use made of war. Both Germany and the United States used war as a mechanism

73. No. 411, Feb. 8, 1954; No. 418, March 27, 1954; No. 580, May 4, 1957; cited in Justus Doenecke, "Lawrence Dennis: Revisionist of the Cold War," pp. 283–84.
74. Lawrence Dennis, *Operational Thinking for Survival* (Colorado Springs, Colo.: Ralph Myles, 1969), p. 209.

for avoiding depression. The only real difference, according to Dennis, was that "America's spending on war preparations is vastly bigger."[75]

As the editor of a fiercely independent private business—itself the model of a laissez-faire venture—Dennis was not subject to editorial pressures, blacklisting, constraints of advertisers, or the dictates of a formal political movement. But writing his thoughts in a journal limited to circulation among a small number of individuals, Dennis paid the price of political irrelevance and intellectual isolation. Unlike Flynn, whose writings achieved some prominence because of his connection with the McCarthy camp and the formal political Right, Dennis did not compromise. McCarthy and MacArthur, Dulles and Acheson, Truman and Eisenhower were equally grist for his mill.

Dennis went against the grain. His refusal to enter the consensus on any level was both a strength and a weakness. His inability to compromise meant that even the Tafts and other conservatives, whom he was most anxious to reach and with whom he constantly thought he shared goals in common, would refuse to accept any advice from him. His persistent laissez-fairism separated him from cold-war opponents on the Left, and so did their general support to the policies of the Soviet Union. He continued to analyze the cold war, reject crusades, and insist upon the practical necessity of neutrality. His estrangement was the nation's loss. The weekly efforts at an appeal to reason were inadequate against the mass media. Only in retrospect, as historians discover what were largely unknown ramblings reserved for the small body of the faithful, can one see what he might have contributed.

75. Ibid., pp. 40–41, 43.

Conclusions

CHARLES A. BEARD, a historian accused of offering writings that "were to become the staple assumptions of the far right wing"; Robert A. Taft, Midwestern political leader accused of reflecting "the public's ambivalent insolationist-aggressive state of emotion" during the 1950s; former *Nation* editor and pacifist Oswald Garrison Villard, described by his biographer as suffering a "spiritual death" after Pearl Harbor, and thereafter producing writing "hardly distinguishable from the utterances of the most reactionary forces in America"; John T. Flynn, a former liberal economist and Nye Committee adviser, accused of "cultivating the radical right front," actually ending as a McCarthy supporter; and Lawrence Dennis, an "intellectual leader and principal adviser of the Fascist groups," as one historian remembered him.

With the exception of Taft, whose political power commanded attention, these men were treated as fighters for a lost cause, whose ideas have been so plainly proven wrong by history that they are irrelevant. When Richard Hofstadter treats Beard's work on foreign policy, he assumes that Beard had lapsed into an "abandonment of objectivity." Michael Wreszin ends his study of Villard with the year 1941, although Villard lived another eight years.

The process in which these men moved closer to an alliance with conservatives began when they were accused of betraying their own principles and going conservative, because they dared to criticize FDR and his interventionist policies.[1] The word "conservative" used as an epithet was a popular attack on those who failed to endorse the politics of expansion. The problem, as

---

1. See, e.g., Oswald Garrison Villard to Richard Koch, Sept. 12, 1946, Oswald Garrison Villard MSS., Houghton Library, Harvard Univ., Cambridge, Mass. Villard admitted to a "basic kinship between my liberal ideas and those upheld by certain honest and fearless conservatives," whom he was able to "get on with so much better of late years than ever before."

Amos Pinchot explained, was also one of changing definitions. "To be a liberal today," he wrote, "you must be a nut. No man now can call himself a liberal unchallenged, unless he is partial, prejudiced, class-conscious, and as intolerant and narrow minded as a backwood Kentucky bishop." If one persisted in calling himself liberal, isolationist leader Pinchot explained, one had to make it clear that the majority of those who professed to be liberal were reactionary, "in that they stand for concentration of power in the executive, destruction of power in the legislative branch of the government, coercion, and various things that heretofore have been correctly assigned to reaction."[2]

In the name of liberalism, modern-day corporate liberals sought to create a Leviathan state. This development has been summarized by Arthur A. Ekirch, Jr., in his classic study *The Decline of American Liberalism:*

> Liberalism in its classic traditional form was the term appropriate to the political philosophy of the eighteenth and nineteenth centuries which stressed the greatest possible freedom of the individual. Liberalism in the United States today, however, is seldom used in this sense—except by a scattering of libertarians and old-fashioned conservatives . . . The modern or new liberal in the United States accepts with very little question the political philosophy of big government. . . . America's largest corporations, kept busy with defense weaponry, are in no position to criticize big government. High government officials, in turn, recognize war economy as a politically convenient support for the idea of a welfare state.[3]

Insofar as such men as Villard and Taft sought to preserve what Ekirch calls the "time honored liberal values," they may be thought of as seeking to conserve traditions. If the values and practices of individual liberty become eroded in the new corporate state, the effort to realize them often becomes a struggle against the repressive powers of the new rulers of the state. Most often those who struggle to achieve political liberties are radicals desiring a new social and economic system. Since both the old

2. Amos Pinchot to Frank E. Gannett, Dec. 28, 1939, Amos Pinchot MSS., Box 66, Library of Congress, Wash., D.C.
3. Arthur A. Ekirch, Jr., *The Decline of American Liberalism* (New York: Atheneum, 1967), p. 2 of new preface.

liberals and the new radicals operate outside the consensus, their activities, and even their writings, are at certain moments conceived as a threat. At those moments the conservative quest for liberty becomes a form of opposition to the *status quo*.

In the early 1950s, as Ekirch explains, cold-war liberals, "in their anxiety lest the United States return to a post World War I intellectual pattern of isolationist pacifism, came to condone and even to abet a resort to the opposite extreme of a militant, interventionist nationalism, masquerading as idealistic internationalism." The new bipartisan consensus to wage cold war hid the reality of a conservative drift in U.S. foreign policy. "In what was really a turn to the right in American diplomacy, war liberals, who had formerly shared in many a leftist cause or program, now vied with conservatives for leadership in the crusade against communism."[4]

Such a turn to the right was taken by the Truman administration. The interventionists had prepared for their new role with the attitudes they had formed in the 1930s, when they were thought of as part of the Left. A thin line divides the Max Lerner who attacked Lawrence Dennis in 1941 from the Max Lerner who supported an aggressive waging of cold-war policy during the 1950s. The approach was the same—only the enemy was different.

These new nationalists, with ties in the world of industry, the armed forces, the State Department, and the corporate liberal policy-making foundations, developed their ties as the cold war continued and the stress of permanent war economy took its toll. These new conservatives were able, as Ekirch concludes, "to assume a dominant position in both major political parties."[5] The result was predicted back in 1947 by C. Wright Mills. "If the sophisticated conservatives," as Mills called them, "have their way, the next New Deal will be a war economy rather than a welfare economy, although the conservative's liberal rhetoric might put the first in the guise of the second."[6]

4. Ibid., pp. 319–320.
5. Ibid., p. 333.
6. C. Wright Mills, *The New Men of Power* (New York: Harcourt, Brace, 1948), pp. 248–249.

The cold-war state had created a new body of sophisticated conservatives—corporate liberal policy makers who employed the rhetoric of the old liberalism. It had also given birth to a new-style right wing. This group, led by the Buckleys and their journal, *National Review,* adopted a policy of support for a global struggle against the Communist menace. Individuals in this group were of a different breed. Conservatives led by the Buckleys, as Murray N. Rothbard had pointed out, "brought to the intellectual leadership of the right-wing a new coalition of traditionalist Catholics and ex-Communists and ex-radicals whose major concern was the destruction of the god that failed them, the Soviet Union and world communism."[7]

The New Right shared the basic assumptions of the cold-war liberals, although they liked to claim that they were protecting the conservative tradition. If anything distinguished their appraisal of U.S. foreign policy, it was an even more militant posture about the need for permanent cold war. When President Nixon announced the bombing resumption in Vietnam and the mining of Haiphong harbor in May 1972, New York Senator James Buckley endorsed the policy and added that the President "would be justified in taking far stronger measures."[8] One does not have to think long to imagine what John T. Flynn, Robert A. Taft, or Oswald Garrison Villard would have had to say about such a blanket endorsement for extending the power of the imperial Presidency.

Unlike the older liberals, who supported Taft's calls for congressional authority on issues of war and peace, today's New Right responds differently. Barry Goldwater argues that "the Founding Fathers vested in the President a discretion to *react* against foreign dangers whenever and wherever he sees a threat to the security of the United States. . . . He responds to a foreign threat already set in motion." The President can send troops "where he chooses in support of America's legal defense commitments." If money exists for an ongoing policy, "the

7. Murray N. Rothbard, "The Foreign Policy of the Old Right," unpub. MS., pp. 28–29.
8. Richard Reeves, "Isn't It Time We Had a Senator?" *New York,* Feb. 25, 1974, p. 45.

President can act on his own authority and is not subject to the policy restrictions of Congress."[9]

The older group of "conservatives" were not always consistent in their opposition to expansionist foreign policy. Taft, shrewd politician that he was, stopped short of outright opposition. Preferring to function within the political mainstream, fearing isolation, Taft steered away from the course urged upon him by George Bender and others. "I have had more criticism for my very mild appeals to look the whole situation over," he once remarked, "than I have had for anything else I have done." Taft wanted to "do everything possible to discourage war excitement," but he did not feel it was possible to oppose "full preparedness."[10]

Some of the conservative critics did not let Taft off the hook. Lawrence Dennis complained about the hypocrisy of supporting a balanced budget and a free market along with a cold-war foreign policy that made necessary state intervention in the economy. When Taft supported the MacArthur policy of escalation in Korea, Dennis attacked him for backing a policy that would increase the danger of war and result in thousands of useless deaths. When Dennis attacked Taft's Korean policy, or when John T. Flynn attacked U.S. intervention in Vietnam, they offered a critique and provided an alternative that was as meaningful as any offered by liberal Democrats. Dennis in particular made the point that the interventionist liberals would not accept: as long as potential opponents of policy accepted the major assumptions of cold-war liberalism, their opposition would be ineffective.

We can only speculate on what criticism Beard would have had about U.S. policy in Asia, or what arguments Villard would have presented about the crises of the sixties. John T. Flynn proved as inconsistent in his commitment to liberty as Taft was in his opposition to globalism. Only Dennis was satisfied to endure total political isolation.

Despite their differences all five men raised critical issues: the

9. Letters to the Editor, *New York Times,* July 30, 1973.
10. Taft to Felix Morley, March 23, 1948, Robert A. Taft MSS., Box 797, Library of Congress, Wash., D.C.

erosion of congressional authority to bring the nation into war; the dangers of concentrated power in the executive; the ability of the President to carry out secret war by executive deception; the assessment that the United States had become some sort of empire, and that the nation's policies revealed this reality; the need for debate on foreign policy; the erosion of civil and political liberties; the menace of crusades and holy wars; the need for attention to the methods used to bring a nation into war; the connections between a permanent war economy, industry, government, and the state.

Few listened. The opposition gives us some understanding of the acceptable limits of dissent. They were charged with serving the interests of foreign powers—the Axis in the 1930s, the Communists in the 1950s. Both charges were sometimes made against the same individual. They were extreme, irresponsible, unconcerned with national security. The rhetoric used against them sounds all too familiar.

Some of these individuals, sadly, ended their careers on the extreme Right. John T. Flynn, who had shed much light on the dangers of foreign expansion, was entrapped by the very conspiracy theories used by the center to create unity for waging cold war. On a personal level, one could hardly blame Flynn for moving into such unkempt company after years of forced isolation from the liberal circles he had been part of. By the time the war liberals had shifted to fighting the new cold war, Flynn was part of the New Right.

Villard and Dennis were stronger. Although they communicated with the Right, they reserved their fire for attacks on the Right's acceptance of the cold war. Some 1970s radicals will not be satisfied with their performance. They would have preferred that such critics as Flynn and Dennis give up their belief that they could return to an age of laissez-faire capitalism, and place the blame for imperial foreign policy on the social structure of American capitalism. But Flynn and Dennis were not won over by those who sought such a solution. The largest political group advocating socialism, the Communist party, had discredited itself in their eyes when it shifted to the interventionist side in 1941.

We have come full circle. Reeling from the pain of the seemingly endless war in Indochina, former practitioners of cold-war liberalism give faint echoes of words familiar in the 1930s and 1950s. Walter Mondale argues that "we no longer can permit the President's war-making powers to go unchecked and unchallenged." Former Assistant Secretary of Defense Paul C. Warnke argues that the Constitution cannot be read to give the President "the right to carry on an air war in a civil conflict in a tiny country on the other side of the world." The Constitution, he says, refutes "the idea that the President is to be a warmaker" or that he has the right "unilaterally to commit American armed force in such combat." Warnke reaches the conclusion that "the President's war in Cambodia is without constitutional support or Congressional endorsement."[11]

Taft in 1950. Beard in 1948. Beard would not be surprised at charges made by Tom Wicker of *The New York Times* when he asserts that Henry Kissinger and Richard M. Nixon "deliberately ordered falsification of the facts of the Cambodian bombing." That an American President had uttered "a deliberate and knowing lie, broadcast in person to the American people," as part of the " 'security' mania that distorts national life," would be no revelation to the historian who spent so long in trying to unravel the duplicities surrounding events at Pearl Harbor.[12] In 1948 such charges were not well received. The "credibility gap" had not yet been discovered.

Most recently the lasting effects of Watergate were described in Beardian terms by one of the earliest senatorial critics of the U.S. war in Vietnam, the late Oregon Senator Wayne L. Morse:

> The trend towards a police state in our country . . . could have been checked years ago if Congress had kept faith with a basic principle of democratic self-government—that in a democracy there is no substitute for full public disclosure of the people's business. The constitutional crisis in which the nation finds itself is largely attributable to the war in Vietnam, which

11. Walter F. Mondale, "Cambodia: Tunnel at the End of the Light," and Paul C. Warnke, "The Dread Responsibility," both in *New York Times,* April 13, 1973, p. 39.
12. Tom Wicker, "The Big Lie Requires Big Liars," *New York Times,* July 24, 1973, p. 35.

has been prosecuted by the usurpation of unconstitutional power on the part of four Presidents—unchecked by Congress and the Supreme Court.

. . . A most dangerous police-state practice is Presidential usurpation of the constitutional power to make war without a declaration of war, as Nixon has done throughout his Presidency and is now doing in Laos and Cambodia. It is nothing less than the exercise of dictatorial power, and amounts to war criminality. The fact that other Presidents before him illegally usurped war making power without a declaration of war does not excuse Nixon's criminality.[13]

Morse's words remind one of Taft's charge on the eve of World War II, and later, at the beginning of the Korean war— that the executive was employing "dictatorial power" to commit troops and wage war. Wayne Morse understands that our "Presidents have been leading us for some years towards a government of unchecked Executive will through usurpation of power not granted them by the Constitution." But like so many other Americans, he believes this development was quite recent. It began, he writes, "in 1953, when [Eisenhower] enunciated the Eisenhower-Nixon-Dulles military-containment policy for Asia without the slightest right of constitutional or international law."[14]

The steady growth of executive power during the Roosevelt and Truman administrations has been conveniently brushed aside in the above remarks, perhaps because Morse stood on the other side of the fence during its rise to power. When Taft raised similar issues during the Korean crisis, Morse attacked him for serving Russian ends. Morse had argued the domino theory: if the U.S. failed to stand firm against Russia, "the rest of the world would fall."[15]

The issue is not Morse's memory; it is the lack of historical perspective we all share. What Morse and others now argue has become part of popular consciousness. In the recent past such

13. Wayne L. Morse, "The Deeper Meaning of Watergate," *Nation*, June 18, 1973, pp. 777–779.
14. Ibid., p. 777.
15. Wayne Morse, "A Reply to Senator Taft's Foreign Policy Proposals," speech to the Senate, Jan. 15, 1951, Taft MSS., Box 1320.

arguments put one beyond the limits of acceptable dissent. When the enemy was Germany, any means could be used to bring the populace into war, and damage done the nation's moral fiber was something very few seemed to consider. By the time a significant number of citizens were ready to examine the prewar isolationist's charges, it was too late; the drift toward globalism, interventionism and concentrated executive power had been institutionalized in the new corporate state. By the time of Korea, opponents were scattered on the Left and the Right. A tiny minority were willing to demand unilateral U.S. withdrawal from Southeast Asia; a smaller number were willing to comment upon the immoral means of warfare waged by the U.S. in Korea. Most were afraid to risk the charge that they were echoing Communist propaganda. Even Taft's mild position on erosion of congressional authority produced cries from the liberal press.

The five men, despite differences, contradictions, and evolution of their thinking, were dedicated and committed. Like John T. Flynn in 1952, they had asked Americans to pause "and take a good, long, cold, sober look at the folly of our whole position." It has taken a long time, but it now seems that a good many Americans are ready to heed Flynn's admonition. While we undertake that task, and attempt to create institutions that will guarantee movement away from the perpetual waging of cold war, we should explore the alternatives advanced by earlier critics who tried, and failed.

These "conservatives"—classical liberals—tried to stop the administration of Harry S. Truman from embarking upon a new global crusade on behalf of American hegemony throughout the world. They opposed many of the programs meant to implement that control. They criticized the assumptions that underlay our interventionist policy. They were charged with disloyalty.

After the war, charges of "Communist" came from the internationalist liberals who had entered upon the alliance with the Soviet Union during World War II. Some of the conservatives responded to that irony in a way that undercut their own position. Flynn, above all, became a bitter domestic anti-Communist, and failed to detect the connection between anti-Communist hysteria and a global crusade. Lawrence Dennis, on the other hand, defended the rights of Communists when many liberals hoped only that Joe McCarthy would carefully distinguish between the real Communists and themselves.

All opposed the postwar Pax Americana. They failed. The isolation they suffered was not theirs alone but also the nation's loss. It was not Villard alone who suffered from being deprived of the right to publish in major journals of opinion. It was more than a personal tragedy that Flynn ended up an ally of Joe McCarthy. It was more than Dennis who suffered from being limited to a tiny group of old friends. He was our earliest and most consistent critic of the cold war.

We have now learned that calls for national unity and security do not justify the suppression of dissent. It is a short step forward to examine the dissenters from a previous consensus. For a number of reasons they were unable to transcend their isolation and reach out and be heard. The times now give us an opportunity to go back and find what had been denied us. The benefit, this time, will be ours.

Index

Dennis, Lawrence (*cont.*)
on corporate state, 281, 284
debate with Lerner and Schuman, 287–88
economic views of, 276–77, 282, 299–301, 305–7
fascism and, 275*ff.*
FDR and, 290
on frontier expansion, 283
on Great Britain, 301
on Hitler, 278, 280, 319, 321
on imperialism, 276–77, 306, 308
on internationalism, 298, 308
on interventionists, 299, 307, 311–12, 316
on Marshall Plan, 304–5
on mass opinion, 297
McCarthy and, 316, 319, 321
on NATO, 310–11
Nazism and, 278, 279, 280, 293
on neutrality, 280–81, 299
New Deal and, 275, 281
newsletter by, 298
Nicaragua and, 276–77
personal background of, 276
on presidential power, 315
Republicans and, 297–98, 302, 306, 308–10, 319
on socialism, 282–83, 286, 300
on Soviet Union, 299*ff.*, 309
Taft and, 312, 315, 319, 327
trial of, 290*ff.*
on Truman, 302–3, 310, 314, 316
on Truman Doctrine, 303–4
Villard and, 294
on war, 284

Depression, 25
Flynn and, 201*ff.*
Determinism, economic, 27
Devil Theory of War, The (Beard), 27
Dewey, John, 219–20
Dewey, Thomas E., 164, 297
Beard on, 61
Dennis on, 309
Flynn on, 242
Dien Bien Phu, 261
Dies, Martin, 249, 279
Dilling, Elizabeth, 290
Dissent, Flynn on, 213
Divine, Robert A., on FDR, 46
Doenecke, Justus D., 9
Domhoff, G. William, 259*n.*
Domino theory, 262
Donell, Forrest C., 168
Dulles, John Foster, 176
Dennis on, 309
Flynn and, 258, 261*ff.*
Taft on, 171
Vietnam and, 261–62
Dynamics of War and Revolution, The (Dennis), 281, 285

Eaton, Horace Ainsworth, 116
Economic Interpretation of the Constitution, An (Beard), 18
Economics
Beard on, 17–19, 20*ff.*, 26–28
Dennis on, 276–77, 282, 299–301, 305–7
determinists and, 27
FDR and, 21–22
Flynn on, 199*ff.*
Villard and, 69, 72

Germany (*cont.*)
  postwar treatment of, 91, 92,
    94*ff.*
  revisionists and, 95
  Soviet Union invaded by, 128–
    129, 224–25
  Soviet Union pact with, 78,
    224, 225
  Taft on, 121, 123–24, 126
  troop buildup by U.S. in,
    177*ff.*
  Villard on, 77, 78, 80
  World War I and, 27, 28, 68,
    69
*Giddy Minds and Foreign Quar-
  rels* (Beard), 33, 35
Gideonse, Harry, 61
Globalism. *See also* Interna-
    tionalism.
  Dennis on, 307
  Flynn and, 258–59
Goldwater, Barry, 192, 271, 326
Great Britain
  Asian policy and, 258
  Beard on, 42, 43–45, 47
  Dennis on, 301
  Flynn on, 207, 218, 224, 236,
    258
  Taft on, 125–26, 140
  Villard on, 78, 80
Great Debate on Foreign Policy,
    176*ff.*, 181
Greece
  Dennis on, 303
  Taft on, 154*ff.*
  Truman Doctrine and, 61–62
  Villard on, 107–8
Green, David, 9
Green, William, 76–77
Greer, U.S.S., 48–49, 127, 131
Guérard, Albert, 77

Hanighen, Frank, 91, 100
Hansen, Alvin, 231, 233
Hart, Merwin K., 249
Hathaway, Clarence, 285
Hay, John, 23
Higham, John, 12
Hillman, Sidney, 231
Hiss, Alger, Dennis on, 318
History, 13–14
Hitler
  Dennis on, 278, 280, 319, 321
  Flynn on, 219
  Taft on, 134
  Villard on, 79, 80
Ho Chi Minh, 253, 256
Hoffman, Nicholas von, 147
Hofstadter, Richard
  on Beard, 25, 27, 39, 40, 64,
    323
  on FDR, 45
  on Japan, 52
Holmes, John Haynes, 216
Hoover, Herbert, 21
  Beard and, 56–57, 65
  Dennis and, 312
  Great Debate on Foreign
    Policy and, 176–77, 181
  on Iceland occupation, 130
  isolationism and, 83
  Japan and, 56–57
  Taft and, 132, 135, 159, 190
Hoover, J. Edgar, 213
Hopkins, Harry, 91, 204
House, Edward M., 26
House Un-American Activities
    Committee, 111, 249
  Dennis on, 279
Hull, Cordell, 59
  Japan and, 54, 55, 56
  Stalin and, 234, 235, 236

Soviet Union (*cont.*)
  Marshall Plan and, 160*ff.*
  New Republic on, 182
  oil supplies for, 88
  postwar plans for, 45
  Taft on, 149–51, 155*ff.*, 160,
    163, 166, 168*ff.*, 175–76,
    182, 193
  troop buildup in Europe and,
    178
  Villard and, 69, 78, 94, 98,
    99, 103, 106, 108, 109
  Wallace on, 104, 105
  Yalta and, 61, 243–44
Spanish-American War, 84
Spanish Civil War
  Beard on, 30
  Villard on, 75
Stalin, Joseph
  Barnes on, 91
  Beard on, 62
  Dennis on, 298, 301, 302
  Flynn on, 225, 234–35, 236,
    243–44, 245, 251
  Truman and, 153, 182
  Villard on, 96, 99, 106
  Yalta and, 243–44
Stark, Harold A., 49
Stassen, Harold, 130
Steel industry, 205
Stevens, Robert, 270
Stimson, Henry L., 93
  Japan and, 56, 57
  Taft against, 125
Stockholders, 198–99
Stolper, Gustav, 214
Strachey, John, Dennis and, 277,
    285–86
Submarine warfare, 27, 28, 68,
    69, 127
Sumner, William Graham, 83

Supreme Court, FDR and, 76
Surpluses, Beard's views on, 23,
    30
Syndicalism, 294

Taft, Robert A., 11, 13, 119*ff.*,
    147*ff.*, 327
  on alliance with British and
    Russians, 140–42
  on arms policy, 169
  Bundy's criticism of, 190–92
  on China, 160, 161, 171–72
  cold war and, 147*ff.*
  on communism, 129, 143,
    149, 154*ff.*, 160, 165–66,
    194
  on containment policy, 186–
    187, 193
  on Czechoslovakia, 162
  Dennis and, 312, 315, 319,
    327
  on domestic peace, 137
  on FDR, 122, 124–25, 132,
    135
  Flynn and, 213, 242
  on Formosa, 171–72, 173
  on Germany, 121, 123–24,
    126
  on Greek aid, 154*ff.*
  on Iceland, 129–30
  on imperialism, 128, 131, 135,
    140–42, 161, 168, 174
  on interventionism, 130, 132,
    142, 169–70
  isolationism and, 130–31, 166
  on justice, 151–52
  on Korean war, 173*ff.*, 184*ff.*,
    194
  on land war, 176, 177, 178,
    184
  on Lend-Lease, 125–26, 131

ABOUT THE AUTHOR

RONALD RADOSH (B.A., University of Wisconsin, 1959; M.A., University of Iowa, 1960; Ph.D., University of Wisconsin, 1967) is an Associate Professor of History at Queensborough Community College of the City University of New York and a member of the graduate faculty of CUNY. The author of *American Labor and United States Foreign Policy,* he contributes to a wide variety of journals, including the *Nation, Liberation,* and the *Monthly Review,* and is a contributing editor of *New Politics.*